THE NEW WEBSTER'S
CONCISE
OFFICE GUIDE

LEXICON PUBLICATIONS, INC.

Written and compiled by: Eugene Ehrlich

Editors: Hayden Carruth
         Jeffrey H. Hacker

Design and composition: Pam Forde Graphics

Copyright © 1993 by
Lexicon Publications, Inc.
Sherman Turnpike
Danbury, CT 06816

ISBN: 0-7172-4660-4

Contents

Section II
WRITING 133-166

Section III
DICTIONARY OF USAGE 167-208

Section IV
READY REFERENCE **209-256**

Section I

UNDERSTANDING GRAMMAR

– 1 –

Glossary

Accusative case. The form of a pronoun indicating that the pronoun is the object of a verb or preposition: *me, her, him, us, them, whom*. Also called **objective case**.

Active voice. See **Voice**.

Adjective. A word or words that are used to modify a noun, pronoun, or verbal: *good* boys, *poor* you, *excellent* hunting.

Adjective clause. A subordinate clause used as an adjective: All *who disagree* may now make their views known.

Adjective phrase. A phrase used as an adjective: We must help all those *in need*.

Adverb. A word or words used to modify a verb, verbal, adjective, adverb, or an entire clause or sentence: read *quickly*; to breathe *heavily*; *quite* stale; *Eventually*, a woman was selected.

Adverbial phrase. A phrase used as an adverb: They moved *to the suburbs*.

Antecedent. A word or words to which a pronoun refers: *Rebecca* (antecedent) asked for *hers* (pronoun).

Apposition. The placement of a noun or noun substitute next to another in order to explain it or identify it: California, *the Golden*

State; Richard *the Lion Hearted*. *The Golden State* and *the Lion Hearted* are called **appositives**.

Article. *A, an,* and *the* are classified as articles. Their function is to modify a noun or noun substitute. *A* and *an* are the **indefinite articles**. *The* is the **definite article**.

Auxiliary verb. A verb used with other verbs to form tense or voice: They *should* find their way; We *were* disappointed.

Case. A form of a noun or pronoun indicating function. The three cases are **nominative (subjective)**, **genitive (possessive)**, and **accusative (objective)**. Nominative: *I* sang. Genitive: That is *mine*. Accusative: The cat bit *them*.

Clause. A group of words containing a subject and verb. Clauses are either **dependent**: The group *that finished lunch* left the dining room; or **independent**: *The executive ordered a cutback in production.*

Collective noun. A noun that appears to be singular but refers to a group. A collective noun is treated as singular when the group is thought of as a unit: The *couple is* attractive. A collective noun is treated as plural when the members of the group are considered individually: The *couple were* happy with *their* apartment.

Comparison. The inflection of adverbs or adjectives to show degrees of quality or amount. **Absolute**: *bad, slowly, notorious*. **Comparative:** *worse, slower, more notorious*. **Superlative**: *worst, slowest, most notorious*.

Complement. A noun or adjective used to complete the meaning of a copulative verb. It is also called a **predicate complement**. I was *sick* (**predicate adjective**). Luciano is a great *tenor* (**predicate noun**).

Complex sentence. A sentence containing one independent clause and one or more dependent clauses.

Compound sentence. A sentence containing two or more independent clauses.

Compound-complex sentence. A sentence containing two or more independent clauses plus one or more dependent clauses.

Conjunction. A word or words used to join words, phrases, or clauses. A **coordinating conjunction** joins elements of equal value. A **subordinating conjunction** joins dependent clauses to independent clauses.

Conjunctive adverb. An adverb used as a conjunction. The most common examples are *however, thus,* and *therefore*.

Coordinate. Elements of equal grammatical or syntactical importance are called *coordinate*: two or more nouns, phrases, clauses, etc.

Copulative verb. A verb, also known as a **linking verb**, that links a subject and its complement. The most common copulative verb is *be*.

Demonstrative adjective. An adjective that indicates a particular noun or pronoun: *this* theme, *that* house, *this* one.

Demonstrative pronoun. A pronoun that specifies a particular referent: *this* is what I resent; *that* will not do.

Dependent clause. See **Subordinate clause**.

Descriptive adjective. An adjective that names the condition or quality of the noun it modifies; *healthy* vegetation, *damaged* goods.

Direct address. A construction in which the writer addresses the reader directly: Sam, please hand me my briefcase. Anne, leave the room.

Direct object. A word or words that receive the action of a verb: The demonstrator struck the *police officer*. We believe *that the economy will improve*.

Gender. This term, of little consequence in English grammar, refers to masculine, feminine, and neuter nouns and pronouns in some other languages. Personal pronouns in English have gender in the third person singular: *he, she, it*.

Genitive case. The form of a noun or pronoun that shows possession: *person's, minute's, hers, his, theirs*, etc. It is also called the **possessive case**.

Gerund. The *-ing* form of a verb that is used as a noun or that performs a noun function: *Flying* is much faster than *sailing*. They both enjoy *hunting* and *fishing*. Gerunds are classified as verbals.

Imperative mood. The verb construction used in giving commands. The subject of the verb in this mood is usually lacking: *Stop* swearing! *Look* lively!

Indefinite pronoun. A pronoun that does not specify a particular referent: *any, anyone, each, everyone,* etc.

Independent clause. A clause that can stand alone and convey meaning when punctuated as a simple sentence: *We invited all our cousins*, even though we had not seen them in years. This type of clause is also known as a *main clause* or a *principal clause*.

Indicative mood. The form of a verb used to make a statement or ask a question: She *speaks* well. *Are* they still *cooking*?

Indirect object. A noun or pronoun receiving a direct object: She gave *him* (**indirect object**) a lecture (**direct object**).

Infinitive. The simple form of a verb, often preceded by *to*: (to) swim, (to) think, (to) hope. Infinitives, which are verbals, function as nouns, adjectives, and adverbs.

Infinitive phrase. A phrase constructed of an infinitive plus its modifiers and object: *to dive gracefully, to prepare food*. Infinitive phrases perform the same functions as infinitives.

Inflection. A change in form to indicate grammatical relationships. Inflection of nouns and pronouns is called *declension*. Inflection of verbs is called *conjugation*. Inflection of adjectives and adverbs is known as *comparison*.

Intensive pronoun. A pronoun used to strengthen a noun or pronoun: The manager *herself*, you *yourselves*, the animal *itself*.

Interjection. An ejaculatory word or expression: *Alas*, there's little water left. *Goodness gracious*, can't we be fair to everybody?

Interrogative adjective. An adjective used in asking a question: *Whose* hat? *Which* boat?

Interrogative pronoun. A pronoun used in asking a question: *Whose* was forgotten? *Which* came in first?

Intransitive verb. A verb that does not take an object: I *laughed* all the way to the bank. They *argue* well. All copulative verbs are intransitive. Many verbs function transitively as well as intransitively.

Irregular verb. A verb, also known as a **strong verb**, that forms its past tense and past participle by a change of vowels: *run, ran, run*; *sing, sang, sung*.

Linking verb. See **Copulative verb**.

Mood. The characteristic of a verb that shows the manner in which a statement is perceived by the writer. See **Indicative mood**, **Imperative mood**, and **Subjunctive mood**.

Nominative case. See **Subjective case**.

Nonrestrictive modifier. A modifier of a word or group of words already limited or restricted: Ruth's father, *who studied Greek in college*, remembers much of what he learned. They have sold the family home, *which still stands in Connecticut*.

Noun. The name of a person, place, thing, quality, action, or idea. Nouns function as subjects, modifiers, objects, objects of prepositions, and objects of verbals.

Noun phrase. A phrase that functions as a noun: *evening meal, the plane to Buffalo*.

Number. The singular and plural aspects of nouns, pronouns, and verbs.

Numerical adjective. An adjective that enumerates the element it modifies: *seven* members of Congress, *first* year.

Objective case. See **Accusative case**.

Parallel construction. The repetition of grammatical construction to achieve coherence or emphasis: *skating* and *sledding*; *I came, I saw, I conquered*.

Participle. The adjectival form of a verb. The *present participle* ends in *ing*: *swimming, thinking*. The past participle ends in *ed* if the verb is regular, changes form if the verb is irregular: *walked, talked*; *swum, thought*. Participles are verbals.

Passive voice. See **Voice**.

Person. The form of a verb or pronoun that indicates the person speaking: *I am, we are* (first person); the person spoken to: *you are* (second person); the person or persons spoken of: *he is, they are* (third person).

Personal pronoun. A pronoun used to indicate people: *I, you, he, she,* etc. *I* saw *her.*

Possessive adjective. An adjective used to indicate possession: *my, your, his, her, its,* etc. *Our* hats, *their* typewriters.

Possessive case. See **Genitive case**.

Predicate. In a clause or sentence, the verb along with its modifiers, object, complement, or indirect object.

Predicate adjective. See **Complement**.

Predicate complement. See **Complement**.

Predicate noun. See **Complement**.

Preposition. A word or words that convey a meaning of position, direction, time, or other abstraction. Together with a noun or pronoun and its modifiers, it forms a **prepositional phrase**, which serves as a modifier: *to the side, from the roof, with her.* In these prepositional phrases, *side, roof,* and *her* function as objects of prepositions.

Principal parts of a verb. The infinitive (*see*), past tense (*saw*), and past participle (*seen*).

Pronoun. A word that takes the place of a noun: *I, she, it,* etc.

Proper adjective. An adjective formed from a proper noun: *French* restaurant, *British* customs.

Proper noun. The name of a specific person, place, or thing: *Hazel, Iceland, Grant's Monument.*

Reciprocal pronoun. *Each other* and *one another.* They are used only as the object of a verb or preposition: Good friends see *each other* regularly. We wrote to *one another* every day.

Regular verb. A verb that forms its past tense and past participle by adding *ed*: I *sweated,* I have *sweated.*

Relative adjective. A limiting adjective introducing a subordinate clause: The people *whose* neighborhood was destroyed are distraught.

Relative pronoun. A pronoun introducing a subordinate clause: The officer *who* hired you has retired. The present *that* you gave me has been lost.

Restrictive modifier. A modifier that limits or restricts a word or group of words: George *the Fifth,* the woman *who works with you.*

Sentence. A group of words normally containing a subject and predicate, expressing an assertion, question, command, wish, or exclamation.

Strong verb. See **Irregular verb**.

Subject. An element in a sentence performing the action indicated by an active verb, or an element in a sentence receiving the action of a passive verb: *Margie* hit her brother. *She* was severely castigated. Infinitives may also take subjects: Dad asked *her* to return on time.

Subjective case. The form of a pronoun showing that the pronoun is the subject of a verb: *I, she, he, it, we, they, who.* This case is also called the **nominative case**.

Subjunctive mood. The form of a verb used to express doubts, possibilities, desires, and conditions contrary to fact: We doubt that they *will ever be elected.* If he *were* still alive, there would be no election.

Subordinate clause. A sentence element consisting of a subject and predicate and functioning as a noun, adjective, or adverb: *That she was chosen* was a complete surprise. The woman *you hired* proved outstanding. We wondered *when we would hear good news.* A subordinate clause, also known as a **dependent clause**, cannot stand alone as a sentence.

Superlative. The highest degree of comparison when comparing three or more entities: my *worst* fear, the *newest* nation, the *smallest* mistake. See **Comparison**.

Tense. The characteristic of verb forms that shows differences in time of the action performed: I *ate,* I *eat,* I *will eat,* I *will have eaten,* etc.

Transitive verb. A verb that takes an object: She *sold* her house. My car *carries* five passengers. See **Copulative verb**.

Verb. A word or group of words used to express action or state of being of the subject: Alfred *read* quickly. Shirley *is* eager to please. We *are going* home. The employees *will have received* bonuses by Friday.

Verbal. A word derived from a verb, but functioning as a noun or modifier. See **Gerund**, **Infinitive**, and **Participle**.

Voice. The characteristic of verbs that differentiates between the subject as performer of the action of a verb (**active voice**) and the subject as receiver of the action of a verb (**passive voice**). Active voice: The lecturer *emphasized* her main points. Passive voice: The main points *were emphasized* by the lecturer.

Weak verb. See **Regular verb**.

– 2 –
Nouns

A noun is the name of a person, place, thing, quality, activity, concept or condition.

Person
> Modern political *leaders* must be skillful *communicators*.
> *Students* of logic study *Socrates*.

Place
> *Lima* is the capital of *Peru*.
> *Colombia* is noted for its marvelous coffee.

Thing
> *Dogs* perform an important function for the blind.
> Russians drink a great deal of *vodka*.

Quality
> A thing of *beauty* is a *joy* forever.
> The *integrity* of the novel was its *strength*.

Activity
> He made his fortune in *manufacturing*.
> One of the best books on *cooking* cannot be found in book-stores.

Concept or Condition
> The movie was credited with reducing adolescent *alcoholism*.
> *Christianity* is one of the great religions of the world.

NOUN FUNCTION

Nouns may perform many functions in a sentence: subject of a verb, direct object of a verb, object of a preposition, object of a verbal (gerund, infinitive, participle), indirect object of a verb, predicate complement, and modifier of another noun.

Subject of a Verb

Beauty is in the eyes of the beholder.

Modern *art* has many admirers.

Direct Object of a Verb

The cattle forced the *crowd* off the road.

Tobacco causes many *deaths*.

Object of a Preposition

I expect to sail my boat after *lunch*.

The attendant parked my car in the *shade*.

Object of a Verbal

Swimming the *lake* was more than he could manage. (Verbal *Swimming*, object of the verbal *lake*.)

All I want now is to see my *granddaughters* again. (Verbal *to see*, object of the verbal *granddaughters*.)

Having lost my *way*, I decided to wait for help. (Verbal *Having lost*, object of the verbal *way*.)

Indirect Object of a Verb

The judge gave her *assistant* a new assignment. (Verb *gave*, indirect object *assistant*.)

We showed the *students* the new textbooks. (Verb *showed*, indirect object *students*.)

Predicate Complement

He is the hottest *performer* in town. (Verb *is*, predicate complement *performer*.)

One problem facing the nation is *illiteracy*. (Verb *is*, predicate complement *illiteracy*.)

Modifier of Another Noun

The *peace* talks seem to be getting nowhere. (Noun *peace* modifies noun *talks*.)

Combative *hockey* teams seem intent on fighting instead of skating. (Noun *hockey* modifies noun *teams*.)

TYPES OF NOUNS

There are two types of nouns, proper nouns and common nouns. A proper noun is the name of a specific person, place, or thing. Capitalize all proper nouns. Capitalize a common noun only when you use it as the first word in sentence:

> *Audrey Hepburn* will long be remembered for her work on behalf of children.
>
> He was a *Democrat* when he first went to *Washington*.
>
> The *Statue of Liberty* holds out hope to the world.

A common noun is the name used for any unspecified member of a class of persons, places, qualities, or concepts:

> *Poets* struggle to gain *recognition*.
>
> Who does not admire *children* in inner *cities* who manage to get a decent *education*?
>
> That *building* is yet another *example* of poor urban *architecture*.
>
> Our principal *aim* was to nurture *democracy* in the *country*.

Collective Nouns

A collective noun may represent a group or class considered as a unit. In this case, treat the collective noun as singular:

> The *band* played uninspiringly. (The *band* as a unit.)
>
> The *jury* was unable to reach a verdict. (The *jury* as a unit.)
>
> The *couple* is without a home. (The *couple* as a unit.)

A collective noun may also represent a group or class of individuals considered as individuals. In this case, treat the collective noun as plural:

> The *audience* are leaving their seats. (The members of the *audience*, as individuals, *are leaving*.)
>
> The *couple* disagree on almost everything. (Both husband and wife, as individuals, *disagree*.)
>
> The *remainder* are going to be left behind. (The remaining members of a group, as individuals, *are going to be left behind*.)

Noun Clauses

A noun clause has a subject and verb and functions as a noun. Noun clauses are usually introduced by *that, which, who, whoever, whatever, why, when, where, how,* or *which.*

As subject:

> *That a daughter can speak so harshly to her mother* is difficult to believe. (Subject of *is.*)
> *Why you ask such questions* befuddles me. (Subject of *befuddles.*)

As object:

> We insist *that our government look after the needy.* (Object of *insist.*)
> They said *that they would change their ways.* (Object of *said.*)

As Predicate Complement

> She at last was *where she always wanted to be.* (Complement of *was.*)
> Life is *whatever you make it.* (Complement of *is.*)

As Object of a Preposition

> I finally acted on the matters to *which you referred.* (Object of *to.*)
> Someone else bought the chair on *which we bid.* (Object of *on.*)

– 3 –
Articles

Articles are considered modifiers of nouns and pronouns. Articles are either definite or indefinite.

Definite Article
The is the definite article. It is used to indicate a specific class of nouns or pronouns, or a specific member of a class of nouns or pronouns:

> *The* leopard is no longer found on our continent. (The *leopard* as distinct from other species.)
>
> She helped me with *the* work I had to complete by this morning. (Specific *work*.)

Omission of the Definite Article
Omit the definite article when you do not specify a particular amount or quantity of the noun:

> Editors assign overtime work as necessary. (An indefinite number of *editors* assign an indefinite amount of *overtime work*.)
>
> *The* editor assigned *the* work on that book without authorization. (A particular *editor*, a particular unit of *work*.)
>
> Sugar is our most important crop. (The amount of *sugar* has not been specified.)
>
> *The* sugar produced last year did not meet our needs. (The amount of sugar *produced last year*.)

19

Indefinite Article

A and *an* are the indefinite articles. They are used as modifiers to indicate an unspecified class or member of a class of nouns:

My daughter gave her department enough work for *a* week. (The *week* is unspecified: any week.)

The price of *a* good meal is rapidly escalating. (The *meal* is unspecified: any good meal.)

Choosing Between *a* and *an*

Use *a* before a word beginning with a consonant sound:

In his family, *a* wake was not the time for mourning. (Consonant sound *w*.)

She will surely become *a* useful citizen again when she is released from prison. (Consonant sound *y* as in *you*.)

Use *an* before a word beginning with a vowel sound;

She was *an* attractive woman. (Vowel sound *a*.)

He spoke for more than *an* hour. (Vowel sound *ow* in *hour*.)

– 4 –
Verbs

A verb is a word or words that describe the action or state of being of the subject of a sentence or clause. A verb makes a statement about its subject:

> Mrs. Jefferson *loves* her son.
> Football players *strive* for excellence.

Predicate

In a clause or sentence, the *predicate* is the verb plus its modifiers and objects or complements. When a verb has no modifiers, no objects, and no complements, the predicate is termed a *simple predicate*. Two verbs that have a single subject are termed a *compound predicate*.

> The car *stalled*. (Simple predicate.)
> The sun *shone brilliantly*. (Predicate consisting of a verb and its modifier.)
> He *read the book*. (Predicate consisting of a verb and its object.)
> They *are renegades*. (Predicate consisting of verb and its complement.)
> Emma *cooks* and *bakes*. (Compound predicate.)

21

Transitive and Intransitive Verbs

A transitive verb must have a direct object. An intransitive verb does not have a direct object. Some verbs function transitively and intransitively:

> We *devoured* dinner. (The verb *devoured* is transitive, since it has a direct object, *dinner*.)
>
> They *studied* for many hours. (The verb *studied* is intransitive, since it lacks a direct object.)
>
> The tree *grew* for many years even though concrete *covered* its roots. (The verb *grew* is intransitive, since it lacks a direct object. The verb *covered* is transitive, since it has a direct object, *roots*.)
>
> My neighbor *grows* azaleas. (The verb *grows* is transitive, since it has a direct object, *azaleas*.)

Linking Verbs

A linking, or copulative, verb does not take an object. Rather, such a verb joins a subject with its complement. The complement is either a predicate noun or a predicate adjective:

> Today I *am* a man. (The linking verb *am* links *I* with *man*, a predicate noun.)
>
> Now it *tastes* good. (The linking verb *tastes* links *it* with *good*, a predicate adjective.)

The most common linking verbs are *be, seem, appear, become, feel, taste, act, sound,* and *grow.* Some of these linking verbs, for example, *feel* and *taste*, may also be used transitively:

> I *felt* ill during dinner. (The linking verb *felt* links *I* with *ill*, a predicate adjective.)
>
> I *felt* the fabric. (The verb *felt* is transitive, with *fabric* as its direct object.)
>
> The cast *acted* depressed. (The linking verb *acted* links *cast* with *depressed*, a predicate adjective.)
>
> The cast *acted* the play professionally. (The verb *acted* is transitive, with *play* as its direct object.)

Auxiliary Verbs

Auxiliary verbs are used with other verbs to form the tenses, voices, and moods of those verbs. The most common auxiliary verbs are *be, do,* and *have.* Less common auxiliary verbs are *can, may, will, shall, must, ought, might, could, should,* and *would.*

Auxiliary verbs alter the meaning or time of the action of the verb:

> I *am going*, I *do go*, I *have gone*, I *ought to go*, I *might go*, I *could go*, I *should go*.
>
> I *may* go to the rally. (A possibility of action.)
>
> I *shall* go to the rally. (An intention to undertake a future action.)
>
> I *will* go the rally. (Firm intention to undertake a future action.)

Shall and Will

Use *shall* in the first person (*I, we*) in asking questions:

> *Shall I* leave lunch money for you?
>
> *Shall we* leave the party now?

Use *will* in the second and third persons (*you; he, she, it, they*) in asking questions:

> *Will you* join us at the reception?
>
> *Will he* have enough information for the report?
>
> *Will she* approve the report when it is in final form?
>
> *Will it* be the last house we look at?
>
> *Will they* be willing to fund your work?

Use *shall* in all persons for emphatic statements:

> *I shall* do no such thing.
>
> *We shall* not be moved!
>
> *You shall* not be allowed to run for office.
>
> *They shall* not pass!

Use *shall* in the first person to express future actions or expectations:

> *I shall* miss the first act because I have to work late.
>
> In all probability, *we shall* meet you at the gallery.

Use *will* in the second and third persons to express future actions or expectations:

> *They will* manage all right on their own.
>
> You *will* have dinner with us as usual, I expect.

Should and Would

Use *should* to express an obligation or condition:

> *I should* repaint the living room without charge. (Obligation.)
> *You should* pay more attention to your children. (Obligation.)
> *They should* leave the apartment in good order. (Obligation.)
> If *we should* cut them off without a penny, they may have to go on public assistance. (Condition.)
> If *you should* disregard all their requests, they will have to go elsewhere. (Condition.)
> If *they should* see no merit in the idea, our fellowships will be withdrawn. (Condition.)

Use *would* to express a wish or customary action:

> *Would* that *we* had spent more time with him. (Wish.)
> *Would* that *you* had spent your money more wisely. (Wish.)
> *Would* that *she* were still with us now. (Wish.)
> *We would* walk together each evening after work. (Customary action.)
> *You would* always remember to call on Father's Day. (Customary action.)
> *They would* turn down any invitation that did not include a full meal. (Customary action.)

Mood

Verbs make statements of fact and what is believed to be fact. They also express wishes, suppositions, doubts, command, and conditions contrary to fact. Mood is the characteristic of a verb that indicates to the reader which of these functions a writer intends.

The three moods in English are the indicative, subjunctive, and imperative. Use the indicative mood to make statements of fact or what is believed to be fact. Use the indicative also to ask questions:

> John Donne *was born* in London. (Indicative mood, used because the writer believes there is ample evidence for making this statement.)
> *Was* John Donne *born* in London? (Indicative mood, used to ask a question.)
> We *believe* our family doctor *is* the best in town. (Whether *we* are correct or not, the verb *is* shows that *we believe* it to be true. The verb *believe* is in the indicative mood because the writer is reporting fact.)

Is a priest present to administer the last rites? (The verb *is* is in the indicative mood because it asks a question.)

The subjunctive mood appears most often in formal writing and in the speech of educated people. The indicative mood almost always replaces the subjunctive mood in informal writing and everyday speech. The subjunctive mood appears in relatively few constructions. You will find it useful most often to express conditions contrary to fact and to express wishes, suppositions, and doubts:

If Babe Ruth *were batting* next, the pennant would be ours. (The conjunction *If* introduces a conditional statement. Since Babe Ruth is not alive, the condition is contrary to fact. The verb *were batting*, in the subjunctive mood, indicates that the condition is contrary to fact.)

I wish my parents *were* still alive. (A wish, because they are not alive.)

Suppose they *were* still alive, would they approve of the way we live our lives? (A supposition, so the verb *were* is in the subjunctive mood.)

If this *be* treason, make the most of it! (The speaker believes he is not guilty of treason, but there may be doubts in the minds of others. The subjunctive *be* expresses this doubt.)

Use the imperative to express a command or make an urgent demand:

Stay in your room!
Call 911!
Let them have their way!

Voice

Voice is the characteristic of a verb that tells the reader whether the subject of the verb is performing the action of the verb (*active voice*) or whether the subject of the verb is acted upon (*passive voice*).

The passive voice is identified by some form of the verb *be* and a past participle:

He *finds* his own way. (Present tense, active voice.)
At this time of day, he usually *is found* in the library. (Present tense, passive voice.)

He *found* the solution. (Past tense, active voice.)
A solution *was found*. (Past tense, passive voice.)
She *will find* a solution. (Future tense, active voice.)
A solution *will be found*. (Future tense, passive voice.)

Number

Verbs, like nouns and pronouns, may be singular or plural in number. In a sentence, the number of the subject determines the number of the verb:

I *try* my best. (The subject *I* is singular, so *try* is singular.)
We *try* our best. (The subject *We* is plural, so *try* is plural.)
She *tries* her best. The subject *She* is singular, so *tries* is singular.)

Make certain that the verbs you employ agree with their subjects:

The *importance* of healthy troops, ample ammunition, and fresh food supplies *was recognized* by the leadership. (Because the subject *importance* is singular, the verb *was recognized* is singular. Do not be confused by the long phrase appearing between the subject and verb.)

In many common constructions, the subject of a verb may follow the verb instead of preceding it. Nevertheless, remember that the subject determines whether the verb will be singular or plural:

There *were* several *women* ahead of me at the unemployment office. (The subject of *were* is *women*, plural, so the plural verb *were* is correct.)

There *is* little *sympathy* for the thousands of homeless people in our city. (The subject of *is* is *sympathy*, singular, so the singular verb *is* is correct.)

Beyond the slums *are* many fine *homes*. (The subject of *are* is *homes*, plural, so the plural verb *are* is correct.)

Beyond the slums *is* a well-maintained *playground*. (The subject of *is* is *playground*, singular, so the singular verb *is* is correct.)

Compound Subjects and Their Verbs

A compound subject consists of two or more nouns, pronouns, or noun phrases acting together as the subject of a verb: *George and I, ruffles and flourishes, health or sickness, pounds of rice or beans*.

Compound subjects connected by *and* usually take a plural verb. Compound subjects connected by *or* or *nor* usually take a singular verb:

> *George and I* are not going to be at the meeting. (The compound subject can be replaced, for example, by *Two of us*, so *George and I* is plural and requires a plural verb, *are going*.)
>
> *Frankfurters and beans* is a lunch that keeps me going until evening. (The compound subject *Frankfurters and beans* is a single dish, so it is treated as singular and requires a singular verb, *is*. Notice that in the subordinate clause *that keeps me going until evening*, the pronoun *that* is treated as a singular because it takes the number of its singular antecedent, *Frankfurters and beans*. Therefore, the singular verb *keeps* is correct.)

When compound subjects are connected by *or*, they are singular unless the parts of the compound subject are themselves plural:

> A *book or newspaper* sees me through the evening. (Both parts of the compound subject *book or newspaper* are singular, so the singular verb *sees* is correct.)
>
> *Fruits or candies* are welcome gifts. (Both parts of the compound subject *Fruits or candies* are plural, so the plural verb *are* is correct.)

Collective Nouns and Their Verbs

A collective noun takes a singular verb when the noun refers to a group as a unit. A collective noun takes a plural verb when the noun refers individually to the members of the group:

> A married *couple* is treated differently than people who are dating. (The collective noun *couple*, although it indicates two people, is considered a single unit in this sentence, so the singular verb *is treated* is correct.)
>
> The *couple* were living in our neighborhood at that time, and we saw much of them. (The collective noun *couple* is considered to be two individuals, so the plural verb *were living* is correct. The pronoun *them* at the end of the sentence emphasizes the plurality of *couple*. Consider how ridiculous the sentence would be if it ended with *we saw much of it*.)

When you use a collective noun, you must decide whether the meaning you intend requires a singular or plural verb.

Person

Person is the characteristic of verbs that indicates the speaker (*first person*), the person spoken to (*second person*), and the person spoken of (*third person*). Personal pronouns also have the characteristic of person:

> *I swim* every day in summer. (First person singular.)
> *We try* to do what's right. (First person plural.)
> *You smile* incessantly. (Second person singular or plural.)
> *He gives* to charity. (Third person singular.)
> *They give* to charity. (Third person plural.)

Tense

Tense is the characteristic of verbs that indicates the time of the action or state of being described. There are six tenses in English: *present, past perfect, past, present perfect, future*, and *future perfect*.

The *present tense* indicates present action, habitual action, simple future action true for all time. The *past perfect tense* indicates action completed before a previous past action. The *past tense* indicates action completed in the past. The *present perfect tense* indicates action begun in the past that continues in the present. The *future tense* indicates simple future action. The *future perfect tense* indicates action completed before a future action. The *progressive forms* of these tenses indicate ongoing action.

Consider the verb *call* in all its tenses and both voices:

> *Present active.* I call.
> *Present passive.* I am called.
> *Present progressive active.* I am calling.
> *Present progressive passive.* I am being called.
>
> *Past perfect active.* I had called.
> *Past perfect passive.* I had been called.
> *Past perfect progressive active.* I had been calling.
> (There is no past perfect progressive passive form.)
>
> *Past active.* I called.
> *Past passive.* I was called.
> *Past progressive active.* I was calling.
> *Past progressive passive.* I was being called.

Present perfect active. I have called.
Present perfect passive. I have been called.
Present perfect progressive active. I have been calling.
(There is no present perfect progressive passive form.)

Future active. I will call.
Future passive. I will be called.
Future progressive active. I will be calling.
(There is no future progressive passive form.)

Future perfect active. I will have called.
Future perfect passive. I will have been called.
Future perfect progressive active. I will have been calling.
(There is no future perfect progressive passive form.)

Agreement of Tenses

The time of the principal action or state of being described in a sentence is established by the tense of the verb in the main clause. Since subordinate clauses depend on the main clause, you must make certain that the verb tenses in subordinate clauses agree logically with the tense of the main verb:

Consider the following sentences:

Many children cry whenever they are hungry. (The main clause is *Many children cry*. The subordinate clause is *whenever they are hungry*. Since *cry* is present tense, indicating habitual action, *are* must also be present tense.)

She coughed because she smoked so much. (Past tense *coughed* in main clause, past tense *smoked* in subordinate clause.)

They cough because they smoke so much. (Present tense *cough* in main clause, present tense *smoke* in subordinate clause.)

They will have finished their dinner before we begin to eat our own. (Future perfect *will have finished* in main clause, present tense *begin* in subordinate clause. The present tense here indicates simple future action. The actions indicated in both clauses will begin in the future, but the future action of the main verb *will have finished* will have been completed before *begin*, the second future action, occurs. The verb in the subordinate clause can also be made future, *will begin*.)

Present Tense for Ideas True for All Time

The present tense is always used to express ideas that are thought to be true for all time:

Truth *is* stranger than fiction.
The earth *revolves* around the sun.

In subordinate clauses as well, the present tense is always used to express ideas that are true for all time:

He proved once again that truth *is* stranger than fiction. (Main clause verb *proved*, past tense.)
Who was the first to point out that the earth *revolves* around the sun? (Main clause verb *was*, past tense.)

– 5 –

Verbals

Verbals—infinitives, participles, and gerunds—are verb forms that can function as nouns, adjectives, and adverbs.

Infinitive

The infinitive is the form of a verb that is seen as a headword in a dictionary. In most uses it is usually preceded by *to*: *to beg, to ask, to play*. The infinitive often appears without *to*, especially after *can, do, may, must, shall,* and *will: can beg, can ask, can play.*

Infinitives have both tense and voice:

> *Present tense, active voice*: (to) beg, (to) be begging.
> *Present tense, passive voice*: (to) be called.
> *Perfect tense, active voice*: (to) have called, (to) have been calling.
> *Perfect tense, passive voice*: (to) have been called.

The infinitive functions as a noun, as an adjective, as an adverb, or as a complement.

Infinitive as Noun

> To marry is my fondest hope. (The infinitive *To marry* is the subject of the verb *is*.)
> They asked to see the car. (The infinitive *to see* is the object of the verb *asked*.)

31

Infinitive as Adjective

    Annie gave me ideas to consider. (The infinitive *to consider* modifies the noun *ideas*.)

    They have expressed the need to be saved. (The infinitive *to be saved* modifies the noun *need*.)

Infinitive as Adverb

    I am happy to wait. (The infinitive *to wait* modifies the adjective *happy*.)

    The patient is well enough to go home. (The infinitive *to go* modifies the adverb *enough*.)

Infinitive as Complement

    Corky's ambition is to be a writer. (The infinitive *to be* is the complement of the verb *is*.)

    Ambition is to be expected of young bankers. (The infinitive *to be expected* is the complement of the verb *is*.)

Infinitive Phrases

    In some instances, the infinitive itself has a subject, object or complement, and modifiers. This type of construction is called an *infinitive phrase*, and it may function as subject, object, complement, or modifier of another sentence element:

    To paint all six rooms in a week required four of us. (The infinitive phrase *To paint all six rooms in a week* is the subject of the verb *required*. Within the infinitive phrase, *rooms* is the object of *to paint*, and *all six* modifies *rooms*.)

    Hazel hoped to swim the lake. (The infinitive phrase *to swim the lake* is the object of the verb *hoped*.)

    Sam is to graduate next year. (The infinitive phrase *to graduate next year* is the complement of the linking verb *is*. Within the infinitive phrase, *next year* modifies *to graduate*, and *next* modifies *year*.)

    We have enough firewood to last the winter. (The infinitive phrase *to last the winter* modifies *enough*. Within the infinitive phrase, *winter* is the object of *to last*. *The* modifies *winter*.)

Participle

    Participles are verbal adjectives that have present and past tenses, for example, *calling, called; laughing, laughed*. They also have active and passive voices: present active *telling*, present passive *being told*; past active *having told*, past passive *told, having been told*.

Laughing at us, he threw us a penny. (The participle *Laughing* modifies *he*. It indicates the condition *he* is in when he performs the action of throwing. *Laughing* is modified by the prepositional phrase *at us*.)

My granddaughter left the room, crying happily and throwing kisses at us all. (The participles *crying* and *throwing* modify *granddaughter*. They describe the condition the granddaughter was in when she left the room. *Crying* is modified by *happily*. *Kisses* is the direct object of *throwing*. *At us all* modifies *throwing*.)

Having received my dismissal notice, I packed all my belongings and left the office. (The participle *Having received* modifies *I*.)

Sustained by his faith, he made his way through the difficult time. (The participle *Sustained* modifies *he*.)

Gerund

A gerund is the *ing* form of a verb used as a noun. A gerund may function as the subject or object of a verb and as the object of a preposition:

Swimming usually relieves tension. (The gerund *swimming* is the subject of the verb *relieves*.)

Harry still likes swimming. (The gerund *swimming* is the object of the verb *likes*.)

That boy is given to lying. (The gerund *lying* is the object of the preposition *to*.)

They use their roof for sunbathing. (The gerund *sunbathing* is the object of the preposition *for*.)

A gerund may also function as a complement, may be modified, and may take an object:

My favorite hobby is golfing. (The gerund *golfing* is the complement of *is*.)

Her latest interest is organic gardening. (The gerund *gardening* is modified by the adjective *organic*.)

Your future depends on working assiduously toward a realistic goal. (The gerund *working* is modified by the adverb *assiduously*.)

Conserving water in times of drought is a sensible practice. (The gerund *Conserving* has as its object the noun *water*.)

Verbals Used as Modifiers

Participles and infinitives are verbals that are used as modifiers. When you use participles or infinitives for this purpose, make certain that these elements are clearly identified with the words they modify:

> Driving for the green, the golfer scored his first birdie. (The participle *driving* modifies the noun *golfer*.)
>
> Having served the general for many years, the sergeant knew all his habits. (The participle *Having served* modifies the noun *sergeant*.)
>
> The teeming rain flooded our basement. (The participle teeming modifies *rain*.)
>
> The storekeeper telephones his wholesaler to order inventory. (The infinitive *to order* modifies the verb *telephones*, so *to order* functions as an adverb.)
>
> Mickey had an assignment to complete. (The infinitive *to complete* modifies the noun *assignment*, so *to complete* functions as an adjective.)

Dangling and Misplaced Modifiers

Modifiers not clearly identified with words they modify are called dangling modifiers or misplaced modifiers.

Dangling Participles

> Having eaten rich food many times before, there was no reason to become ill. (*Having eaten* is a participle that is part of the participial phrase *Having eaten rich food many times before*. The entire phrase acts as a modifier, but has nothing to modify in the main clause *there was no reason to become ill*. For this reason, the phrase is called a dangling modifier.)

You can repair the construction by supplying a noun, pronoun, or noun phrase for the participle to modify. Here are three corrected versions of the offending sentence:

> Having eaten rich food many times before, I had no reason to become ill.
>
> Since I had eaten rich food many times before, I had no reason to become ill.
>
> Since I had eaten rich food many times before, there was no reason for me to become ill.

Misplaced Modifiers

Even when modifiers have a noun, pronoun, or noun phrase to modify, the reader can be misled if the modified element is not clearly identifiable. Such a modifier is called a misplaced modifier. The construction must be corrected.

Consider the following sentence:

Swimming as fast as possible, I saw the boy ahead of me. (Who was swimming as fast as possible, *the boy* or *I?*)

Here are two ways to repair the faulty construction:

I saw the boy ahead of me, swimming as fast as possible. (Now we know *the boy* is swimming as fast as possible.)
I swam as fast as possible and finally saw the boy ahead of me.

Dangling Infinitives

What is true for participles applies as well to infinitives. Consider the following sentence:

To convey information understandably, the needs of the reader must be considered. (*To convey information* does not modify anything in the sentence.)

Here are two ways to correct the construction:

To convey information understandably, the writer must consider the needs of the reader.
A writer who wishes to convey information understandably must consider the needs of the reader.

AUXILIARY VERBS AND INFINITIVES IN COMPOUND CONSTRUCTIONS

Auxiliary Verbs

When different tenses are used within a compound construction, the auxiliary verbs must usually be supplied in full. When the same tense is used throughout a compound construction, repetition of the auxiliary verbs is not usually necessary. Consider the following sentences:

Basketball has become and probably will always be the favorite sport of Americans. (The first part of the compound verb, *has become*, is in the perfect tense. The second part is in the future tense, *will be*. Because the two tenses used are different, the auxiliary verbs *has* and *will* must be supplied.)

All players will be eligible for league play if they *have studied* and *practiced* consistently. (The auxiliary *have* is not needed before *practiced*, because *have studied* and [*have*] *practiced* are both in the perfect tense.)

Infinitives

In compound constructions employing infinitives, *to* can be used before each infinitive in order to emphasize the parallel structure:

He was asked *to submit* his application and *to report* for a physical examination.

The second *to* can be omitted if the emphasis is not desirable:

He was asked *to submit* his application and *report* for a physical examination.

In a series employing infinitives, the first infinitive is always preceded by *to*. If the second infinitive is also preceded by *to*, then all the rest must be preceded by *to*. In most series, however, the initial *to* is usually sufficient. Consider the following sentences:

He was asked *to submit* his application, *report* for a physical examination, and *present* suitable references from his previous employers.

He was asked *to submit* his application, *to report* for a physical examination, and *to present* references from his previous employers.

PARALLEL STRUCTURE AND VERB FORMS

Parallel grammatical constructions are used to express parallel ideas. This means that compound constructions must contain grammatically identical forms. This requirement is especially important for verbs and verbals. It is easy to recognize a compound construction by the presence of a coordinating conjunction: *and, but, or, nor*.

Be sure to preserve parallel structure when using two or more verbs or verbals:

I often *swim, fish,* and *hunt.* (The three verbs are in identical form, present indicative.)

I like *swimming, fishing,* and *hunting.* (Three gerunds.)

I like to *swim, fish,* and *hunt.* (Three infinitives.)

Paradoxically, the helicopter has been used *to save* lives and *to kill* the innocent. (Two infinitives.)

The coach stressed two ideas: *play* hard and *win.* (Two imperatives, second person: *play* and *win.*)

The coach stressed two ideas: *playing* hard and *winning.* (Two participles modifying *ideas.*)

– 6 –

Pronouns

A pronoun is a word or words used in place of a noun, a noun and its modifiers, or another pronoun. The element replaced is called the *antecedent* of the pronoun.

Consider the following sentences:

Secrecy characterizes every action of the leading political parties. *It* is accepted unquestioningly by the voters. (The pronoun *It* substitutes for the noun *Secrecy* of the first sentence. *Secrecy* is the antecedent of the pronoun *It*.)

He worked so well that his boss promoted *him*. (The pronoun *him* has the pronoun *He* as its antecedent.)

The voters of the community refused to approve the bond issue. *They* vowed to vote no additional funds. (The pronoun *They* substitutes for the noun *voters* and its modifier *of the community*. The antecedent of *They* is *The voters of the community*.)

Sally baked bread so well that *she* rapidly built a thriving business. (The antecedent of the pronoun *she* is *Sally*.)

TYPES OF PRONOUNS

There are nine principal types of pronouns:

Personal pronouns: *I, you, he, she, we, they, one*
Impersonal pronouns: *it, they*
Relative pronouns: *who, which, that, whoever, whichever*
Demonstrative pronouns: *this, that, these, those*
Interrogative pronouns: *who, which, what, whoever, whatever*
Reflexive pronouns: *myself, yourself, himself, herself, itself, ourselves, yourselves, themselves*
Intensive pronouns: *myself, yourself, himself, herself, itself, ourselves, yourselves, themselves*
Reciprocal pronouns: *each other, one another*
Indefinite pronouns: *each, either, any, anyone, some, someone, all*

Personal and Impersonal Pronouns

Personal pronouns refer to people. Impersonal pronouns refer to everyone and everything but people. Both these types of pronouns can be singular or plural. They can also be in the subjective, possessive, or objective case. Personal pronouns also indicate gender.

The following table summarizes personal and impersonal pronouns in number, case, and gender:

	Subjective	Possessive	Objective
First person			
Singular	I	mine	me
Plural	we	ours	us
Second person			
Singular	you	yours	you
Plural	you	yours	you
Third person			
Singular			
Masculine	he	his	him
Feminine	she	hers	her
Neuter	it	its	it
Any gender	one	one's	one
Plural			
All genders	they	theirs	them

The following sentences illustrate the uses of personal and impersonal pronouns in each of the three cases:

Subjective Case

I (We, You, They) enjoy television.
He (She, It, One) can do no better.

Possessive Case

The problem was *mine (ours, yours, hers, his, theirs)*.
Mine (Ours, Yours, His, Hers, Theirs) was the only work selected for a second reading.

Objective Case

The leader recommended *me (us, him, her, one, it, them)*.

Relative Pronouns

Relative pronouns—*who, which, that*—refer to people and objects. *Who* refers to people; *that* to people or objects; *which* to animals, objects, or collective nouns.

Who, that, and *which* are used in the three cases:

Subjective	Possessive	Objective
who	whose	whom
that	of that	that
which	of which, those	that

The following sentences illustrate the uses of *who, that,* and *which* in all their cases:

Subjective Case

A person *who* wants to succeed in life must work hard.
The horse *that* came in first was overlooked by most bettors.
Which of the signatures were forged?

Possessive Case

Whose was never found?
I would like more *of that*.
The discussion *of which* you disapprove will continue.
Any problem *whose* solution is difficult will be eliminated.

Objective Case

The artists to *whom* you wish to award prizes are not present.
Whom did you select?
You must agree to *that.*
The newspapers *of which* he disapproves have enormous
readership.

Whoever, whomever, whichever, and *whatever* are also classified
as relative pronouns:

Whoever thought that Chelsea would attend a private school?
Whomever you nominate will surely be turned down.
They had three choices: *whichever* they decide on will surely
be wrong.
Whatever people do in anger will prove to be mistaken.

Demonstrative Pronouns

Demonstrative pronoun—*this, that, these, those*—replace nouns
and function in the same manner as nouns. Demonstrative pronouns
do not have gender, but they do have case:

Subjunctive	Possessive	Objective
this	of this	this
that	of that	that
these	of these	these
those	of those	those

The following sentences illustrate the uses of the demonstrative
pronouns in all their cases:

Subjective Case

This is more than I can eat.
That will be enough.
These can be found in the reference section.
Those can be found in the stacks.

Possessive Case

The principal drawbacks of *this* are high cost, shoddy work-
manship, and weak consumer interest.
Of that I will say no more.
Of these, a great number will be found useful.
Of those, few will be found acceptable.

Objective Case

We agree to give *this* speedy consideration.
They decided against *that* a long time ago.
Despite our complaints, the censors dropped *those*.
Read *those* and tell me which ones you like.

Other common demonstrative pronouns are *former, latter, other, such,* and the ordinal numbers: *first, second, third,* etc.

The following sentences illustrate the uses of these demonstrative pronouns:

The *former* was the one I chose, not the *latter*.
Such is not the case, despite all our hopes.
Now fix the *other*.
The *first* was not my choice. I favored the *third*.

Interrogative Pronouns

Interrogative pronouns are used in asking questions. The principal interrogative pronouns are *who, which,* and *what. Whoever* and *whatever* are less common.

Who is used for people. *Which* and *that* are used for things. These pronouns do not have gender:

Subjective	Possessive	Objective
who	whose	whom
which	of which	which
what	of what	what

The following sentences illustrate the uses of interrogative pronouns in all their cases:

Subjective Case

Who ate the turkey dressing?
Which will not be needed?
What is the matter with me?

Possessive Case

Whose do you prefer?
Which can be discarded?
What do you do first after arising?

Objective Case

Whom do you like best?
Which did you like best?
What do you think?

Reflexive Pronouns

Reflexive pronouns are used in sentences containing verbs whose actions are directed toward the subjects of the verbs. These pronouns are formed by adding *-self* or *-selves* to the personal pronouns *my, your, him, her, one, our, them,* and the impersonal pronoun *it.*

The following sentences illustrate the uses of reflexive pronouns:

I cut *myself* while shaving this morning.
You are hurting *yourself* by acting selfishly toward others.
He supported *himself* by teaching music theory.
Sarah discovered *herself* during the retreat.
If one could only know what was exactly right for *oneself.*
We neglect *ourselves* when we neglect others.
Ask *yourselves* what your true intentions are.
They convinced *themselves* that their plan was infallible.
The bull elephant found *itself* in quicksand.

Intensive Pronouns

Intensive pronouns are used as appositives to strengthen the subject of a verb. Intensive pronouns have the same forms as reflexive pronouns: *myself, yourself, himself, herself, oneself, itself, ourselves, yourselves,* and *themselves.*

The following sentences illustrate the uses of the intensive pronouns:

I *myself* see nothing advantageous in their ideas.
I see nothing advantageous in their ideas *myself.*
Your *yourself* will have the major burden.
You will have the major burden *yourself.*
Alfred *himself* was at fault.
Alfred was at fault *himself.*
Erica *herself* found little of interest in the proposal.
Erica found little of interest in the proposal *herself.*
What can one *oneself* do?
What can one do *oneself*?
The report *itself* offers little.

The report offers little *itself*.
We *ourselves* are eager to go along with the suggestion.
We are eager to go along with the suggestion *ourselves*.
You *yourselves* will be held fully responsible.
You will be held fully responsible *yourselves*.
Americans *themselves* are abusing their civil rights.
Americans are abusing their civil rights *themselves*.

Reciprocal Pronouns

The reciprocal pronouns are *one another* and *each other*. Both are used when writing of two people. *One another* is generally used when writing of more than two people. Both reciprocal pronouns have possessive and objective cases.

The following sentences illustrate uses of these pronouns:

Tom and Jerry found *one another's* company satisfying.
All the musicians habitually sought *one another's* advice.
Ethel and her husband perceived themselves as loving *each other*.
Ethel and her children caught themselves shouting at *one another*.
Neighbors on both sides of the street stopped speaking to *one another*.

Indefinite Pronouns

Indefinite pronouns constitute a large number of imprecise words that can function as pronouns. The most frequently used are *all, another, any, anybody, anyone, anything, both, each one, either, everybody, everything, few, little, many, more, much, neither, nobody, none, no one, nothing, oneself, other, others, several, some, somebody, someone, something,* and *such.*

The following sentences illustrate some uses of indefinite pronouns:

All I can do is accept the jury's verdict.
All are recycled after use.
This dress fits *anybody* who weighs two hundred pounds or more.
Each is discarded after use.
He paid me *nothing* for the paint job.
If *others* cared as much you, the situation would be resolved.
Someone must be held responsible for the mistake.

I gave the child *something* to keep her happy.
The crowd was *such* that the riot squad was called out.

Pronoun Agreement

Pronouns must agree in number with their antecedents.

A pronoun is singular when its antecedent is singular, plural when its antecedent is plural:

> Any *woman who* is friendly with her neighbors will be well re-garded. (The pronoun *who* is singular because its antecedent, *woman*, is singular.)
>
> The interesting thing about *John* is that *he* always finishes telling a joke whether or not *he* has an appreciative audience. (The pronouns *he* and *he* are singular because their common antecedent, *John*, is singular.)
>
> All three *judges* stated that *they* believed the convict had been accused unjustly. (The pronoun *they* is plural because its antecedent, *judges*, is plural.)

A pronoun is plural when its antecedent consists of two or more words joined by *and*:

> *Tim and Frank* are completing graduate degrees *they* hope will enable *them* to teach.
>
> *Boys and girls* are finding *themselves* disenchanted with *their* school routine.

A pronoun is singular when its antecedent consists of two or more singular words joined by *or* or *nor*:

> I doubt whether *Bridget* or *Ann* made *herself* clear in the debate.
>
> Neither *Jimmy Carter* nor *Ronald Reagan* has received *his* final historical appraisal.

When a singular antecedent and a plural antecedent are joined by *or* or *nor*, the pronoun agrees in number with the antecedent that is closer. Few sentences can be found in which the plural antecedent is placed before the singular antecedent:

> Either *Jane or* her *brothers* will have to do what *they* can to support the family. (The two antecedents are joined by *or*. Because the plural antecedent *brothers* is closer to the pronoun that follows, *they* is plural.)

Neither *Jeffrey* nor his *brothers* found *themselves* completely satisfied.

Collective Nouns and Their Pronouns
If an antecedent is a collective noun that is treated as singular, the associated pronoun must be singular:

The *board of directors is* meeting next week to reach a decision *it* can live with. (The antecedent *board of directors* is treated as singular, as is shown by the use of the singular verb *is*, so the singular pronoun *it* is correct.)

If an antecedent is a collective noun that is treated as plural, the associated pronoun must be plural:

The *board of directors are* deliberating at this very moment and so far have not identified the chairperson *they* have chosen. (The antecedent *board of directors* is treated as plural, as is shown by the use of the plural verb *are deliberating*, so the plural pronoun *they* is correct.)

Be sure you treat collective nouns consistently in a single piece of your writing. Once you have established in a paper that a particular collective noun is singular, make certain it is singular throughout. Once you have established it as plural in a paper, make it plural throughout.

Singular Pronouns as Antecedents
A singular pronoun is used when the antecedent of the pronoun is any one of the following pronouns: *one, anyone, anybody, someone, somebody, everyone, everybody, each, either, neither, no one,* and *nobody*:

Everyone who thinks *he* or *she* can write professionally needs a literary agent. (*Everyone* is the antecedent of *he* or *she*.)
Each of the actresses recited the lines *she* knew best. (*Each* is the antecedent of *she*.)

– 7 –

Adjectives

Adjectives have two functions: They modify nouns and pronouns, and they may also be used to complete linking, or copulative, verbs:

A *happy person* faces each new day optimistically. (The adjective *happy* modifies the noun *person*.)

The *last one* to finish the race will receive a consolation prize. (The adjective *last* modifies the pronoun *one*.)

Ruth is content after she finishes a good meal and a full bottle of milk. (The adjective *content* completes the linking verb *is*. Such an adjective is called a predicate adjective.)

TYPES OF ADJECTIVES

There are three principal types of adjectives: *descriptive, limiting*, and *proper*. Descriptive adjectives name a quality or condition of the element modified: an *unhappy* marriage, a *blue* dress, a *capable* attorney, a *broken* axle. Limiting adjectives identify or enumerate the element modified: *our* table, *present* company, *most* people, *his* fiancee, *eight* days, *second* stanza. Proper adjectives are descriptive adjectives that derive from proper names: *Shinto* customs, *California* wine, *Chinese* checkers, *North American* rivers.

Adjectives that are used to complete linking, or copulative, verbs are called *predicate adjectives*. Common linking verbs include *act, be, become, feel, prove,* and *seem.* Linking verbs can also be completed by *predicate nouns.*

Together, predicate adjectives and predicate nouns are called *predicate complements.* Both types of predicate complements are illustrated in the following sentences:

Many people *act sick* on Monday mornings. (The linking verb *act* has the predicate complement *sick.* Since *sick* is an adjective, it is classified as a predicate adjective.)

She *is a radiologist.* (Because *radiologist* is a noun, it is classified as a predicate noun.)

They *seem content.* (Because *content* is an adjective, it is classified as a predicate adjective.)

Position of Adjectives

Except for predicate adjectives, adjectives are usually placed next to the nouns or pronouns they modify, and the most common position of all is immediately before the element modified:

red herring, *superior* children, *senior* citizens (descriptive adjectives)

that book, *many* novels, *twenty-four* weeks (limiting adjectives)

Spanish grammar, *German* cooking, *Greek* wine (proper adjectives)

In some constructions adjectives may also be placed immediately after the element modified:

The President delivered a speech *brief* and *eloquent.* (The writer has chosen this construction to achieve a desired rhythm.)

The actress delivered a monologue so *personal* that all who heard it were deeply affected. (Because the adjective *personal* is itself modified by the clause that follows, the normal position has been discarded.)

attorney *general,* court-*martial* (These terms were expressed in this order in French and are accepted as English expressions.)

Except in rare constructions, predicate adjectives follow the linking verbs they complete:

They looked *doubtful.*

He seemed *irrational*.
My teacher feels *hopeless*.
Happy was she. *Innocent* was the Child. (Such inverted constructions are reserved for special stylistic effect.)

Comparison of Adjectives

Adjectives have three comparative forms—*absolute, comparative,* and *superlative*—to indicate greater or lesser degrees of the quality described:

Absolute	Comparative	Superlative
fat	fatter	fattest
fine	finer	finest
beautiful	more beautiful	most beautiful
intelligent	more intelligent	most intelligent

The comparative form of most adjectives can be achieved in two ways: by adding *er* to the absolute form or by adding the adverb *more*.

The superlative form of most adjectives can be achieved in two ways: by adding *est* to the absolute form or by adding the adverb *most*.

Some adjectives change forms radically to express comparison: *good, better, best; bad, worse, worst.*

Use the comparative form when discussing two items or individuals, the superlative when discussing three or more:

Of the two brothers, Fred is the *more personable*.
Of all his novels, the first was by far the *most successful*.
Hazel is a *better* swimmer than her brother.
She is the *best* writer I know.

Use the comparative form when comparing a single item or individual with a class of items or individuals:

Anne was a *better* student than any of the men in her class.
Our town library has a *poorer* selection of fiction than any of the libraries in your town.

Adjective Phrases

An adjective phrase is a phrase used to modify a noun or pronoun. Adjective phrases are formed by combining a preposition with a noun or pronoun plus the modifiers of the noun or pronoun:

The sofa *in the dressing room* needs repairs. (The adjective phrase *in the dressing room* modifies the noun *sofa*. The preposition *in* has *room* as its object. The noun *room* is modified by *the dressing*.)

Anyone *in the room* can be elected. (The adjective phrase *in the room* modifies the pronoun *Anyone*.)

To ensure clarity, place adjective phrases close to the word or words that the phrases modify. In most constructions, this means placing the adjective phrases immediately after the element modified.

Adjective Clauses

An adjective clause is a clause used to modify a noun or pronoun. Like all clauses, adjective clauses consist of subject, verb, modifiers, and object when appropriate:

Every alteration *that is made between tonight and opening night* may create problems for the actors. (The adjective clause *that is made between tonight and opening night* modifies the noun *alteration*.)

Anyone *who refuses early retirement* may live to regret the decision. (The adjective clause *who refuses early retirement* modifies the pronoun *Anyone*.)

The two examples of adjective clauses just given are introduced by relative pronouns, *that* and *who*. Many times, adjective clauses are not introduced by relative pronouns:

The partner *with whom I wrote many books* died a few years ago. (The adjective clause modifies the noun *partner*.)

Murals *she worked on in her youth* established her reputation as a first-class artist. (The adjective clause *she worked on in her youth* modifies the noun *Murals*.)

To ensure clarity, keep adjective clauses close to the word or words they modify. Adjective clauses usually are placed immediately after the words they modify.

Restrictive and Nonrestrictive Adjective Clauses

Adjective clauses are either restrictive or nonrestrictive. A restrictive adjective clause is a clause that is essential in defining or limiting a noun or pronoun:

Students *I admire most* are those who know where they are going and never let up in their pursuit of their lifetime goals.
(The adjective clause *I admire most* limits the general noun
students to one particular group of students. Without the
adjective clause, the sentence would not have the intended
meaning.)

A nonrestrictive adjective clause is a clause that defines or limits
a noun or pronoun but is not essential in giving the sentence its intended meaning. Nonrestrictive modifiers give useful, but not essential information:

This one, *which I have carefully tended all summer*, has proven
disappointing. (The pronoun *one* is modified by the adjective clause *which I have carefully tended all summer*, but
this clause does not identify *one* in a way that makes *one*
distinctive. The modifier *This* has already made *one* distinctive. Thus, the sentence *This one has proven disappointing*,
without the adjective clause, conveys all the essential meaning, making *which I have carefully tended all summer* a
nonrestrictive clause.)

Nonrestrictive modifiers are set off by punctuation, while restrictive modifiers are not set off. Consider the following sentences:

The word processor *I bought* meets all my expectations. (The
restrictive modifier *I bought* is not set off by commas, indicating that it cannot be omitted from the sentence without
changing its meaning in a critical way. *I bought* is needed to
identify the word processor being discussed.)
My word processor, *which cost $2000 at the time I bought it*,
now sells for less than $1000. (The nonrestrictive modify-
ing clause *which cost $2000 at the time I bought it* is set off
by commas, indicating that it can be omitted without damaging the essential meaning of the sentence, *My word processor now sells for less than $1000*.)

That and *Which* with Adjective Clauses
It is best practice to use the relative pronoun *that* to introduce
restrictive adjective clauses, *which* to introduce nonrestrictive adjective clauses.

If you have trouble differentiating restrictive adjective clauses
from nonrestrictive adjective clauses, here is a good tip: When the

relative pronoun can be omitted before an adjective clause, the clause is restrictive. When the relative pronoun cannot be omitted before an adjective clause, the clause is nonrestrictive.

Consider the following sentences:

> The purse *that I bought yesterday* has been stolen. (The adjective clause *that I bought yesterday* is restrictive, since it cannot be omitted without making *purse* unidentifiable. As a restrictive clause, it is introduced by *that*, and commas are not used to set it off. Because the clause is restrictive, *that* can be omitted: The purse *I bought yesterday* has been stolen.)
> I have mislaid my brown purse, *which my mother gave me*. The adjective clause *which my mother gave me* is nonrestrictive, since *my brown* has already identified *purse*. For this reason the clause is introduced by *which* and set off by commas. The relative pronoun *which* cannot be omitted. Read the sentence without *which* and you will see that it cannot be omitted.)

Nouns Used as Adjectives

Nouns often function as adjectives: the *Reagan* years, the *Clinton* White House, the *clothing* store, the *toy* store, *college* life, *street* smarts:

> Give me the *bachelor* life.
> *Book* learning counts for little in some circles.

Adjectives Used as Nouns

Just as nouns may function as adjectives, many adjectives may function as nouns: the *high* and *mighty*, *The Naked and the Dead*, the *rich*, the *privileged*, the *destitute*, the *homeless*:

> The race is not always to the *swift*.
> The *lame* and the *halt* were received warmly.

Participles Used as Adjectives

Present and past participles are often used as adjectives: *growing* disillusionment, *leaning* tower; *used* cars, *tired* phrases:

> *Watching* closely, he was able to see everything that happened. (The present participle *Watching* modifies the pronoun *he* and is itself modified by the adverb *closely*.)

A turkey *roasting* slowly gives off marvelous aromas. (The present participle *roasting* modifies the noun *turkey* and is itself modified by the adverb *slowly*.)

Audrey Hepburn, fondly *remembered* by thousands of us, will be sorely missed. (The past participle *remembered* modifies *Audrey Hepburn* and is itself modified by the adverb *fondly* and by the phrase *by thousands of us*.)

Participles used as adjectives may also take an object:

Watching her closely, he quickly learned the secret of her tennis serve. (The present participle *Watching* modifies the pronoun *he* and has as its object the pronoun *her. Watching* is itself modified by the adverb *closely*.)

Poirot, carefully *pursuing* every clue, finally decided that the chief suspect was innocent of the crime. (The present participle *pursuing* modifies *Poirot* and has as its object the noun *clue*. The participle is itself modified by the adverb *carefully*.)

Dangling Participles

When you use a participle as an adjective, you must make certain that the reader can easily identify the noun or pronoun that the participle modifies. When your construction makes the reader uncertain of what is being modified, the mistake is called a dangling participle:

Consider the following sentences:

While watching closely, my purse was stolen. (A dangling participle: Obviously, *my purse* was not *watching* anything. Who was *watching*? *I* was watching. But *I* is not in the sentence.)

While I was watching closely, my purse was stolen. (Correct.)

Cooked rare, I could not chew my steak. (A dangling participle: Obviously, *I* was not *cooked rare*. The *steak* was. But *rare* is too far from *steak*.)

I could not chew the steak, because it was cooked rare. (Correct.)

Infinitives as Adjectives

Infinitives and infinitive phrases often function as adjectives. Infinitive phrases consist of infinitives together with their modifiers and objects or complements.

Consider the following sentences:

The way *to win* has not yet been made clear. (The infinitive *to win* modifies the noun *way*.)

Sabrina's determination *to succeed* overpowered her. (The infinitive *to succeed* modifies the noun *determination*.)

Alice has the most *to lose* by joining the strike. (The infinitive *to lose* modifies the noun *most*.)

The President sent elements of our forces into action *to provide food for the starving Somalians*. (The infinitive phrase *to provide food for the starving Somalians* modifies *action*.)

For his birthday, he was given a knife *to use in shucking oysters*. (The infinitive phrase *to use in shucking oysters* modifies *knife*.)

Many computer stores sell software *to meet every need of computer buffs*. (The infinitive phrase *to meet every need of computer buffs* modifies *software*.)

– 8 –
Adverbs

Adverbs modify verbs, adjectives, and other adverbs:

> She agreed *readily*. (The adverb *readily* modifies the verb *agreed*.)
>
> He spoke *disagreeably*. (The adverb *disagreeably* modifies the verb *spoke*.)
>
> My mother was *really* happy. (The adverb *really* modifies the adjective *happy*.)
>
> My daughter is *completely* fearless. (The adverb *completely* modifies the adjective *fearless*.)
>
> Alfred cares for his orchard *very* well. (The adverb *very* modifies the adverb *well*.)
>
> Her grandchildren are *almost* always hungry. (The adverb *almost* modifies the adverb *always*. The adverb *always* modifies the adjective *hungry*.)

Adverbs may also modify entire clauses:

> *Obviously* he is wrong, but I will hear him out. (The adverb *Obviously* modifies the clause *he is wrong*.)
>
> *Surely* the plane will be late, but I will not count on it. (The adverb *Surely* modifies the clause *the plane will be late*.)

Adverbs may also modify all the rest of a sentence:

Perhaps you are the only person in the class who knows the answer to my question.

Certainly she will find that other attorneys in her department have also been harassed.

Recognizing Adverbs

The adverbs easiest to recognize are those that end in *-ly*. The only pitfall to avoid is confusing adverbs that end in *-ly* with adjectives that end in *-ly*.

Remember that adjectives modify nouns and pronouns and that adverbs modify everything else. Thus, when you wish to determine whether you are dealing with an adverb or an adjective, identify the element modified. If it is a noun or pronoun, the modifier is an adjective. If the element modified is any other part of speech, the modifier is an adverb. (This subject is dealt with further in the next two sections.)

The modifiers in the following sentences are adverbs:

She stared *hatefully.* (The adverb *hatefully* modifies the verb *stared.*)

He will be *supremely* happy when the verdict is announced. (The adverb *supremely* modifies the adjective *happy.*)

Eventually they will reach an agreement, but I do not know when. (The adverb *Eventually* modifies the clause *they will reach an agreement.*)

It is important to keep in mind that there are adjectives that end in *-ly*, for example, *comely, costly, early, lively, lovely,* and *surly.* Consider how these adjectives are used in the following sentences:

My father described her as a *comely* lass. (The adjective *comely* modifies the noun *lass.*)

Above all, *costly* purchases should be avoided when you are unemployed. (The adjective *costly* modifies the noun *purchases.*)

The *early* bird does not always catch the worm. (The adjective *early* modifies the noun *bird.*)

Our chorus specializes in *lively* songs. (The adjective *lively* modifies the noun *songs.*)

My sister was a *lovely* woman. (The adjective *lovely* modifies the noun *woman.*)

A *surly* bartender will not last long in my establishment. (The adjective *surly* modifies the noun *bartender*.)

Recognizing Adverbs by Their Functions

Always remember that adverbs may answer the following questions: *how? how much? when? where? why? true or false?* This means that you may classify adverbs as adverbs of manner, degree, time, place, cause or purpose, or assertion.

Adverbs of manner answer the question *how?*

They study *carefully*.
Dick cooks *well*.

Adverbs of degree answer the question *how much?*

You must be *adequately* prepared for college.
Our finances were *completely* exhausted.

Adverbs of time answer the question *when?*

We will arrive *late*.
I have not sung *recently*.

Adverbs of place answer the question *where?*

I cannot run *upstairs*.
They went *north* for the summer.

Adverbs of cause or purpose answer the question *why?*

I will *therefore* refuse my party's nomination.
She will *consequently* be denied promotion.

Adverbs of assertion answer the question *true or false?*

He will *certainly* be hired.
He will *surely* grant parole to the convict.

Differentiating Adverbs from Adjectives

Many English words function both as adjectives and adverbs. As has already been said, the surest way for you to tell whether a word is an adjective or an adverb is to examine the sentence in which it appears and determine what the function of the word is. For this, you must go back to the fundamental distinction between an adjective and an adverb: Adjectives modify nouns and pronouns; adverbs modify everything else.

The following list presents some of the words that are used both as adjectives and adverbs:

bad	early	hard	much	slow
better	enough	high	near	smooth
bright	even	late	quick	straight
cheap	fair	little	right	tight
close	far	loose	rough	well
deep	fast	loud	second	worse
doubtless	first	low	sharp	wrong

Many of these words also have forms ending in *-ly,* among them: *badly, brightly, cheaply, deeply,* and others. Some people prefer the *-ly* forms in formal writing, and the *-ly* forms in many instances are used exclusively in certain idiomatic constructions:

The bullet hit *close to the mark.*
Watch them *closely.*
The team plays *hard* all the time.
The violinist could *hardly* flex his fingers.

In both these pairs of sentences, the modifiers *close, closely, hard,* and *hardly* perform adverbial functions. *Close* modifies the verb *hit; closely* modifies the verb *watch. Hard* modifies the verb *plays; hardly* modifies the verb *flex.* Thus, they are all adverbs.

By way of contrast, consider how *close* and *hard* function as adjectives in the following sentences:

The work is so *close* that it strains my eyes.
I think *hard* times are still ahead of us.

Closely and *hardly* are never used as adjectives but, as shown in the previous examples, *close* functions as the complement of the linking verb *is,* and *hard* modifies the noun *times.* Thus, they are both adjectives.

Comparison of Adverbs

Like adjectives, adverbs have three comparative forms—*absolute, comparative,* and *superlative*—to indicate greater or lesser degrees of the characteristics described.

Adverbs that are identical with adjectives form their comparatives and superlatives in the same manner, for example, *bad, worse, worst; well, better, best,* etc. Even when the absolute form of an adverb ends in *-ly,* the comparative and superlative are identical with the corresponding forms of the adjective: *badly, worse, worst.*

Adverbs also add *er* and *est* to the absolute form to make their comparatives and superlatives:

> *sad, sadder, saddest*
> *sadly, sadder, saddest*

Adverbs also employ *more* and *most* before the absolute form to make comparatives and superlatives. *More* and *most* are commonly used with adverbs of more than one syllable:

> *privately, more privately, most privately*
> *happily, more happily, most happily*

When you are not certain of how to construct a comparative or superlative form of an adverb, consult your dictionary.

Nouns and Phrases Used as Adverbs

Nouns and phrases are often used as adverbs, particularly to indicate time and degree:

> They stayed home *evenings*. (The verb *stayed* is modified by the noun *evenings*.)
> The President jogged *three miles*. (The verb *jogged* is modified by the noun phrase *three miles*.)
> She swam *three hundred meters*. (The verb *swam* is modified by the noun phrase *three hundred meters*.)
> He swam *two miles* farther than any other swimmer. (The adverb *farther* is modified by the noun phrase *two miles*.)
> The dress is not worth *a thousand dollars*. (The adjective *worth* is modified by the noun phrase *a thousand dollars*.)

Adverbial Clauses

Adverbial clauses modify verbs, adverbs, and adjectives, but they most often modify other clauses. Adverbial clauses are best classified according to the type of modification they provide: *cause, comparison, concession, condition, manner, place, purpose, result,* and *time*:

Cause—introduced by *as, because,* or *since*:

As there was no other way to accomplish her purpose, she finally decided to mount a full-scale attack. (The adverbial clause answers the question *why*? The adverbial clause modifies the entire main clause.)

They left *because the party was so dull*. (The adverbial clause answers the question *why*? The adverbial clause modifies the verb *left*.)

Comparison—introduced by *as* and *than*:

Nuclear energy has proven as expensive *as fossil fuel*. (The verb *is* is understood in the adverbial clause *as fossil fuel [is]*. The adverbial clause modifies the adjective *expensive*.)

That house costs more *than we had expected to pay*. (The adverbial clause modifies the adverb *more*.)

Concession—introduced by *although, even if, even though, though*:

Although my novel failed, I am still optimistic. (The adverbial clause modifies the entire main clause.)

I shall go on studying *even though my parents refuse to help me*. The adverbial clause modifies the entire main clause.)

Condition—introduced by *if, on condition that, provided that, unless*:

We will go along with the plan *if the others are all agreeable to giving us full support*. (The adverbial clause modifies the entire main clause.)

She agreed to work on the project *on condition that the publisher agree to improve the terms offered*. (The adverbial clause modifies the entire main clause.)

Had Joseph brought up his ideas earlier, they would have prevailed. (The adverbial clause modifies the verb *would have prevailed*. The subject and verb in the adverbial clause are inverted—*Had Joseph* instead of *Joseph had*.)

Manner—introduced by *as, as if, as though*:

Most company officials act *as they are told to act*. (The adverbial clause modifies the verb *act* in the main clause.)

He runs *as if the police were after him*. (The adverbial clause modifies the verb *runs*.)

Place—introduced by *where* and *wherever*:

Where there's a will, there's a way. (The adverbial clause modifies the entire main clause.)
I see homeless people *wherever I walk in the city*. (The adverbial clause modifies the entire main clause.)

Purpose—introduced by *in order that, so, that*:

We arranged an early dinner *in order that the game would not be held up*. (The adverbial clause modifies the entire main clause.)
They sent the child to live with his aunt *so that he would experience the advantages of growing up on a farm*. (The adverbial clause modifies the entire main clause.)

Result—introduced by *so* and *that*:

Our supply of oil ran out, *so we shivered all week long*. (The adverbial clause modifies the entire main clause.)
He delayed for so long *that we decided to proceed without him*. (The adverbial clause modifies the entire main clause.)

Time—introduced by *after, as, before, since, when, while, until*:

After the book was finished, John left for a long vacation in Florida. (The adverbial clause modifies the verb *left*.)
As I walked along, I dreamed of a better life. (The adverbial clause modifies the verb *walked*.)

Conjunctive Adverbs

Conjunctive adverbs are adverbs used as conjunctions. The most common conjunctive adverbs are *accordingly, also, anyhow, besides, consequently, furthermore, hence, henceforth, however, indeed, instead, likewise, moreover, meanwhile, namely, nevertheless, otherwise, still, therefore,* and *thus.* Conjunctive adverbs join elements of a sentence and influence meaning in a way that conjunctions cannot:

The board had formally rejected her application; *however*, she decided to exercise her right of appeal. (While *however* joins two independent clauses in this sentence, *however* indicates a relationship between the clauses that is absent with the most commonly used conjunctions: *and, or, but, so*, etc. The word *however* is a conjunctive adverb.)

He relinquished his position as chief executive officer; *moreover*, he sold all his stock in the company and resigned from the board of directors. (The conjunctive adverb *moreover* joins two independent clauses and indicates a special relationship between the two clauses.)

When used between independent clauses, as in the two examples above, a semicolon is required before a conjunctive adverb and a comma after it.

When a conjunctive adverb is placed within a clause, commas are used to set it off:

I will, *therefore*, insist on hearing the charges before my interrogation begins. (This use of a conjunctive adverb within a clause suggests that something has been said in the preceding sentence that justifies the use of *therefore*. For example, the preceding sentence may have said: *The rules of interrogation are rigorous in providing a witness with a full understanding of the reasons for the interrogation.* I will, *therefore*, insist etc.)

A conjunctive adverb used at the beginning of a sentence is set off by a comma:

The rules of interrogation are rigorous in providing a witness with a full understanding of the reasons for the interrogation. *Therefore*, I will insist on etc.

Intensifiers

Certain adverbs, such as *certainly, extremely, highly, least, much, quite, somewhat, such, too, tremendously,* and *very,* may be used to heighten the meaning of an adjective or adverb. Intensifiers may do little to enrich adjectives and adverbs that are already meaningful. Consider the following sentences:

She is a *very* beautiful woman. (Does *very* add much to *beautiful*?)

I am not *too* interested in that book. (Why not *I am not interested?* Why not *I am uninterested?*)

Even so, intensifiers sometimes convey important meaning:

I am *too* fat to get into my clothes.
He is *too* big for his britches.

Use intensifiers when they add to meaning. Omit them when they do not.

Infinitives as Adverbs

Infinitives and infinitive phrases function as adverbs in many sentences:

She works *to exist* and paints *to live*. (The infinitive *to exist* modifies the verb *works*. The infinitive *to live* modifies the verb *paints*.)

Jon speaks French well enough *to pass as a native speaker*. (The infinitive phrase *to pass as a native speaker* modifies the adverb *enough*.)

The nominee returned to Connecticut *to pursue her previous career*. (The infinitive phrase *to pursue her previous career* modifies the verb *returned*.)

– 9 –

Prepositions and Prepositional Phrases

A preposition is a word that conveys a meaning of position, direction, time, or other abstraction. It functions to relate its object to another sentence element.

A great number of prepositions will be supplied shortly. For now, consider the most commonly used prepositions: *at, by, for, from, in, of, on, to,* and *with*:

> *at* work, *by* then, *for* children, *from* them, *in* secret, *of* value, *on* top, *to* you, *with* us

A prepositional phrase consists of a preposition, its object, and any modifiers of the object. In the prepositional phrase *by the foremost American athletes*, the preposition is *by*, the object of the preposition is *athletes*, and the modifier of the object is *the foremost American*.

Prepositional phrases are used to modify verbs, nouns, pronouns, and adjectives:

Modifiers of Verbs
   Granny *left* the child *in his crib*. (Where did Granny leave the baby? *In his crib*.)

64

We *keep* our disks *on the personal computer.* (Where do we keep our disks? *On the personal computer.*)

Modifiers of Nouns and Pronouns

She feels the *love of her extended family.* (Whose love? The love *of her extended family.*)

They want *something by their favorite composer.* (What do they want *by their favorite composer*? Something.)

Modifiers of Adjectives

My brothers are *young in spirit.* (Young in what sense? Young *in spirit.*)

Her message was *simple in content, profound in implication.* (Simple in what sense? Simple *in content.* Profound in what sense? *Profound* in implication.)

Commonly Used Prepositions

The following list identifies many commonly used prepositions and provides examples of their use. In addition to the single words that are given, phrases are listed that also function as prepositions:

aboard	aboard the plane, aboard the bandwagon
about	about town, about dogs
above	above life itself, above all
according to	according to experts, according to convention
across	across the street, across our property
after	after dinner, after an accident
against	against everything dear, against our wishes
ahead of	ahead of our time, ahead of the mob
along	along the road, along the moat
alongside	alongside the float, alongside the building
amid	amid the crowd, amid our protests
amidst	amidst my work, amidst the meeting
among	among their objections, among the nations
apart from	apart from her injuries, apart from the reward
apropos	apropos your credentials, apropos his beliefs
around	around his head, around the table
as far as	as far as Boston, as far as the market
aside from	aside from his inaugural address, aside from my own thoughts

as to	as to your objections, as to the letter you wrote
at	at no point, at the end
back of	back of the bank, back of his objections
because of	because of his good looks, because of what they said
before	before lunch, before finishing
behind	behind her smile, behind closed minds
behind in	behind in his payments, behind in their projections
below	below expectations, below the arch
beneath	beneath my dignity, beneath the ridge
beside	beside himself, beside a garden wall
besides	besides the bank president herself, besides the committee
between	between the two us, between Monday and Friday
beyond	beyond his understanding, beyond the state line
but	but him, but a few of us
by	by the same sculptor, by next week
concerning	concerning good works, concerning human rights
contrary to	contrary to expert opinion, contrary to law
despite	despite everything, despite his good intentions
down	down the river bank, down the street
due to	due to lack of food, due to cutbacks
during	during her reign, during the war
except	except the brothers, except me
for	for the child's safety, for the sake of justice
from	from that country, from a large family
in	in advance, in front
in addition to	in addition to her legacy, in addition to hard work
in back of	in back of the building, in back of her plan
in front of	in front of his mind, in front of the museum
in lieu of	in lieu of salary, in lieu of a paid staff
in light of	in light of what they claimed, in light of the child's age
in place of	in place of flowers, in place of the sofa
in regard to	in regard to your claim, in regard to the letter you sent

inside	inside the secret organization, inside his mind
in spite of	in spite of instructions to the contrary, in spite of her crime
instead of	instead of armed conflict, instead of returning the wallet
into	into an acute depression, into the walled city
in view of	in view of her sentiments, in view of your request
like	like a monkey, like a professional
near	near the motel, near despair
of	of immigrant parents, of little value
off	off the mark, off his form
on	on no account, on occasion
on account of	on account of the long delay, on account of the riots
onto	onto the dais, onto the loading dock
out	out the window, out the back door
out of	out of sight, out of mind
over	over your house, over the assembly
owing to	owing to your condition, owing to his experience
past	past the corner house, past the mall
round	round the class, round her head
since	since birth, since the start of the fiscal year
through	through my dreams, through the book
throughout	throughout the day, throughout his career
till	till death do us part, till today
to	to best use, to the theater entrance
toward	toward deeper love, toward the end of the month
towards	towards greater understanding, towards our goals
under	under the Liberian flag, under suspension
until	until we meet again, until her departure
unto	unto one another, unto others
up	up the wall, up the ladder
via	via the transatlantic route, via the traffic circle
with	with regret, with the entire family
within	within his means, within our abilities
without	without care, without armed intervention

Object of a Preposition

The object of a preposition is always in the objective case. The only part of speech that shows case is the pronoun. Subjective: *I, you, he, she, it, we, you, they; who.* Objective: *me, you, him, her, it, us, you, them; whom.* Possessive: *mine, yours, his, hers, its, ours, yours, theirs; whose.*

The case of immediate interest here is the objective case. In each of the following examples, the object of the preposition *to* is a pronoun in the objective case:

> They gave their furniture *to me.*
> We will give it *to you.*
> Francis gave the book *to him.*
> We spoke *to her.*
> We offered dog biscuits *to it.*
> They gave money *to us.*
> The minister will soon speak *to you.*
> We will say nothing *to them.*
> *Whom* did you speak *to?*

Prepositional Phrases as Modifiers

A prepositional phrase, which consists of a preposition, the object of the preposition, and the modifiers of the object, functions as an adverb or adjective:

> They withdrew *at the eleventh hour.* (Adverb modifying the verb *withdrew.*)
> They came *from Peru.* (Adverb modifying the verb *came.*)
> Many politicians speak *without due caution.* (Adverb modifying the verb *speak.*)
> The Pooles are vacationing *at the spa.* (Adverb modifying the verb *are vacationing.*)
> Many families *in mourning* wear black clothing. (Adjective modifying the noun *families.*)
> The oldest son, *as the most respected family member*, delivered the eulogy. (Adjective modifying the noun *son.*)
> Training *in veterinary medicine* is provided at Cornell University. (Adjective modifying *Training.*)

Differentiating Prepositions from Other Parts of Speech

Many words that are classified as prepositions, for example, *after, but, for,* and *since*, are also used as other parts of speech:

adverbs, adjectives, or conjunctions. The way to determine the part of speech you are dealing with is to examine its role in a sentence.

Consider the following sentences:

> Boys marched to the blackboard, one *after* another. (Preposition.)
> Do not follow *after* your children. (Preposition.)
> *After* dinner, all the men smoked cigars. (Preposition.)
> She named her son *after* her father. (Preposition.)
> Jill tumbled *after*. (Adverb.)
> They lived happily ever *after*. (Adverb.)
> Does she still take an *after* dinner drink? (Adjective.)
> *After* I find a suitable apartment, I will move all my furniture. (Conjunction.)

– 10 –

Conjunctions

Conjunctions join words, phrases, or clauses and are classified as coordinating conjunctions or subordinating conjunctions.

Coordinating Conjunctions

The most common coordinating conjunctions are *and, but, for, nor, or, so,* and *yet*. Note that *so* and *yet* may also act as subordinating conjunctions.

Consider the following sentences, each of which has a coordinating conjunction:

She *and* I are bridge partners. (Coordinating conjunction joining pronouns.)

He *or* I will stay behind. (Coordinating conjunction joining pronouns.)

The bed in our room *or* the one in the guest room should be replaced. (Coordinating conjunction joining phrases.)

He quickly decided to run for mayor, *but* just as quickly withdrew. (Coordinating conjunction joining clauses.)

There is enough time to finish the book, *for* we still have an hour before dinner. (Coordinating conjunction joining clauses.)

Other coordinating conjunctions are the so-called *correlatives*, which occur in pairs: *either . . . or, neither . . . nor, not only . . . but also,* and *both . . . and.* The *correlatives* are used to join sentence elements having equivalent value.

Consider the following sentences:

> *Either* you do the dishes now *or* I will do them later.
> *Neither* my mother *nor* my father saw much of me from then on.
> *Not only* has the Security Council imposed sanctions, *but* many countries are suggesting armed intervention.
> *Not only* does she write poetry, *but* she *also* writes short stories.
> *Both* sushi *and* broiled fish were served to the guests.

Subordinating Conjunctions

Subordinating conjunctions connect clauses of less than equivalent value. The most common subordinating conjunctions are *after, although, as, as if, as long as, because, before, how, if, in order that, since, so, so that, though, till, unless, until, when, where, wherever, while, why,* and *yet.* The relative pronouns *that, what, which,* and *who* also act as subordinating conjunctions.

Consider the following sentences:

> I will take over the nursing duties *after* the nurse leaves.
> You and I cannot take all the credit for our success, *although* we did a great deal of the work.
> The Kenners arrived at the party *before* most of the other guests showed up.
> All students have been studying Spanish *since* they entered third grade.
> The sad day will surely arrive *when* the mortgage interest will increase.
> Mickey sat in the library *while* Sam was out on the tennis court.

–11–

Punctuation

THE COMMA

Items in Series

Use commas to separate items in a series, whether the series is made of words, phrases, or clauses. The last item is usually preceded by a conjunction, such as *and* or *or*. When no conjunction is used to connect the last item in a series, the last item is still set off by a comma: *a, b, c.*

Words in Series

Our Mayor did not recommend *experienced, reliable, qualified* contractors for work on public housing projects.
We arrived home *exhausted, hungry,* and *ill-tempered.*

Phrases in Series

Out of money, disappointed in love, afraid to face the future alone, the man decided to return home.

Clauses in Series

Tamara wrote newspaper releases, Jon wrote copy for radio broadcasts, *and* the rest of us helped the candidate prepare her speeches.
My company is ready to hire fifty more programmers, other companies have announced plans for expansion, and the new shopping center needs many additional sales clerks, *yet* our town still has a high rate of unemployment.

Independent Clauses

Use a comma between two independent clauses joined by a coordinating conjunction:

> They fought for the rights of the homeless for many years, but most people showed no interest in the endless struggle.

To form a compound sentence of two or more independent clauses, a coordinating conjunction—*and, but, for, nor, or, so,* or *yet*—is usually used before the final independent clause. Use a comma before the conjunction:

> With his remaining strength Jeff fought the powerful sailor, and a police officer who was passing by came finally to his aid. (Without the comma after *sailor*, readers may think Jeff *fought* the *police officer* as well as the *sailor*.)

With two brief independent clauses, do not use a comma as long as there is no risk of misleading readers:

> Paul left for home early but Avis stayed all evening.
> The bird flew to the feeder and the cat prepared to spring.

With more than two independent clauses, the rule for use of commas for items in series applies:

> The wind howled, the rain fell steadily, but we kept warm before the welcome fire.

Introductory Phrases and Clauses

Use a comma to separate a long introductory phrase or subordinate clause from the rest of the sentence:

Phrases

> *For many days that week,* the children wondered why their parents had decided to divorce.

Subordinate Clauses

> *While all the passengers waited impatiently,* the pilot did his best to restart the airplane engines.

Verbal Phrases

Use a comma to separate an introductory verbal phrase from the rest of a sentence. A *verbal phrase* is a phrase that contains an infinitive, gerund, or participle:

- infinitives: *(to) teach, (to) work*
- gerunds: *teaching, working* (used as nouns)
- participles: *teaching, working* (used as adjectives)

Infinitive Phrases

To be sure, all the professors decided to wait until the chair announced her ruling.

Gerund Phrases

In reaching its decision, the city council appeared to respect complaints coming from all parts of the community.

Participial Phrases

Finding herself alone in her position on the matter, she decided to give in to her opponents.

Coordinate Adjectives

Use a comma to separate coordinate adjectives that appear before a noun and are not joined by *and*. Two or more adjectives that independently modify the same noun can be joined by *and*. Such adjectives, often describing age, color, education, or number, are classified as coordinate.

Experienced writers apply the *and* test to determine whether adjectives are coordinate. When *and* can be used between adjectives, the adjectives are coordinate, and a comma can replace the *and*. When *and* cannot be used between adjectives, the adjectives are not coordinate, and a comma cannot be used.

Here are examples of phrases consisting of nouns and coordinate adjectives:

with *and*:	without *and*:
dank and dark nights	dank, dark nights
bright and happy kids	bright, happy kids

Here are examples of phrases consisting of nouns and adjectives that are not coordinate—that is, the adjectives cannot be joined by *and*:

four dark nights	honest local governments
many superior children	small blue hat
expensive chrome furniture	economical sports cars

Splitting the Unsplittable

Do not split a final modifier and the element it modifies:

> Joan found she could not concentrate yesterday, even though she usually likes to work on warm, dry days. (There must not be a comma between *dry* and *days*.)
>
> The most valuable, reliable volume in any writer's library is a good dictionary. (There must not be a comma between *reliable* and *volume*.)

Introductory Modifiers

Use a comma to set off all introductory modifiers. Adjectives, adverbs, participles, and participial phrases—all modifiers—often are placed at the beginning of a sentence to give them special emphasis. In some cases these words or phrases modify the entire sentence. In other cases they modify a particular element of the sentence. No matter what they modify, they are set off from the rest of the sentence by a comma.

Adjective

> *Alive*, beef cattle are worth a great deal of money. (*Alive* is set off by a comma.)

Adverb

> *Legally*, neither candidate had any right to institute legal action. (*Legally* is set off by a comma.)

Participle

> *Defeated*, the President went off to Camp David. (*Defeated* is set off by a comma.)

Participial Phrase

> *Seeking interesting employment*, the young couple left California. (*Seeking interesting employment* is set off by a comma.)

Nonrestrictive Phrases and Clauses

Use commas to set off nonrestrictive phrases and clauses. Modifiers are either restrictive or nonrestrictive. Restrictive modifiers *are not* set off by punctuation; nonrestrictive modifiers *are* set off.

A *restrictive* modifier identifies, defines, or limits the term it modifies. A restrictive modifier *cannot* be removed from the sentence in which it appears without significantly changing the intended meaning of the sentence.

A *nonrestrictive* modifier adds information concerning a term already identified, defined, or limited. A nonrestrictive modifier *can* be removed from the sentence in which it appears without changing the intended meaning of the sentence.

Restrictive Phrases

Henry *the Eighth* ruled England from 1509 to 1547. (The phrase *the Eighth* is restrictive. No commas.)

The couch *in my office* came from a Salvation Army store. (The phrase *in my office* is restrictive. No commas.)

Nonrestrictive Phrases

Our cat, *almost seventeen years old*, is still in good health. (The phrase *almost seventeen years old* is nonrestrictive. Commas.)

Any unabridged dictionary, *no matter how old*, provides useful information and should never be discarded. The phrase *no matter how old* is nonrestrictive. Commas.)

Restrictive Clauses

My wife and I are interested in buying paintings *that we will be proud of.* (The clause *that we will be proud of* is restrictive. No commas.)

Bill Clinton has always been seen as a person *who cares deeply about people.* (The clause *who cares deeply about people* is restrictive. No comma.)

Nonrestrictive Clauses

Thousands of Vermont cows, *which feed all summer on ample supplies of grass,* supply milk for many Bostonians. (The clause *which feed all summer on ample supplies of grass* is nonrestrictive. Commas.)

Appositives

Use commas to set off nonrestrictive appositives. Appositives may be described as noun repeaters. They point out or identify the nouns with which they are in apposition. Like modifying clauses and phrases, appositives are either restrictive or nonrestrictive.

Appositives are usually nouns, noun phrases, or noun clauses:

Noun

My brother *Lenny* spent six months in the Civilian Conservation Corps. (The noun *Lenny* is a restrictive appositive in apposition with *brother*. No commas.)

Noun Phrase

My children look forward each year to eating Alfred's apples, *the most delicious fruit available in autumn.* (The noun phrase *the most delicious fruit available in autumn* is a nonrestrictive appositive in apposition with *apples*. Comma.)

Noun Clause

The President's declaration *that we will defend democracy everywhere* caused me to wonder whether we were about to go to war. (The noun clause *that we will defend democracy everywhere* is a restrictive appositive in apposition with *declaration*. No commas.)

Gerund phrases can also be used as appositives:

Joseph's principal interest, *learning all he can about writing,* absorbs all his waking hours. (The gerund phrase *learning all he can about writing* is a nonrestrictive appositive in apposition with *interest*. Commas.)

As in the case of modifiers, *restrictive appositives* cannot be omitted from a sentence without severely altering the meaning of the sentence, while *nonrestrictive appositives* can be omitted. The rule is the same as for modifiers—restrictive appositives, no commas; nonrestrictive appositives, commas.

Restrictive

My brother *Al* has spent fifty years as a lawyer. (The implication is that I have more than one brother. Without the appositive *Al*, the reader cannot tell which brother I am discussing.)

Nonrestrictive

My oldest sister, *Tamara*, will take a new job this year. (I have only one oldest sister. The appositive *Tamara* can be omitted from the sentence without damaging its meaning.)

THE PERIOD

At the End of a Sentence

A period is used to indicate the end of a declarative sentence, an imperative sentence, and certain sentence fragments.

A *declarative* sentence is one that makes a statement:

All the candidates agreed to participate in the debate.

An *imperative* sentence is one that states a command:

Cooperate or leave the class.

A *sentence fragment* is an incomplete sentence that is punctuated as though it were a sentence:

Who caused most of the trouble? The oldest child. (*The oldest child* lacks a predicate —a complete verb—and so it is classified as a sentence fragment.)

In Abbreviations

A period is used to indicate an abbreviation. With few exceptions abbreviations must be marked by periods:

Ms. Barolini missed the party.
Carolyn was awarded the *Ph.D.* degree. (Notice that no extra space is needed after the period following *Ph.*)
I will be ready at seven *a.m.* (The abbreviation a.m. can also be written A.M.)

A sentence ending in an abbreviation that is followed by a period does not require a second period:

Her card identifies her as Jane Hoffman, *M.D.*

A sentence that requires a question mark or an exclamation point must have the appropriate mark even if the sentence ends in an abbreviation followed by a period:

Where did your brother receive his *M.D.*?
What an opportunity for someone without a *B.A.*!

Scholarly abbreviations employ periods:

l. (line)
ll. (lines)

op. cit. (*opere citato*, in the work cited)
viz. (*videlicet*, namely)

Units of measurement do not use periods when abbreviated:

mph (miles per hour)
rpm (revolutions per minute)

With Quotations

When a sentence ends in a quotation and requires quotation marks, a single period serves the quotation and the sentence. Required periods are placed *inside* final quotation marks:

The President said, "We have too many mouths to feed."
Last year they read one of Joseph Conrad's best stories, "Youth."

When a sentence ends in a quotation but requires a final question mark, no period is used:

Did you hear the judge say, "We will do nothing for the defendant"?

When a quotation at the end of a sentence requires a question mark, no final period is used:

Mr. Churchill then asked, "Is England asleep at this fateful moment in history?"

When a sentence ends in a quotation but requires a final exclamation point, no final period is used:

What a mess was made by "the people's choice"!

When a quotation at the end of a sentence requires an exclamation point, no final period is used:

We will never forget "Read my lips!"

With Commas

When a sentence includes an abbreviation that immediately precedes a comma, the period required in the abbreviation is retained:

We will welcome Joan Attucks, *M.A.*, at a luncheon next week.

THE SEMICOLON

Many writers consider the semicolon a mark of formal style and avoid using it. By doing so, they miss out on opportunities to clarify meaning and heighten the effectiveness of their ideas. Instead of writing mature sentences that enhance complex thoughts, they deal in childish sentences that may well mask sophisticated thinking.

With Independent Clauses

The general rule is: Use a semicolon to separate independent clauses that are not connected by a coordinating conjunction.

To understand this practice fully, it is worthwhile to review the use of commas and conjunctions in dealing with independent clauses. You will recall that a comma is used between independent clauses connected by a coordinating conjunction: *and, or, for, but,* etc.:

Peggy has an office job, and Jim works at home. (Independent clauses connected by a coordinating conjunction, *and.*)

When a coordinating conjunction is not present, a semicolon must be used:

Peggy has an office job; Jim works at home. (Independent clauses separated by a semicolon. A semicolon is not ordinarily used in a sentence as simple as this, although it is acceptable to do so.)

The semicolon can also be thought of as replacing the period that would be used if the two independent clauses stood as separate sentences:

Peggy has an office job. Jim works at home. (Two sentences.)

Now see how the semicolon is used in more realistic examples:

"The only guide to a man is his conscience; the only shield to his memory is the rectitude and sincerity of his actions." (The semicolon heightens the effectiveness of two closely related thoughts that are presented in parallel grammatical form.)

"While there is a lower class, I am in it; while there is a criminal element, I am of it; while there is a soul in prison, I am not free." (This sentence has three independent clauses plus three dependent clauses. The dependent clauses all require commas to set them off from the independent clauses: *While there is a lower class, while there is a criminal element, while there is a soul in prison.* Semicolons are needed because no coordinating conjunctions are present: *I am in it; I am of it; I am not free.*)

The key to use of the semicolon with independent clauses, then, is to ask whether the thoughts in independent clauses are so closely related that they might best stand in a single sentence and whether a semicolon is more effective than a coordinating conjunction plus a comma.

With Conjunctive Adverbs

Use a semicolon before a conjunctive adverb that connects two independent clauses. In addition, use a comma after the conjunctive adverb.

The most common conjunctive adverbs are *however, therefore,* and *thus.* They serve to connect independent clauses, just as coordinating conjunctions do. However, the relationship they imply between the clauses is different from that implied by the coordinating conjunctions. (See page 62 for the explanation of how to use commas with conjunctive adverbs.)

Consider the following sentences:

Several European countries established colonies in the New World during the sixteenth century; *however,* by the twentieth century, the influence of these countries all but disappeared. (Two independent clauses connected by the conjunctive adverb *however.*)

Throughout the nineties, fast food will continue to find favor with working parents and harried executives; *nevertheless,* not all types of establishments that provide quick-bite burgers and shakes will thrive equally. (Two independent clauses connected by the conjunctive adverb *nevertheless.*)

As you can see, in both these sentences the conjunctive adverbs are followed by commas. Some writers are beginning to drop the comma after a conjunctive adverb, but careful writers retain it. If the comma is dropped, there is the risk of confusing readers, who may not notice that the conjunctive adverb is functioning as a conjunction rather than as an adverb. This risk is greatest with *however*, because *however* is frequently used as an adverb:

> *However* hard we tried, we could find no way out of our troubles. (The adverb *however* modifies *hard*.)

> The American League voted to retain the designated hitter; *however*, many fans continued to voice their disapproval of the practice. (The conjunctive adverb *however* connects two independent clauses: *The American League voted to retain the designated hitter* and *many fans continued to voice their disapproval of the practice*.)

You would do well to continue to use a comma after a conjunctive adverb that connects two independent clauses.

As Comma Substitute

Use a semicolon to replace a comma in sentences containing other commas, in order to differentiate between the uses of the commas and the semicolon:

> Some voters, though conscientious about going to the polls, frequently find themselves at a loss when confronted by a long, complex, closely printed paper ballot; yet others, with no more education or experience, can work their way intelligently down such a ballot and hardly ever make an error.

Commas are needed for two reasons in this long sentence: (1) to set off the long modifiers *though conscientious about going to the polls* and *with no more education or experience*, and (2) to separate a series of modifiers, *long, complex, closely printed*. Because these commas are necessary, the conjunction *yet*, which normally would require only a comma before it, is preceded by a semicolon.

> During the course of a long career in the military, thirty-five years of exceptional devotion to duty, even heroism on several occasions, General Dyer was recognized as a leader in aviation, artillery tactics, and strategic planning; but outside the military this exceptional man, always modest in behavior, goes unnoticed by his fellow citizens, who take pains to ignore all achievements but those directed toward accumulation of wealth, prestige, and power.

Commas are needed in this long sentence (1) to separate a series of long modifiers: *During the course of a long career in the military, thirty-five years of exceptional devotion to duty,* and *even heroism on several occasions.* (2) To separate two other series: *aviation, artillery tactics, and strategic planning* and *wealth, prestige, and power.* (3) To set off the modifiers *always modest in behavior* and *who take pains to ignore all achievements but those directed toward accumulation of wealth, prestige, and power.* Because these commas are necessary, the conjunction *but,* which normally would require only a comma before it, is preceded by a semicolon.

Within a Series

Use semicolons between elements in a series when any of the elements have internal commas.

Ordinarily, commas are used between elements in a series: *Many countries of Europe export grain, dairy products, and vegetables.* The series can be separated by commas because the elements of the series are themselves not punctuated internally: *grain, dairy products, and vegetables.* When the elements of a series are internally punctuated, however, semicolons are needed between the elements to prevent confusion:

> I enjoy several types of films: westerns, primarily because I love simple stories that always end happily; romances, which take me out of the real world for ninety minutes; and detective mysteries, because I never can guess who the guilty person is.

Each of the elements of the series—*westerns, romances,* and *detective mysteries*—is itself modified by elements that must be set off by commas: *primarily because I love simple stories that always end happily, which take me out of the real world for ninety minutes,* and *because I never can guess who the guilty person is.* Therefore, the first two elements of the full series must be set off by semicolons.

> Everyone present was a gourmet except for my mother, who never did learn how to cook properly; my father, who cared little about food; and my oldest brother, who would always eat anything put in front of him.

Because each element of the series—*mother, father,* and *oldest brother*—is itself modified by elements set off by a comma, a semicolon is needed after the first two full elements of the series.

THE COLON

The colon is a mark that is helpful in certain conventional uses, primarily in introducing enumerations and lists. In certain sentences, it is used as an alternative to the semicolon when providing explanatory material. Beyond these uses the colon is seen infrequently.

With Enumerations

Use a colon to introduce an enumeration when the enumeration is preceded by a noun or noun phrase. The enumeration in that case is in apposition with the element preceding the colon:

> The Pentateuch consists of five books: Genesis, Exodus, Leviticus, Numbers, and Deuteronomy. (The titles of the books are in apposition to *books*.)
>
> They decided to cut expenses by eliminating unproductive privileges: *first-class flights on short trips, private offices for middle-level managers,* and *executive use of limousines.* (The italicized noun phrases are in apposition to *privileges*.)

When an enumeration follows a verb, the enumeration is the object or complement of the verb and must not be separated from the verb by punctuation:

> The three guiding qualities of his life are faith, hope, and charity. (*Faith, hope,* and *charity* are complements of the linking verb *are*.)

When an enumeration follows a preposition, a colon is not needed. The enumeration is the object of the preposition:

> They distributed food to children, homeless adults, and senior citizens. (*Children, homeless adults,* and *senior citizens* are objects of the preposition *to*.)

With Formal Statements, Quotations, Questions

A colon sets off expressions that introduce formal statements, quotations, and questions. As a rule introductory expressions before direct quotations are set off by commas. Now we are dealing with the punctuation of introductory expressions that occur before formal statements.

A formal statement is defined by the setting in which the statement is made, for example, a meeting of a professional group, a campaign address, a published book or article; or by the status of the person being quoted, for example, a public official, an important company officer, a distinguished scholar, and the like.

The statement may be a direct quotation or a paraphrase. It may also take the form of a question. Notice that in all the following examples the first word after the colon is capitalized:

> This is the issue on which her campaign is based: "All people must be housed with dignity, suitably employed, and educated to the extent of their ability. Nothing less than this will do for a nation as wealthy as ours."
>
> As Rousseau said in *The Social Contract*: "As soon as public service ceases to be the chief business of the citizens, and they would rather serve with their money than with their persons, the State is not far from its fall."
>
> The Detection Club, Miss Sayers reported, asks this question in its membership oath: "Do you promise that your Detectives shall well and truly detect the Crimes presented to them, using those Wits which it shall please you to bestow upon them and not placing reliance upon, nor making use of, Divine Revelation, Feminine Intuition, Mumbo-Jumbo, Jiggery-Pokery, Coincidence, or the Act of God?"
>
> I am interested in only two questions: Is the club membership prepared to oust all officers who betray their official trust? Is the membership prepared to act promptly on submittal of conclusive evidence?
>
> The Dean concluded her lengthy remarks by forcefully restating her position: The College was organized to educate. Conditions on campus are making education impossible. Unless conditions change quickly, there will be no alternative to shutting the campus down.

With Independent Clauses

A colon separates two independent clauses when no conjunction is used and the second clause explains, amplifies, or illustrates the first clause.

A semicolon is often used to separate two independent clauses when no conjunction is used. With a semicolon, the clauses are considered to have approximately equal value.

When a colon is used between two independent clauses, the colon signals that a special relationship exists between the two clauses: the second clause explains the meaning of the first clause or expands or illustrates its meaning. Notice that some of the following sentences are compound-complex, that is, they consist of two or more independent clauses plus any dependent clauses. The punctuation rule still holds:

> The married couples had no intention of going to the party: they were bored by such affairs and preferred staying home.
> The Korean language shares a characteristic with Japanese and Chinese: it has no inflections for plurals or tense.
> San Francisco attracts many visitors each year: cable cars are fun to ride and watch, the waterfront brings fishing boats rich with fresh sea life, and Chinatown beguiles the gourmet tourist and collector of *objets d'art*.

Miscellaneous Uses of the Colon

1. A colon is used between hours and minutes in expressions of time: 12:45 p.m. 1:10 a.m.

2. A colon is used after the speaker's name in a play:

> Iago: Sir, would she give you so much of her lips As of her tongue she oft bestows on me, You would have enough.
> Desdemona: Alas, she has no speech!
> Iago: In faith, too much.

THE QUESTION MARK

Direct Questions

A question mark is used after a direct question. A direct question is one that is quoted verbatim or is addressed directly to the reader:

> Has anybody here seen George?

A question mark is used for a question phrased as a declarative sentence but spoken with the rising intonation of a question:

> You really are six years old? (A question in the form of a declarative sentence.)

Indirect Questions

An indirect question is a question that is not quoted verbatim or addressed directly to the reader. It is written as a subordinate element of a sentence and does not require a question mark or quotation marks:

> She asked whether I could help her son find a job.

Polite Requests

To phrase requests or commands politely, speakers and writers may use a word order that usually is employed for questions, but periods are used rather than question marks:

> Will you please check to see whether you have all the necessary forms before you leave the room.
> May I hear a round of applause for this excellent speaker.

These sentences do not require question marks, because they are not questions. The first one is a polite request, and the second one may be thought of as a polite command.

Questions Within Sentences

Writers occasionally construct sentences containing a series of questions. These questions can all be punctuated by question marks to emphasize the individual questions. Because the questions are all part of a single sentence, however, the first word of each question is not capitalized:

> The attorney asked the witness where he was born? where he grew up? how much formal education he had? where he worked? whether he was married or single?

Such questions can also be punctuated with commas. Notice that if the sentence itself is not a question, then the final punctuation is a period. If the sentence itself is a question, the final punctuation is a question mark:

> The prosecutor asked the witness where he was born, where he grew up, how much formal education he had, where he worked, whether he was married or single, where he lived, and how long he had known the accused.
> Did the prosecutor ask the witness where he was born, where he grew up, how much formal education he had, where he worked, whether he was married or single, where he lived, and how long he had known the accused?

The questions in the above sentences are not direct quotations. In the following sentence, the questions are quoted directly:

> The prosecutor submitted a series of written questions to the witness: "Where were you born?" "Where did you grow up?" "How much formal education have you had?" "Are you married or single?" "Where do you live?" "How long have you known the accused?"

Uncertain Information

A question mark enclosed in parentheses shows that information is open to question. When the best available sources cannot supply a date, a number, or any other asserted fact with full certainty, the writer indicates this by inserting a question mark enclosed in parentheses after the item open to question:

> Geoffrey Chaucer was born in 1340(?) and died in 1400. (The best scholarship indicates Chaucer was born in 1340, but no one is certain of the date.)

If the uncertain item is place inside parentheses, the question mark is not enclosed in its own parentheses:

> Johann Gutenberg (1398?-1468) was the inventor of movable printing types.

Inside or Outside Quotation Marks?

When question marks are combined with quotation marks, a little thought is needed: Is the question part of the quote? Then the question mark goes inside the final quotation mark. Is the sentence itself a question? Then the question mark goes outside the final quotation mark.

> Did he really say, "I would rather be dead than hungry"? (The sentence is a question, not the quoted material.)
> She asked, "Are you so hungry that you cannot wait another minute or so for dinner?" (The quotation is the question.)

When a question mark is used after a quotation at the end of a sentence, a question mark is not needed after the final quotation mark even though the sentence enclosing the quotation is itself a question:

> Did she really ask, "Are you so hungry that you cannot wait another minute for dinner?"

Notice also that a sentence that ends in a question mark does not require a final period, nor is a comma needed when a question mark appears.

"Is Alice coming to dinner?" my mother asked.

THE EXCLAMATION POINT

Emphatic Interjections
An exclamation point is used after an emphatic interjection. Interjections can be expressed with great emphasis or with little emphasis, depending on the feelings of the speaker or writer. When little emphasis is intended, the appropriate punctuation is a period:

"Oh. I didn't know you called me."

If the interjection is made part of a sentence and little emphasis is intended, a comma is appropriate:

"Oh, I didn't know you called me."

When the interjection is intended to show great emphasis, an exclamation point—never more than one—is used:

"No! I will never give up!"

Exclamatory Phrases, Clauses, and Sentences
An exclamation point is used after any truly exclamatory sentence element.

Typical correct uses include exclamatory sentences containing *what* or *how*:

What a beautiful woman!
How I suffered!

Curses and blessings:

Damn you!
May your life be happy!

Accusations and characterizations:

Thief! Cheat!
You cowardly liar!

Forceful Commands

An exclamation point is used after forceful commands. You must differentiate between forceful commands and mere requests. The former require exclamation points, the latter only periods.

Inside or Outside Quotation Marks?

When an exclamation is part of a quotation, the exclamation point goes inside the final quotation mark. If the sentence itself is the exclamation, rather than the quotation, the exclamation point goes outside the final quotation mark:

> She waited the required four minutes and then cried, "Fire!"
> (The quotation is the exclamation.)
> How disappointing that he has never read "The Bells"!
> (The sentence is the exclamation.)

THE HYPHEN

Book publishers, editors of current magazines and newspapers, and teachers of composition disagree with one another on use of the troublesome hyphen mark more than they agree. Although certain rules can be offered for your guidance, you will have to become accustomed to relying—as most writers do—on an up-to-date standard dictionary for whatever comfort it can give. It is ironic that a mark intended to prevent confusion causes so much dispute.

In Numbers and Fractions

Hyphens are used with spelled-out numbers from twenty-one through ninety-nine and with spelled-out fractions. Numbers from zero through twenty are single words, so they are not hyphenated: *two, eight, nineteen.*

Numbers above one hundred are usually written as numerals, except for two hundred, three hundred, etc.: *104, 675, 892, 1166; six hundred, twelve hundred, one thousand, two million.* We never hyphenate numerals, and we never hyphenate multipliers; in the number five hundred, for example, *five* is the multiplier of *hundred.*

Numbers between twenty-one and ninety-nine that consist of two words can be thought of as having the word *and* understood between them: *thirty-four* can be thought of as *thirty and four* (the hyphen replaces the *and*); *sixty-seven* is *sixty and seven*. Contrast this with *seven hundred*, in which what we have is *seven times one hundred*.

In fractions written as words, the sign of the fraction—which means *divided by*—is usually replaced by a hyphen: *1/6* is written as *one-sixth; 3/4* is written as *three-fourths*. A hyphen is not used for the division sign when the numerator or denominator requires a hyphen: *3/32* is written as *three thirty-seconds; 31/64* is written as *thirty-one sixty-fourths*. Needless to say, few writers find a need for writing such fractions.

Compounds with Self-

Hyphens are used in compounds employing *self-*. One unabridged dictionary includes more than nine hundred words employing *self-*.

Most of the *self-* words are hyphenated. Two common exceptions are *selfish* and *selfless*. There are other prefixes, such as *all-, ex-, auto-, non-,* and *anti-*, that are occasionally hyphenated. The dictionary is your best source when you are not certain of whether to hyphenate.

Family Relationships

Hyphens are used in terms that express family relationships, such as *in-laws*. Some family members are designated in two-word expressions: *half sister, half brother, kissing cousin*. Others are designated in single words: *sister, brother, grandmother*.

Family relationships employing *in-law* are hyphenated: *sister-in-law, brother-in-law*. Some expressions preceded by *great* are also hyphenated: *great-aunt, great-grandmother*.

Awkward Combinations

Hyphens are used between syllables of words to prevent harsh or misleading combinations of letters. Words made of two words—*red-hot, secretary-general*—or of a prefix and root word—*anti-imperialistic, semi-independent*—sometimes can be difficult to pronounce without a hyphen. When no problem of pronunciation exists, the words are spelled without a hyphen: *redhead, antihuman, semifinal*. But how would you like to read *red-hot* as *redhot, secretary-general* as *secretarygeneral, anti-imperialistic* as *antiimperialistic*?

Would you know what a *halllike* room looks like? You know what a *fireman* is, but can you tell what a *fireeater* is? The hyphen makes *hall-like* and *fire-eater* easy to understand.

Don't trust your judgment in this use of the hyphen. If you are not certain, check your dictionary. But be advised that dictionary editors do not always agree on when to spell words with hyphens.

With Compound Modifiers Before a Noun

Hyphens are used in compound modifiers that appear directly before the nouns they modify. Many modifiers are made of two or more words acting as a single word: *clear-sighted* observers, *first-rate* performers, *up-to-date* writing. When modifiers such as these appear before nouns they modify, a hyphen is usually required.

> A *clear-minded* individual with a good grasp of the language will have no trouble making a good grade on the Law School Aptitude Test.
> Clarissa is a *second-rate* tennis player.
> He alternated between using *first-person* and *third-person* pronouns throughout his story.

When a modifier is made of an adverb that ends in *-ly* plus another adverb or adjective, the term is not hyphenated, even when the modifier appears before the noun it modifies:

> A *clearly addressed* envelope is essential.
> Have you enclosed a *clearly written* self-addressed envelope?

With Prefixes and Capitalized Root Words

Hyphens are used in words consisting of prefixes and capitalized root words. Many terms in English are made of prefixes and capitalized root words, or proper nouns. The capital letter is often retained in the new word. When it is, a hyphen is required: *trans-Siberian, pro-Somali.* When the capital letter is not retained, no hyphen is required: *transatlantic, transpacific, prepaleolithic.*

Suspension Hyphen

Hyphens are used with incomplete modifiers whose meanings are in suspense. When two or more modifiers employing hyphens precede a noun, writers will often leave incomplete all but the final modifier. When they do, they must retain the hyphens within the modifiers.

We would like to buy tourist-class or second-class tickets. (The modifiers are complete: *tourist-class, second-class.*)
We would like to buy tourist- or second-class tickets. (The modifier *tourist-* is in suspense and so retains its hyphen.)

Notice that a space is left after *tourist-* in the second example. The practice of retaining the hyphen ensures that readers see that a modifier in suspense is completed by the same term as the next modifier.

Linked Numerals and Letters

Hyphens are used with numerals that are part of a modifier, and with letters that are linked to nouns. Numerals often appear as part of a modifier: *10-inch planks, 50-cent lollipops.* The hyphen attaches the numeral firmly to the rest of the modifier (*inch, cent*).

Letters used as part of a noun also are attached to the rest of the noun by hyphens: *X-rays, D-day.*

Word Division at the End of a Line

It is customary to hyphenate between syllables when you wish to divide a word at the end of a line. This rule is simple to state but hard to follow, since logic sometimes appears to fall apart in deciding where syllables begin and end. Consider *de·moc·ra·cy* and *dem·o·crat·ic, bar·ba·rism* and *bar·bar·i·ty.* If a long word appears at the end of a line and cannot be completed on that line, you may divide it and use a hyphen to show the division. You can see that your dictionary will not last long if you use it to verify syllabication as often as you may have to in following this rule.

But there is more to the problem than has yet been presented. The following practices should also be observed:

- Never divide a word to leave a single letter at the end of a line or at the beginning of a new line.

- Never divide an already hyphenated word except at the hyphen, so that you will not have more than one hyphen in the word.

- Never divide a hyphenated expression except at one of the hyphens: *up-to-date.*

- Never divide a word of one syllable. This would seem to be obvious if you follow the hyphen rule given for hyphenating words between syllables, but you may forget that adding the suffix *ed*, for example, to words of one syllable does not always change the word from one syllable to two. *Watch* and *watched* are both one-syllable words, as are *patch* and *patched*. But *head* and *headed*, and *lead* and *leaded* are different.

- You may always divide words between double consonants: *com-mit, pat-tern, suf-fer*.

THE DASH

The dash may have many uses, but it is almost never used by some writers, seldom used by most writers, and overused by inexperienced writers. The problem with amateurish writing is that it substitutes careless use of dashes for good diction and effective sentence structure.

Modern writing does not often require use of the dash. Yet, when a dash is needed, there is nothing better. Notice that a dash is made on a typewriter by two hyphens, with no spacing either before or after.

Dashes indicate greater separation of elements of a sentence than can be accomplished with commas. In this sense the dash is a supercomma. Dashes can also play the same role as parentheses in setting off material not central to the thought of a sentence. Where parentheses tend to deemphasize enclosed material, dashes tend to emphasize it and thus are useful marks.

For Abrupt Breaks in Thought

A dash is used to indicate an abrupt break in thought within a sentence. For stylistic effect writers may use a dash to break off suddenly within a sentence and change subjects or end a sentence completely.

During the campaign the underdog spoke constantly of the role of her opponent in recent Washington scandals, the waste and corruption in the legislature, the personal habits of leading officials—you know the whole story. (By breaking off at the dash, the writer of this sentence implies there is much more to be told. The reader may fill in the rest. The reader becomes an assenting insider, privy to shameful secrets.)

Imagine a situation like this, so degrading for the individuals involved, so damaging for their families—how can anyone but a novelist intent on revealing the sordid nature of humanity do justice to it?

They said they could not find suitable jobs—had they really looked hard?—so we continued to support them.

"Jimmy, please don't lean out so far—." Too late. The boy had already begun to slide down the face of the sharp cliff.

Now I shall tell you the entire story of how the affair started and died—but first have another cup of coffee.

As you can see, such sentences are not often needed, so the dash is not often needed to indicate an abrupt break in thought within a sentence. But the dash stands ready to do the job when needed.

With Appositives

Dashes are used to set off nonrestrictive appositives worthy of greater emphasis than is achieved with commas and to set off appositives that contain commas. Ordinarily, commas are used with nonrestrictive appositives, as noun repeaters that point out or identify the nouns with which they are in apposition. You will recall that nonrestrictive appositives are appositives that can be omitted without damaging the meaning of a sentence. (See pages 76-77 for full discussion of commas with appositives.)

I like romances, fictional accounts of heroic achievement, and often read myself to sleep with a paperback that takes me far away from today's troubled world. (The commas enclose the nonrestrictive appositive *fictional accounts of heroic achievement*.

The problems—unemployment and inflation—perplex economists and mystify the public. (Use of dashes gives greater emphasis to the nonrestrictive appositive *unemployment and inflation* than would be achieved through use of commas. Commas would not be incorrect, merely less emphatic.)

The role of the Securities Investigating Commission proposed in the bill—seeking out corruption among investment bankers, recommending new securities legislation, and checking abuse of securities practices—was poorly understood by most investors. (The commas used within the nonrestrictive appositive *seeking out corruption among investment bankers, recommending new securities legislation, and checking abuse of securities practices* make it mandatory to set off the appositive in dashes rather than commas. Use of commas to set off the appositive would confuse readers.)

Notice that when a nonrestrictive appositive occurs at the end of a sentence, a single dash is used.

> She asked me to buy three things at the supermarket, and I forgot all three of them—bread, hamburger, and tuna fish.

A comma would suffice if there were no internal commas.

> She asked me to buy two things at the supermarket, and I forgot both of them, bread and hamburger.

For Parenthetic Elements

Dashes are used to set off parenthetic elements when commas are insufficient and parentheses inappropriate.

Commas are used ordinarily to set off interrupters, parenthetic elements that break into the expected movement of a sentence.

> Bernice is, however, concerned with the administration of student affairs at her high school.

A parenthetic element that can stand logically and grammatically as a sentence or that is internally punctuated requires more than commas. When a parenthetic element is not part of the main thought, yet sufficiently pertinent to include in a sentence, parentheses are used:

> I frequently consult *The Reader Over Your Shoulder* (Macmillan, New York, 1943) to find out what Robert Graves and Alan Hodge have to say about sentence structure. (Bibliographic information is a good example of parenthetic information that is usually enclosed in parentheses within a sentence.)

When a parenthetic element is too closely related to the main thought of a sentence to justify use of parentheses and can stand logically and grammatically as a sentence, dashes are used. As pointed out above, dashes give greater emphasis than parentheses give to the material they set off:

> Her final examinations—may I never have to take another one!—are legendary instruments of student torture. (Notice that exclamation points can be used with dashes.)

Corky's usual appearance—I'm not sure it's what you expect in one so talented—attracts a great deal of interest wherever he goes.

Ned's earnings as a stockbroker—he made more than $200,000 last year—scarcely qualify him for welfare payments by our current standards.

With Summaries Following a Series

A dash is used to set off a summary statement following a series of words, phrases, or clauses. Writers sometimes vary sentence structure to place a summary or assertion after a series. This is an excellent way to achieve variety of sentence structure and to emphasize the elements of the series. A dash is used before the summary statement.

The first sentence in each of the following pairs of sentences illustrates the sentence structure usually used with a series. The second sentence in each pair illustrates the use of a dash to emphasize the elements of the series:

The three elements of the trivium leading to a bachelor's degree in medieval universities were grammar, logic, and rhetoric.

Grammar, logic, and rhetoric—these were the three elements of the trivium leading to a bachelor's degree in medieval universities.

The ability to write clearly, speak effectively, and work hard do more for an engineer's career than technical knowledge.

Clear writing, effective speech, and willingness to work hard—these attributes do more for an engineer's career than technical knowledge.

My English professor spends her summers enjoying hard work and good exercise: she works on her research; she swims, rides, and runs daily; and she perfects her knowledge of fine cooking and dining.

Hard work and good exercise fill my English professor's summers—working on her research; swimming, riding, and running daily; and perfecting her knowledge of fine cooking and dining.

The use of the dash to set off summaries and assertions after a series is a rare one, since such constructions are rare. Used sparingly, these inversions of the usual structure of a sentence achieve variety and emphasize the elements of the series.

With Other Marks

Dashes are used when necessary to set off sentence elements punctuated as questions or exclamations. When a question is set off by dashes within a sentence, the question mark precedes the second dash:

> My sister-in-law—why was I home when she called?—asked me once again about the money we owe her.

When the question is set off at the end of a sentence, only a single dash is needed in addition to the question mark:

> I have always had trouble with mathematics—do you know anyone who hasn't?

When an exclamation is set off by dashes within a sentence, the exclamation point precedes the second dash:

> The Dodgers won the pennant in the last game of the season— what a season it was!—leaving their fans emotionally drained but happy.

When an exclamation is set off at the end of a sentence, only a single dash is needed in addition to the exclamation point.

> Despite many initial difficulties, our marriage has turned out to be the happiest I can imagine—how few of my friends still are married!

Notice that the exclamation point in this example serves as punctuation for the entire sentence as well as for the exclamation.

A dash can also be followed by a period:

> I asked her where she would find the book if she could not—.
> Again she interrupted me.
> They were about to go to the old woman's rescue, but when they saw the gun in the assailant's hand—.

The Double Dash

A double dash is used to indicate deleted expressions and to suggest hesitant speech. We live in times of relaxed rules of decorum, so writers tend to use so-called explicit language in their work. Yet family newspapers and some magazines still use dashes from time to time to replace offensive expressions.

> The candidate then used the word ——, leaving his partisan audience unwilling to believe their ears but certain that the

outcome of the election was in greater jeopardy than ever. (Some newspapers hypocritically show such omissions by a series of hyphens, carefully counting out each letter of the omission so that the reader will know exactly what has been omitted, for example, --- -- - -----. They may as well spell out the offending item.)

A double dash (——) is sufficient, no matter how the offender is spelled. In print a double dash appears as a solid bar twice the length of a dash. Notice that the double dash in this use is spaced as a word; a dash normally does not have a space before it or after it.

Double dashes are also used to indicate that part of a name has been omitted from an account. We see this usage most often in works of fiction, such as spy novels. Some writers of serious fiction also use the dash this way to heighten the effect of their work:

Colonel L—— drew his pistol from its holster and carefully pointed it at his right temple. (This is a double dash no matter how long the full name is. Notice that there is no space after the first letter of the name, but there is a space after the dash.)

In the novel she is always referred to as Mlle. P—l. (Writers usually use a single dash when supplying the last letter of the name. Notice the spacing of the dash.)

The Half Dash
A half dash is used to indicate inclusive dates, times, and page references.

The convention was scheduled for Philadelphia, Pennsylvania, November 23–25, 1996.

The meeting will be held in the manager's office, 6:30–8:30 p.m.

For a fuller discussion, I refer you to *The Christian Science Monitor* of April 19, 1992, pp. 52–54.

QUOTATION MARKS

In American usage quotation marks normally are double quotes (" *and* "). Single quotes (' *and* ') are used only for quotations within quotations. In British usage quotation marks are normally single quotes, with double quotes used for quotations within quotations. (See *Quotes Within Quotes* on pages 104-105.)

Quotation marks have several uses, principally to indicate quoted speech and material quoted from another printed source. They are also used to indicate titles of certain literary works or reports and to indicate that particular words are to be understood as words rather than as meanings conveyed by the words. (The use of words as words is explained on pages 107-108.)

Two problems that face many writers are the use of quotation marks in combination with other marks of punctuation, and the abuse of quotation marks in what appears to be an attempt to imply that certain words mean more they normally mean.

Quoted Speech

Quotation marks are used to indicate directly quoted speech. Many examples of this use of quotation marks have already been provided:

> Alfred said, "If I can build a greenhouse large enough to accommodate thousands of seedlings, I will be able to establish myself in the nursery business." (This is a direct quotation. *Alfred* said every word enclosed in quotation marks.)

An indirect quotation does not quote the exact words of a speaker and, therefore, is not enclosed in quotation marks:

> Alfred said that he will be able to get started in the nursery business if he can build a greenhouse large enough to accommodate thousands of seedlings. (Even though some of these words are *Alfred's*, others are not. Obviously *Alfred* would not refer to himself as *he* and *himself.* The quotation, therefore, is indirect and is not punctuated with quotation marks. Direct quotations are completely, not partially, direct.)

When speech is quoted directly, the speaker may be identified before the quotation, after the quotation, within the quotation, or not at all if the identity of the speaker is already clear to readers. This last situation occurs most frequently in dialogue. Notice that each time a new speaker is quoted, a new paragraph is needed:

> "Can you tell me where I can find the Director of Clerical Services?"
>
> "She's right down the hall. I'm going that way myself."
>
> "Thank you."

When quoted speech of a single speaker runs to more than a single paragraph, each paragraph is preceded by quotes, but only the final paragraph has final quotes. Indentation and spacing between lines are the same as for regular text:

So Jesus spoke again:

"In truth, in very truth I tell you, I am the door of the sheepfold. The sheep paid no heed to any who came before me, for these are all thieves and robbers. I am the door; anyone who comes into the fold through me shall be safe. He shall go in and out and shall find pasturage.

"The thief comes only to steal, to kill, to destroy; I have come that men may have life, and may have it in all its fullness. I am the good shepherd; the good shepherd lays down his life for the sheep. The hireling, when he sees the wolf coming, abandons the sheep and runs away, because he is no shepherd and the sheep are not his. Then the wolf harries the flock and scatters the sheep. The man runs away because he is a hireling and cares nothing for the sheep.

"I am the good shepherd; I know my own sheep and my sheep know me—as the Father knows me and I know the Father—and I lay down my life for the sheep. But there are other sheep of mine, not belonging to this fold, whom I must bring in; and they too will listen to my voice. There will then be one flock, one shepherd. The father loves me because I lay down my life, to receive it back again. No one has robbed me of it; I am laying it down of my own free will. I have the right to lay it down, and I have the right to receive it back again; this charge I have received from my Father."

When a speaker must be identified, you must take care in deciding where to place the other required marks of punctuation:

He asked, "Are you going to stay at your desk all night?" (Comma before quotation. Question mark before final quote, because the quotation is a question. *He asked* is not enclosed in quotation marks because it is not part of the quotation.)

Did the manager really say, "I am sick of this mess; we must find a solution for the production bottleneck or we will be in deep trouble"? (The entire sentence is a question, so the question mark appears outside the final quote. The quotation needs no other final punctuation. The question mark serves to complete both the sentence and the quotation.)

"Can you remember what she asked you?" Richard said. (Question mark inside final quote, because the quotation is a question.)

"I hope you can find your way home easily," the police officer said. (Comma before final quote.)

"I must tell you," my boss said, "that if you are late once more you will be fired." (The quotation is a single sentence interrupted by *my boss said*. Comma before final quote in the first part of the quotation, period before final quote in the second part.)

"There are many ways to solve this problem," Professor Morris said. "If you think through the directions already given, you will surely find the correct answer." (The quotation is in two sentences. Comma before final quote of the first sentence. Period before final quote of the second sentence.)

"You must recall that I told you I had found evidence of embezzlement," I insisted; "moreover, I advised you of your legal responsibility to take action." (Semicolon after *insisted*, because a semicolon would be required even if *I insisted* were not present. The conjunctive adverb *moreover* must be preceded by a semicolon and followed by a comma when it joins two clauses.) (See pages 61-62.)

Printed Sources

Quotation marks are used to indicate direct quotation from printed sources except when the material quoted is lengthy.

With one exception, material quoted word-for-word from literature, newspapers, magazines, journals, or any other published source must be enclosed in quotation marks. The exception is quoted material running longer than five lines for prose and longer than two lines for poetry. These longer quotations are given special indentation and are single-spaced rather than double-spaced.

The man, turning his back upon the setting sun, looked along the empty and broad expanse of the sea-reach. For the last three miles of its course the wandering, hesitant river, as if enticed irresistibly by the freedom of an open horizon, flows straight to the east—to the east that harbours both light and darkness. Astern of the boat the repeated call of some bird, a cry discordant and feeble, skipped along the smooth water and lost itself, before it could reach the other shore, in the breathless silence of the world.

—Joseph Conrad, "Tropical River"

Up! up! my friend, and quit your books,
Or surely you'll grow double;
Up! up! my friend, and clear your looks;
Why all this toil and trouble?

—William Wordsworth, "The Tables Turned"

When material is quoted from printed sources, short quotations—like short quoted speech—are not set off in special indentation, but are run in with the text:

The ringing phrase "Life, Liberty and the pursuit of Happiness" may not have been intended to ensure that all Americans have the right to work and support their families. (The quotation marks enclose a phrase from the Declaration of Independence.)

In light of recent exposures of corruption among attorneys, one can rightly wonder whether de Tocqueville would still stand with his characterization of the profession of law as "the only aristocratic element" in American life. (The quotation is from *Democracy in America*.)

Do you know the name of the vessel in the Oliver Wendell Holmes poem that begins: "Ay, tear her tattered ensign down! Long has it waved on high"? (This quotation supplies two lines from "Old Ironsides." If the writer of the sentence wished to show that the first two lines were separate, the lines would appear this way: " Ay, tear her tattered ensign down!/Long has it waved on high," with the slash mark indicating the break between the two lines.)

Notice that the opening words in these three quotations do not require capitalization unless they are already capitalized, as with *Life* in the first example and *Ay* in the two lines from Holmes. In addition, there is no need for a comma to introduce the quotations in the first two examples. The quoted material is run into the sentences containing the quotations. In the example quoting Holmes, the colon is used in accordance with the rule governing use of the colon to set off formal statements, quotations, and questions (see pages 84-85).

As the following sentences show, commas or periods needed after quotations are placed inside the final quotes:

> Like Mrs. Malaprop you have "proof controvertible," and I shall now proceed to "extirpate you." (In *The Rivals* Sheridan's famous Mrs. Malaprop massacres the language in a most engaging fashion. Both *proof controvertible* and *extirpate you* are examples of her delightful way with the wrong words. Comma after *controvertible*, period after *you*.)
>
> Medicine can learn a great deal from Nietzsche, who said: "Contentment preserves one even from catching cold. Has a woman who knew that she was well dressed ever caught cold? No, not even when she had scarcely a rag to her back." (Period inside final quotes.)

Quotes Within Quotes

Single quotes are used to enclose a quotation within a quotation. While not a common occurrence, quotations may themselves include quotations. When they do, single quotes are used for the enclosed quotation, and double quotes are used for the enclosing quotation:

> "Have you read the article in the *Los Angeles Times* that speaks of 'possible corruption in the legislature'? It goes on to say that only the leadership is under suspicion." (This entire example is conversation, and so it is enclosed in quotation marks. The words *possible corruption in the legislature* are an exact quotation from a newspaper. They must be enclosed in single quotes, since they are inside a quotation.)
>
> At that time a number of Pharisees came to him and said, "You should leave this place and go your way; Herod is out to kill you." He replied, "Go and tell that fox, 'Listen: today and tomorrow I shall be casting our devils and working cures; on the third day I reach my goal.' However, I must be on my way today and tomorrow and the next day, because it is unthinkable for a prophet to meet his death anywhere but in Jerusalem."

In the opening sentence of this excerpt from *Luke*, the warning of the Pharisees is reported word-for-word and enclosed in double quotes. In the second sentence Jesus replies, and the reply is enclosed in double quotes until the word *Listen*, which opens the exact words the Pharisees are instructed to use in responding to Herod.

Everything from *Listen* to *goal* must be enclosed within single quotes. These words constitute the direct quotation of the instructions to the Pharisees. The double quotes after *Jerusalem* end the direct quotation from Jesus.)

When a single quote is used just before a final double quote, any accompanying punctuation must appear either inside the single quote or outside the double quote. You already know that periods and commas are placed inside quotation marks, and the quotation mark rules on pages 114-116 govern the use of quotes with all the marks. The following examples illustrate the use of periods and commas with single and double quotes:

> I wrote Vera to invite her to attend the concert with us, saying, "You surely can steal time from your painting to spend an hour listening to Beethoven's Fifth, that 'most sublime noise that has ever penetrated into the ear of man.'" (The single quotes enclose a line from E.M. Forster's novel *Howards End*.)
> "I must have your answer by tonight. You are not the only candidate for the position. In fact, I must tell you there are 'Multitudes in the valley of decision,'" the dean said in her letter. (The single quotes enclose words from the Old Testament, which capitalizes *Multitudes*. Otherwise there would be no need to capitalize the word.)

Remember that other marks of punctuation are treated the same when a single quote appears just before a final double quote. The rules about the positioning of other marks with quotation marks apply directly to single quotes that appear just before final double quotes.

Titles of Works of Art

Quotation marks are used when referring to titles of works included within other works—stories in a collection of stories, magazine articles, book chapters, individual poems in a collection of poems—and for paintings, sculptures, speeches, and song titles.

In typing a paper, quoted titles of books, magazines, newspapers, operas, symphonies, and long poems are underscored; in printing, these titles are italicized. Quotation marks are used for parts of books, magazines, and newspapers, and for speeches, parts of musical works, paintings, and single poems of less than volume length.

Usage varies. Some editors prefer italics for paintings and sculpture. In any case no comma is used before a title unless there is some other valid requirement for one.

> In Joyce's collection *Dubliners*, "A Little Cloud" recounts the sad realization of a less than talented man that he will never write good poetry. (The collection of stories is italicized. The single story is enclosed in quotes.)
>
> I came across a copy of *The Saturday Evening Post* of June 9, 1962, which contained an account of how Senator Joseph McCarthy was trapped by his own underhanded tactics. "The Final Irony of Joe McCarthy" is good reading for all of us. (Magazine title italicized, article title in quotes.)
>
> "The Last Days of Peace" is a particularly gripping chapter of William L. Shirer's *The Rise and Fall of the Third Reich.*
>
> Have you read Edwin Arlington Robinson's poem "Richard Cory"?
>
> My favorite song in the musical *South Pacific* is "Some Enchanted Evening."
>
> You ought to hear her sing "The Bell Song," from Delibes' *Lakmé.*

Notice that the rules governing use of punctuation marks with other marks apply equally when quotation marks are used to enclose titles. The last three examples above show quotation marks with a question mark, quotation marks with a period, and quotation marks with a comma. The question mark is outside the quote, because the entire sentence—not the quotation—is a question. The period and the comma are inside the quotes, as they always are.

When quotation marks are needed for a title that appears inside a sentence that is itself a quotation, single quotes are used for the title, since the quotation is enclosed in double quotes:

> The critic wrote: "I find no fault with this production of *My Fair Lady* except for some sloppiness in enunciation. For example, in 'Get Me to the Church on Time,' I was not at all certain whether I heard the singers or was singing to myself the words I know so well."

Titles of works such as plays and novels, which would normally be italicized, are enclosed in quotation marks when the works are cited as parts of larger volumes, for example, anthologies of plays or novels.

Yeats's play "The Countess Cathleen" can be read in *The Collected Plays of W.B. Yeats.* (Because *The Countess Cathleen* is a play, it is normally italicized.)

You can read "Nostromo, A Tale of the Seaboard" in *The Collected Works of Joseph Conrad.* (*Nostromo, A Tale of the Seaboard* is a novel and, therefore, is normally italicized.)

Words Used as Words

Quotation marks are used to indicate words used as words rather than for their meaning. (In this book, as in most books, italics are used to indicate words that are intended to be understood as words rather than as conveyors of meaning.) What do we mean by "words as conveyors of meaning" and "words intended to be understood as words"? The sentence you have just read should indicate what is meant, but the following illustrations will make the distinction clear:

Words as Meanings

Children play happily with bicycles. (All the words in this simple sentence convey meaning. If you had read them in an ordinary paragraph, you would have understood the thought intended.)

Words as Words

Children play happily with bicycles. In this sentence "bicycles" is the object of the preposition "with." (The words *bicycles* and *with* in the second sentence are understood as words. Notice that *bicycles* in the second sentence is not plural. It is the subject of the verb *is.* When *bicycles* is used for its meaning, it is plural: *Bicycles are* commonly used for transportation in many European countries.)

Many people confuse "affect" and "effect" in their writing. (These are the words *affect* and *effect*, not the meanings of *affect* and *effect*.)

We wonder whether "at that point in time" means anything more than "then." (The phrase in quotes and the single word in quotes are words used as words. If the quotation marks were removed, this sentence would be a hopeless jumble. Notice that *at that point in time* and *then* require only two sets of quotation marks, since both the phrase and the word are intended to be perceived as individual verbal units.)

Are you always correct in your spelling of "to," "two," and "too"? (Here, three sets of quotes are needed for three individual words used as words.)

Audrey used ten "uh's" in a single sentence and five "and's."

Misuse of Quotation Marks

Quotation marks are commonly used by writers to apologize for the words they enclose. This is poor practice. Punctuation marks cannot make up for improper or imprecise usage.

Good speakers and writers do their best to choose words appropriate for the audience they are addressing and the degree of formality of the communication. For one audience a writer may use slang or even profanity; in another situation the same writer will deliberately avoid vocabulary that could give offense. (Candidates for public office know the importance of speaking carefully to potential supporters.) What applies to choice of words also applies to grammatical constructions. In one situation no care is given to such matters as agreement of subject and verb or to reference of pronouns; in another situation great pains are taken to ensure correctness of sentence structure, spelling, and punctuation.

These considerations relate to the levels of English usage, reflecting the educational background of the users of English and the situations in which they employ language. Many authorities identify four levels, or varieties, of usage: *nonstandard, informal, general*, and *formal*. Since these levels overlap somewhat, all but the nonstandard may be used in various situations by people of the same educational background.

Nonstandard English is the language used by relatively uneducated people in the conversations they carry on in everyday life. Writing plays a small part in their lives:

I ain't gonna do this nohow.
He got no right to put me down like that.

Informal English is the language employed by better-educated people in relaxed conversation with friends and associates and in informal writing, such as personal letters. It may contain slang and the specialized jargon of occupational groups and social groups. Informal English is generally closer in correctness of grammar and structure to what is taught in most schools than is nonstandard English. In addition the user of informal English—unlike the user of nonstandard English—can move easily into general or formal English when the situation calls for it.

Did you see the thirty-second spots that advertisers ran during
the Superbowl game last night?

Maggie sure gave the kids whatfor yesterday when they told her
the brakes froze while they were driving on Interstate 91.

General English is the language employed by better-educated
people in business correspondence, newspaper articles, books, and
magazines, and in conversation and public talks. General English is
the language of people on their best behavior, cautious in selecting
words and careful to observe as best they can all the rules they were
taught in school.

My subject today is a matter of great concern to all groups
within our community.

Whether we continue to operate successfully in the next five
years depends on action we take now to build sales, improve
the quality of our product, and develop the managerial skills
necessary to compete successfully under present and future
conditions.

Formal English is the language employed by educated people in
a formal setting when they are speaking before audiences of similar
background and when they are writing for such audiences. Technical, scientific, academic, and professional writing almost always
employs formal English. Vocabulary may be specialized and beyond
the grasp of people who lack special training. All rules of grammar
and syntax are scrupulously observed by writers and editors to the
best of their ability. The difference between general English and
formal English lies primarily in the writers' perceptions of their
audiences.

The dynamism of the construct impairs our perception of the
essential interior organic whole.

During the most recent quarter the company made important
strides in overcoming market factors that heretofore precluded quantifiable economic gains, at the same time laying
the groundwork for future capture of export markets in areas of burgeoning growth and capital accumulation accomplished primarily through more efficient use of natural
resources exploited and exchanged with manufacturing
economies at increasingly higher prices.

Educated people, then, employ informal, general, and formal
English at various times, going from one level to another in
response to the situation in which they find themselves. If they

occasionally lapse into incomprehensible gobbledygook when employing formal English, their failure is human. Nonstandard English may also be incomprehensible at times to those who do not use it every day.

Even those who have never studied linguistics are aware that differences in usage mark the speech and writing of educated and uneducated users of English. This insight shows itself when writers employing a particular level of English become self-conscious when they use a word or phrase from another level. To indicate to their readers that, as writers, they know better, they will enclose the offending words in quotation marks. They want the strength that comes from the word or phrase they have chosen, but they do not want to be accused of ignorance. Not only do they do this in writing, but also in speech. How many times have you heard speakers say "quote unquote" to impart a special message to audiences about words they are using?

This practice is useless and patronizing. There is no master list of language approved for any particular level of usage, even though some dictionaries supply their readers with discussions of good and bad usage. If, in the mind of a writer, slang or jargon or profanity is the most effective way to convey an idea, then that writer must take the chance. There is no point in apologizing for use of a word. If a word is inappropriate for an audience or a topic under discussion, it should not be used. Quotation marks do not make the unacceptable acceptable.

The message for you as a writer is clear: Select the best expression you can find for any thought you are discussing and use it without apology. Reserve quotation marks for their legitimate uses:

Wrong: Frank Lloyd Wright frequently designed "cantilevered" structures for his buildings. (They were cantilevered, were they not? What purpose is served by quotation marks?)
Right: Frank Lloyd Wright frequently designed cantilevered structures for his buildings.

Wrong: The "perpetrator" was "apprehended" by the other officer and I.
Right: The perpetrator was apprehended by the other officer and me.
Right: Two of us arrested the suspect.

Wrong: Jackie was a member of the "fast" set in our high school, always smoking "grass" and "popping" pills. (We know that *fast* in this sentence has nothing to do with acceleration or velocity. We also know that *Jackie* did not smoke lawn clippings and that *popping* means swallowing. If these words are inappropriate for the audience, they should not be used. If they are appropriate, why apologize?)

Right: Jackie was a member of the fast set in our high school, smoking grass and popping pills almost every day.

Right: Jackie was a member of the fast set in our high school, given to smoking marijuana and taking psychic energizers and depressants.

Wrong: A "hip chick" really "knows her way around." (Does the audience know what a *hip chick* is? What about *knows her way around*? If the audience does not know these terms, quotation marks will not help. Neither expression should be enclosed in quotation marks if the writer wants to write the sentence this way. If the audience does know these terms, what purpose is served by the quotation marks?)

Right: A really hip chick knows her way around.

Right: A sophisticated young woman needs no guidance.

Inexperienced writers and bumblers sometimes try to invest words with shades of meaning by enclosing them in quotation marks. These misguided writers send a coded message, telling readers that the words in quotation marks are entitled to special treatment. It is as though the writers are winking conspiratorially as they write, with the idea of letting their readers in on the conspiracy so the readers can share the secret message and understand the words precisely as the writers intend.

The problem is that quotation marks have no secret powers. They convey no more meaning than the enclosed material already conveys. They do not contribute to the humor of what is said. They do not convey irony. They do not add emphasis. They merely mark their users as inept.

If a word is intended to mean something other than what it means, another word should be used in its place. If the word conveys the meaning intended, the word may stay, but the quotation marks must go. A "beauty" is no more than a beauty. A "bargain" is only a bargain. If something else is meant, other words must be found.

Find the words that express your meaning. Do not use words that mean less and then decorate them with quotation marks.

Wrong: My mother-in-law always thought she was the "district attorney" in our "conversations." (We know the role of a *district attorney* and we probably know that the *conversations*, therefore, were less than pleasant. In short we understand the humor intended, heavy-handed as it is. We do not need quotation marks to get the point. Does the writer of this sentence think we would miss it without the quotation marks?)

Right: My mother-in-law always thought she was the district attorney in the grillings she conducted every time we met.

Right: My mother-in-law always thought she was the district attorney when we held our so-called conversations.

Wrong: Jack was acting "funny" when I saw him. (If *Jack* was *funny*, no quotation marks are needed. If not, then *funny* is the wrong word.

Right: Jack was acting funny when I saw him.

Right: Jack was acting strangely when I saw him.

Right: Jack was incoherent when I saw him, appearing to be under the influence of drugs or alcohol.

Wrong: You seem to consider yourself a member of the "intelligentsia." (The dictionary provides an excellent definition of *intelligentsia*. What more do quotation marks add? If the writer means to convey irony, perhaps a better expression can be found.)

Right: You seem to consider yourself a member of the intelligentsia.

Right: You think you are more intellectual than you really are.

Wrong: I "really" hate you. (What is stronger than *hate*? Even if we need *really*, it requires no quotation marks. Nothing can be more real than hate.)

Right: I hate you. I really do.

Wrong: He "bombarded" us with facts until we were ready to "scream." (Of course there was no bombardment employing jet airplanes and napalm. In this sentence *bombarded* is used metaphorically and effectively. And what more is conveyed by *scream* enclosed in quotation marks than is conveyed without them?)

Right: He bombarded us with facts until we were ready to scream.

Two other common misuses of quotation marks are found in much writing:

1. Quotation marks are not used with foreign language words or expressions unless they are quoted. Italics, or underscorings in writing or typing, call attention to foreign language words and expressions.

Wrong: She had a certain "je ne sais quoi."
Right: She had a certain *je ne sais quoi*. (French for "indescribable something.")

Wrong: The "Weltschmerz" in the works of Goethe is not always apparent to young readers today.
Right: The *Weltschmerz* in the works of Goethe is not always apparent to young readers today. (*Weltschmerz* is a German noun meaning "sentimental pessimism." It is capitalized because German nouns are capitalized.)

Wrong: The lecturer concluded her statement in a memorable sentence: "If you cannot see the significance of 'ego et meus rex' in the attitude of the Secretary of State, you will never understand the foreign policy we pursue today."
Right: The lecturer concluded her statement in a memorable sentence: "If you cannot see the significance of *ego et meus rex* in the attitude of the Secretary of State, you will never understand the foreign policy we pursue today." (The Latin expression *ego et meus rex* translates as "I and my king," the implication being that the Secretary of State puts himself before the President he serves.)

2. Quotation marks are not used by students writing the titles of their own papers. They are not used by any writer in titling any article, story, song, or the like of which he or she is the author or composer. The rule governing use of quotation marks when referring to the work of others does not apply to titles written for one's own work and appearing on the title page or first page of that work.

Quotation Marks with Other Marks

No mark of punctuation is used immediately after opening quotes.

- Place a comma or a colon before opening quotes.

- Place periods and commas immediately before final quotes.

- Place colons and semicolons immediately after final quotes.

- Place exclamation points and question marks before final quotes if the quotation is an exclamation or question.

- Place exclamation points and question marks after final quotes at the end of a sentence if the sentence is an exclamation or question.

Taken together, this is the longest rule in this book and one that gives many writers trouble. Read carefully through the examples and the discussions that follow. This lengthy rule is really not difficult to learn.

Wrong: Jessie said "There's nothing I can do for you." (No discussion is needed. A comma must be placed before the opening quotes to set off the introductory element *Jessie said*. Nobody has trouble with this part of the rule.)

Right: Jessie said, "There's nothing I can do for you."

Right: The foreman of the jury announced the terrible verdict: "Guilty of murder in the first degree."

Wrong: One chapter of *The Russians*, by Hedrick Smith, is entitled "Patriotism: World War II Was Only Yesterday". (Under no condition may a writer of American English place a period outside the final quotes and be correct. This restriction does not concern logic. It is standard practice.)

Right: One chapter of *The Russians*, by Hedrick Smith, is entitled "Patriotism: World War II Was Only Yesterday."

Wrong: In his chapter "Patriotism: World War II Was Only Yesterday", Hedrick Smith describes Russians as "perhaps the world's most passionate patriots." (Now the final period appears inside the final quotes, where it belongs, but the comma after the chapter title is mistakenly placed outside the final quotes. Under no conditions may a writer of American English place a comma outside final quotes and be correct. This practice has nothing to do with logic.)

Right: In his chapter "Patriotism: World War II Was Only Yesterday," Hedrick Smith describes Russians as "perhaps the world's most passionate patriots."

Wrong: In our childhood Joe Louis was known as the "Brown Bomber:" this affectionate term reflected our respect for his ability to deliver a punch yet suggests we perceived him as a member of another race rather than as a man. (Another violation of standard practice: the colon must never appear before final quotes.)

Right: In our childhood Joe Louis was known as the "Brown Bomber": this affectionate term reflected our respect for his ability to deliver a punch yet suggests we perceived him as a member of another race rather than as a man.

Wrong: He and I finally had a chance to study Emily's new story, "A Wild Goose Chase;" we found it lacking in character development but strong in plot and details of locale, so we accepted it for immediate publication. (Again a violation of standard practice: semicolons must never appear before final quotes.)

Right: He and I finally had a chance to study Emily's new story, "A Wild Goose Chase"; we found it lacking in character development but strong in plot and details of locale, so we accepted it for immediate publication.

Although the rules for periods and commas (inside final quotes) and for colons and semicolons (outside) are strict and without exception, exclamation points and question marks require some thought:

Wrong: Would that I could write something half as good as "The Fall of the House of Usher!" (The title of Poe's famous story does not contain an exclamation point. The sentence in which it is named is itself the exclamation, so the exclamation point must be moved.)

Right: Would that I could write something half as good as "The Fall of the House of Usher"!

Wrong: She was sufficiently angry to say, "To hell with your job"! (The exclamation in this construction is the quotation, not the sentence. The sentence, a declarative statement, would normally require only a period. Since we do not use an exclamation point together with a period, the exclamation point serves in place of the period. But the exclamation point must be placed inside the final quotes.)

Right: She was sufficiently angry to say, "To hell with your job!"

Wrong: Has Joan completed her report on Picasso's "Guernica?" (This title of this great painting is not a question. The sentence is a question. The question mark must be moved.)

Right: Has Joan completed her report on Picasso's "Guernica"?

Wrong: The new minister delivered a sensational sermon entitled "Is God Only Half Alive"? (This sentence is not a question. The title of the sermon is. The question mark must be moved.)

Right: The new minister delivered a sensational sermon entitled "Is God Only Half Alive?"

Placement of an exclamation point or a question mark depends on whether the material within quotes is an exclamation or a question, or whether the sentence including the quotation is an exclamation or a question.

Thus, the exclamation point goes *inside* quotes if the *quotation* is an exclamation, *outside* quotes if the *sentence* is an exclamation.

Likewise, the question mark is placed *inside* quotes if the *quotation* is a question, *outside* quotes if the *sentence* is a question.

PARENTHESES

Parentheses are used within sentences, around entire sentences, and even around entire paragraphs. Parentheses are used most often to set off elements that interrupt the grammatical and logical flow of a sentence.

When are parentheses preferred over commas and dashes to set off parenthetic elements? Parentheses are used when the elements to be set off are too relevant to omit but are not part of the sentences or paragraphs in which they are found. Readers see material enclosed in parentheses as less important, at least for the moment, than material that is enclosed in dashes or commas. They consider material enclosed in dashes and, to an even greater extent, material enclosed in commas as true parts of the sentence they are reading.

The greatest users of parentheses are scholars who want to tell their readers everything they know about a subject and to supply readers with as much related information as their editors will permit. Most writing, however, requires parentheses only occasionally, primarily for such conventional uses as enclosing numerals and letters in an enumeration. Parentheses are sometimes used in this book to set off discussions from sentences used as illustrations. This is a convention of textbook publishing. Another occasional use in this book is to set off cross-references for the reader's convenience.

With Relevant but Not Vital Information

Parentheses are used to set off material that is too relevant to omit but is not truly part of the sentence or paragraph in which it appears. Somewhat like the actor in a Shakespearian play who addresses asides to the audience, abruptly leaving off speaking with the other actors to communicate confidentially with the audience, a writer may wish to refer to something that is not central to the topic under discussion. Knowing that the reader deserves an explanation for the sudden interruption, the writer encloses the interrupting material in parentheses. Material within parentheses is usually an illustration, a definition, an explanation, or a reference to other writing:

> Theodore Dreiser's novels are no longer popular (even though a film made of *An American Tragedy* enjoyed great commercial success some years ago), but some critics rank Dreiser among the best American novelists and anticipate a revival of interest in his work.

You can see that the reference to the film in this example is relevant to the sentence but not truly part of it. The claim for Dreiser's ability has little to do with the film made of one of his novels. The material is worthy of inclusion in the sentence only because the subject of Dreiser's popularity was introduced. Parentheses are the correct mark to use in setting off the parenthetic element. Notice that the comma before *but* comes outside the final parenthesis, because the comma is not part of the parenthetical material.

> Many of the early colonists fled their homes to avoid the fighting that erupted in New England (and later in other areas as well).

This material is enclosed in parentheses because the principal discussion concerns events that occurred at a particular time and place. What happened elsewhere is not of immediate concern, but the writer wishes to call attention to the fact that colonists also fled their homes in other areas. Parentheses are the correct mark. Notice that the period comes outside the final parenthesis because the parenthetical material is not a complete sentence.

> Television journalists enjoy great personal reputations and extremely high salaries. (David Brinkley even today is mentioned in lists of most-admired and most-trusted Americans.) Their counterparts in print journalism remain relatively unknown by the general public and are paid substantially less than TV news people.

Introducing Brinkley's name gives us an interesting bit of information that is insufficient to offer as conclusive proof of the claim made in the first sentence. The writer knows this and offers the sentence enclosed in parentheses as information that is relevant but not truly a part of the paragraph. Notice that the material enclosed within parentheses is a complete sentence, so its period is placed inside the final parenthesis.

When parentheses include only part of a sentence, the punctuation of the sentence is not affected by the parentheses.

> All the information on substantial lawsuits outstanding is included in the company's annual report (reproduced here as Appendix A).
>
> The composer refuses to state where she was born (three countries claim her as a native), but birth records indicate she was born on October 4, 1946, in Brooklyn, New York.
>
> Funding for the program falls far short of what was anticipated (newspaper accounts suggest the original amount exceeded $2,000,000); every indication at present is that the program will terminate in this coming fiscal year.

In these three sentences the final parenthesis falls inside the regular sentence punctuation. In the first sentence a period is needed to end the sentence. In the second a comma is needed before the conjunction *but*, which connects the two independent clauses. In the third a semicolon is needed between the two independent clauses.

> Dramatic expressionism is a term applied to plays that emphasize emotional content, subjective reactions of characters, and symbolic representations of reality. (O'Neill's *The*

Emperor Jones is an excellent example of this genre.) In painting, expressionism suggests exaggeration and distortion of forms derived from nature combined with the intensification of color to express emotion. Thus, while the relationship of the two forms of expressionism can be perceived, the terms have differing meanings that must be explored fully for complete understanding.

Collage employs materials that classical artists would have thought alien to art. (What use would Rubens or Rembrandt have made of old newspapers and bottle caps?) Yet the principles of composition and the appreciation of color relationships in the best collages retain their resemblance to the composition and color of the older art.

These two examples show punctuation internal to parenthetic material. In the first case the parentheses set off an entire sentence punctuated by a period. In the second the parentheses set off a question. An exclamatory sentence, of course, can also be set off by parentheses. In all complete parenthetical sentences, the final parenthesis follows the period, the question mark, or the exclamation point. Notice that in such constructions no period is needed after the parenthesis.

Miscellaneous Uses

Parentheses are used to set off numerals and letters used in enumerations and in numerical figures that confirm a spelled-out number.

To qualify for bidding, a defense contractor is required to show evidence of (1) financial stability, (2) technical competence, (3) qualified personnel in adequate numbers, and (4) full understanding of the problem.

Before undertaking the doctoral examinations, students must be certain they can demonstrate (a) reading knowledge of one classical and two modern languages in addition to English, (b) broad competence in American and English literature, and (c) thorough knowledge of the centuries in which they intend to specialize.

The check must be made out in the amount of five hundred dollars ($500.00) and must be certified by the bank on which it is drawn. (This use of parentheses goes back to a time when transactions were recorded in pen and ink. The purpose was to clarify what often was indecipherable handwriting. With the advent of the typewriter, the convention lost its purpose.)

Brackets

Just as writers use parentheses to set off explanations or comments within their own sentences, they use brackets to set off explanations, corrections, or comments they wish to make in material that they are quoting. In this latter situation writers act as editors of words spoken or written by someone else.

Brackets are also used to set off parenthetic material within parenthetic material already enclosed in parentheses. We see such punctuation primarily in legal documents, footnotes, and complex bibliographic entries, infrequently in other writing.

Editorial Changes and Comments

Brackets are used to set off explanations, corrections, expansions, and comments inserted in quoted material. A quotation introduced into an essay may require slight alteration before it can be used in the sentence or paragraph for which it is intended. The writer using the quoted material is free to make any change necessary as long as the change does not alter the intended meaning of the quoted material, but the readers must be informed that changes have been made. Brackets around the changes are the conventional means of informing readers of the changes. These changes may take the form of explanations, corrections, expansions, or comments:

"F. Scott Fitzgerald wrote amusing lyrics for *Safety First* [the Princeton 1916-1917 Triangle show] as well as for two other operettas." (The writer using this quotation thinks it important to supply proper identification of *Safety First*, something the writer being quoted did not choose to do.)

"The process of disentanglement from art is clearly final when *Malone Dies* [Samuel Beckett's novel, published as *Malone meurt* in 1948] ends." (The writer using this quotation identifies *Malone Dies* for the convenience of readers.)

"Is it [Kafka's "The Metamorphosis"] the whine of an irretrievable neurotic or is it a beautiful lament?" (The pronoun *it* is explained by the writer using this quotation.)

"From the day the Korean War began [June 25, 1950] until the day it ended [July 27, 1953], there was substantial opposition to the operation within important segments of the press." (The writer supplies the dates for the convenience of readers.)

"Critical acclaim came quickly for the poet from all sides [one notable exception was Diana Trilling] and with the acclaim a measure of financial security." (The writer inserts a correction in the quotation.)

As Alexander Pope put it: "Authors are partial to their wit, 'tis true/But are not critics [partial] to their judgment too?" (The writer quoting Pope has added *partial* to clarify the thought for modern readers.)

Sophocles warns against excessive self-pride in these words: "Wisdom is the supreme part of happiness; and reverence toward the gods must be inviolate. *Great words of prideful men are ever punished with great blows* and, in old age, teach the chastened to be wise." [The emphasis is the author's, not Sophocles'.] (The writer explains the use of italics to indicate emphasis, lest readers think the original text of the opening clause of the second sentence appeared in italics.)

As you can see, a writer has considerable leeway in amplifying and correcting quotations. The intention of the original must not be altered, however, and readers must be shown clearly that the changes made are not those of the writer being quoted.

Another use of brackets is different from the uses described previously. This use is commonly seen and often misunderstood. The Latin word *sic* means *thus*. It appears in brackets when it is used as an editorial comment, and it is italicized because it is a foreign word. *Sic* in brackets after an apparent mistake in a quotation indicates that the mistake is not the fault of the writer who uses the quotation, but an error or deviation from standard practice in the text being quoted:

The letter from the kidnapper consisted of one sentence: "You better git [*sic*] the $250,000 dollars rite [*sic*] away and hide it ware [*sic*] I tell you soon." (Misspellings in the letter are explained as the kidnapper's errors, not the writer's.)

"I don't know where you're from, but I'm from Brooklyn, Vermont, [*sic*] and damned proud of it." (The brackets indicate that "Brooklyn, Vermont" is accurately quoted.)

Parenthetic Material Within Parenthetic Material

Brackets are used instead of parentheses to set off parenthetic material that occurs within material already enclosed in parentheses. This rule is rarely applied except by lawyers and scholars:

> The party of the first part (in this case the lessor [the lessee is the party of the second part] unless the lessor is a corporation) is responsible for delivering to the party of the second part a building in good operating condition.
>
> For fuller discussion, see Perrin's article on *echo phrases* (Porter G. Perrin, *Writer's Guide and Index to English* [Chicago, 1942]).

– 12 –

Capitalization

There are many uses for capitalization, some clearly understood by most writers and some not so clearly understood. The review that follows begins with the easiest rule of all and then presents all the other requirements for capital letters.

SENTENCES

The first letter of every word of every grammatical unit punctuated as a sentence is capitalized. Notice that the rule speaks of *every grammatical unit punctuated as a sentence*. Why? Everyone who has had even a few years of formal instruction knows that the first word of a sentence is capitalized:

> *Now* is the time for all good men to come to the aid of their party.
> *Let* there be peace all over the world!
> *Can* anyone doubt that people anywhere who are hungry must be fed?

A sentence is normally defined as a group of words expressing a complete thought and containing a subject and a predicate. But what about a sentence that contains only one word? There are many examples of this:

> Homeless persons abound on many of our city streets. *Why?*
> Whom did you meet at the party? *Jane.*

Neither *Why* nor *Jane* contains both a subject and a predicate. Such units are commonly called *fragments* or *incomplete sentences*, and they are punctuated and used as sentences by professional writers as well as the rest of us. For this reason, the rule given governs capitalization of the first letter of the first word of any grammatical unit punctuated as a sentence.

Consider the following examples, none of which is called a complete sentence:

At last!
Now!
Now?
No.

Now consider this dialogue:

"Which do you like?"
"Neither."
"Which will you buy?"
"Both."
"Now?"
"Right now."

The first and third examples are complete sentences in the traditional sense. The remaining examples are fragments. Yet all are treated as sentences, with the first letter of the first word of each capitalized.

POETRY

The first letter of the first word in conventional poetry is capitalized.

The great majority of poets start each line of their poems in this way, but a small number of poets choose to ignore this convention. Thus, when quoting a line or more of conventional poetry, you must capitalize conventionally. When quoting a poet who ignores this convention, follow the lead of the poet:

One impulse from a vernal wood
May teach you more of man,
Of moral evil and of good,
Than all the sages can.
　　　　—William Wordsworth

QUOTATIONS

The first word of a quotation is capitalized, unless the quotation is less than a sentence long.

Quoted material sometimes does not consist of complete sentence. When this is so, the first word is not capitalized unless there is some other reason for capitalizing. Consider first two quotations that are complete sentences:

> Harry's mother said, "*You* must keep your room clean."
> "*We* will not help you with your work," the older children said.

Now consider two quotations that are not complete sentences:

> Hobbes's famous phrase "a kind of sudden glory" describes the feeling of an onlooker seeing misfortune befall another person. (The first letter of the quotation is not capitalized, because the quotation is not a sentence.)
> Will we ever hear the word *expletive* again without recalling "expletive deleted," of Watergate fame? (The first letter of the quotation is not capitalized, because the quotation is not a sentence.)

When a quotation of a complete sentence is broken into two parts in the sentence quoting it, the first word of the second part is not usually capitalized:

> "You will," he went on, "do exactly what I tell you to do."

The second part of quotation may well be a complete sentence. If so, its first word must be capitalized:

> "You will do exactly what I tell you to do," he went on. "You will leave for the airport immediately and bring your sister home."

THE WORDS *O* AND *I*

The pronoun *I* and the interjection *O* are capitalized. Except for *I*, pronouns are not capitalized unless they are used as the first word of a sentence or a line of poetry. Do not confuse the pronoun *I* with the letter *i*:

She and I are going together. (*She* is capitalized because it is the first word of a sentence, *I* because it is *I*.)

Please see that she and I are seated together.

There are three i's in the word *invidious*.

The interjection *O*, seen mainly in literature and in prayer books but rarely used today, is always capitalized, even though the interjection *oh* is not capitalized. Do not confuse the interjection *O* with the letter *o*:

Ben Jonson wrote the famous line: "O me no O's."

Hear me, O Israel!

The word *cooperate* has two o's and is spelled three different ways: cooperate, co-operate, and coöperate.

NAMES

Proper nouns and adjectives are capitalized. A proper noun is the name of a person, place, or thing. A proper adjective is an adjective derived from a proper noun.

Frank asked *Lucy* for a dinner date. (Proper nouns.)

The scenery of *Italy* attracts many thousands of tourists from all over the world. (Proper noun.)

The *Oval Office* is synonymous with political power in the *United States*. (Proper nouns.)

After a long absence from the finest tables, *Portuguese* wines are making a comeback. (*Portuguese* is a proper adjective, modifying *wines*. In the sentence *He is a Portuguese*, *Portuguese* is a proper noun.)

Her second child was delivered by *Caesarean* section. (*Caesarean* is a proper adjective, derived from the name *Julius Caesar*.)

The swimming team practiced the *Australian* crawl. (*Australian* is a proper adjective. In the sentence *She is an Australian*, *Australian* is a proper noun.)

When you deal with words such as *china* (the ceramic used for dishes) and *China* (the country), be certain that you do not confuse common nouns with proper nouns. The rule given here for capitalizing affects only proper nouns and proper adjectives.

PARTICLES

Capitalize American family names beginning with the particles *Van, Von, De, Du,* or *Da.* Do not capitalize foreign family names beginning with the particles *van* or *von.* Do not capitalize foreign family names beginning with the particles *de, du, di,* or *da* unless the names appear without first names or titles.

Many family names of foreign origin include particles. *Van* is of Dutch origin. *Von* is of German origin. *De* and *du* are of French origin. *De* is also of Spanish origin. *Di* and *da* are of Italian origin. All have the same meaning: *from* or *place of origin.* Thus, someone named *Simon de Versailles* would literally be *Simon of Versailles.*

As names employing the various particles become Americanized, the particles often are treated as separate and capitalized parts of the names rather than as particles with the meaning of *of:*

> The *Van Cortlandt* family,
> Agnes and Cecil *De Mille.*

Names of foreign families are given special treatment following European custom:

> Ferdinand *de* Lesseps, builder of the Suez Canal
> Paul *von* Hindenburg, President of Germany from 1925 to 1934

In the European custom, with first names and titles omitted, these two names would be given as *Lesseps* and *Hindenburg.* In the American custom they would be given as *De Lesseps* and *Von Hindenburg:*

> One of the best engineers I knew in Connecticut was Paul Von Hardenburgh. (An American name.)
> The Van Doren family boasted two distinguished literary men: Carl and Mark. (An American name.)
> Most branches of the Du Pont family still reside in Delaware. (An American name.)
> Do you know the novels of Pietro di Donato? (An Italian name.)
> Have you read Donato's novels? (An Italian name appearing without a first name.)
> Wernher von Braun started his career as a rocketeer at Dortmund, Germany. (A German name.)
> We know that Braun later lived in Alabama and died there. (A German name appearing without a first name.)

GEOGRAPHICAL NAMES

Since geographical names are proper nouns, they are capitalized. There are several conventions that are followed when using geographic names, however, that make additional discussion worthwhile.

Before beginning, be certain you understand that words such as *river, ocean, mountain,* and *gorge* are geographical terms that are used both alone and as parts of of the names of of geographical features: *Mississippi River, Atlantic Ocean, Doe Mountain, Quechee Gorge.* When *river* and other terms occur as parts of geographical names, they are capitalized. Otherwise, they are not capitalized.

In all the examples given thus far, the geographical term has been singular. Other terms are often plural, for example, *Harbor Hills, Thousand Islands, Rocky Mountains,* and *Verrazano Narrows.* Again, since *Hills* and the other terms are parts of a geographical name, they are capitalized. Otherwise, these plurals are not capitalized.

The final group of geographical terms to be considered consists of singular words that are used both before and after place names: *Bay of Fundy, Cape of Good Hope, Lake Louise* and *Mount Rainier; Baffin Bay, Howe Cape, Churchill Lake,* and *Rocky Mount.* These terms follow the same practice. When they are part of a geographical name, they are capitalized. When they are not, they are not capitalized:

> I have seen many mountains in my long life, but none to rival the Rocky Mountains.
> Of all the rivers in the United States, there is none to rival the Mississippi River.
> If I had one wish that would be fulfilled, I would wish to own one of the islands of the Thousand Islands or one of the lakes of the Finger Lakes.

COMPASS DIRECTIONS

Compass directions are capitalized when they are parts of the names of specific regions. Do not capitalize *east, west,* and so on when these terms merely indicate directions: *Travel north on I-95 to see the beauties of the season.* Capitalize compass directions when they serve as parts of the names of places or regions:

> An old song referred the region just a little bit *south* of *South Carolina.* (A direction, *south*, and a place name, *South Carolina.*)
> In national elections voters in *South Dakota* do not often vote differently from voters to the *north.*

REGIONAL NAMES AND NICKNAMES

The names and nicknames of geographic regions and political units are capitalized:

> Columbus set forth from the *Old World* to find China and actually found what turned out to be the *New World.*
> Mystery writers never seem to tire of setting their tales in the *Orient.*
> John Steinbeck's most memorable novel dealt with the people who fled the *Dust Bowl* in the 1930's.

STREETS, BUILDINGS, PARKS, AND COMPANIES

The names of all formally designated streets, buildings, parks, public places, and companies are capitalized:

> All the world has heard of New York City's *Fifth Avenue.*
> The *World Trade Center* is the tallest structure in New York City.
> Have you ever visited *Yellowstone Park*?
> Lenin's tomb in Moscow's *Red Square* has outlived the Soviet Union.
> *American Airlines* is still the premier American airline company.
> The *United Nations* appears to be taking on new functions.

ORGANIZATIONS AND OTHER GROUPS

The proper names of all organizations, religions, races, nationalities, orchestras, and other groups are capitalized. This convention is another specific expansion of the rules of capitalization governing proper names: *Princeton University, Seventh-Day Adventists, Asians, Poles, Department of State, Chicago Police Department, The Salvation Army*, and countless other organizations and groups.

When anything but the proper name of such a group is used, no capitals are required: *university departments, fundamentalists, bureaucrats, government departments, charities, rock groups*.

When a phrase is used that could serve as the proper name of an organization but does not, the phrase is not capitalized. Only official names are capitalized:

> We decided to form a *cheerleaders' club*.
> The Tenafly, New Jersey, *Cheerleaders' Club* is popular with students.
> In the 1930's our political leaders recognized that the government had a responsibility to organize a *commission* that would regulate the securities business.
> The *Securities and Exchange Commission* oversees the public sale of securities.

DEITY AND SACRED WRITINGS

Nouns and pronouns referring to God and writings held to be sacred are capitalized. American usage requires that all references to God, members of the Trinity, religious observances, and the books sacred to religious traditions be capitalized:

> God, the Father, the Son, and the Holy Spirit were celebrated in a special Mass.
> The reading of the Haggadah during the Passover Seder is a reminder of the deliverance of the Israelites from Egypt.
> Many Muslims know the Koran by heart.

EVENTS, ERAS, PRIZES, DOCUMENTS

The proper names of all wars, battles, historic events, treaties, documents, prizes, and historical periods are capitalized. This convention is an extension of the general practice governing capitalization of proper names:

A *civil war* is the saddest of wars.

The onset of the *Spanish Civil War* presaged the end of democracy in that land.

The *Nobel Prize for Literature* is awarded for a lifetime of literary work.

People who lived through the *Great Depression* will never recover completely from the experience.

TITLES; ACADEMIC DEGREES; AND TITLES OF BOOKS, PLAYS, AND PERIODICALS

Capitalize military and civil titles when they precede a name, indicate high rank, or are used as substitutes for the names of individuals:

Did you know that *Consul* Burton was in danger of losing his job at that point in his career? (Title preceding a name.)

The *Secretary of Defense* now admits that he misled the Congress in his testimony. (Title of high rank. Notice that *of* is not capitalized. Articles, prepositions, and conjunctions are not capitalized unless—in the case of prepositions and conjunctions—they are five letters or more in length.)

After André was apprehended, the *Major* was kept captive until his trial. (Title used as a substitute for the full title and name of a person: *Major John André*.)

The mortality rate for lieutenants in World War I was shockingly high. (No capital letter for *lieutenants*. The word is not used as a substitute for someone's name.)

Capitalize all academic degrees and their abbreviations:

The degrees *Doctor of Law* and *Juris Doctor*, abbreviated (*J.D.*), are now awarded commonly in American law schools.

Eloise is the only person I know who may write *R.N.* and *M.D.* after her name.

Capitalize the first word and all unimportant words of five letters or more in titles of literary works, music, journals, magazines, and newspapers:

The House of Seven Gables (*The* is the first word; *of* is only two letters long.)

Much Ado About Nothing (All the words are important, even *Ado*.)

Consider all the following examples, which are correctly given:

The Way of All Flesh
All's Well That Ends Well
For Whom the Bell Tolls
Long Day's Journey into Night,
The Importance of Being Earnest
"Recent Additions to the Morgan Library"
"Dover Beach"
Gypsy
"Happy Days Are Here Again"
Statistical Abstracts
Journal of the National Association of Deans of Women
Playboy
National Review
The Daily News

Section II

WRITING

– 1 –

The Act of Writing

All writers must begin at the same place: the first word. The page is always blank before you begin, and if the empty page frightens you, rest assured that many who make their living with the pen or typewriter or word processor find it just as threatening.

Inexperienced writers are often inhibited by the belief that they must know everything they are going to say before they begin to write. Professional writers do not make this mistake. While a succinct thesis statement and an outline are useful, ideas and their organization can develop during the writing itself. Experienced writers know this.

The act of writing is a process of discovery. Good writing does not depend on thinking everything through in advance. As you write and rewrite, you will find out how much or how little you already know about your chosen subject. You will realize that some of the ideas you thought would be easy to explain and support are in fact not so clear. On the other hand, as you write, vague ideas may blossom into concrete and heartfelt convictions.

You may find that you have much more to say on a subject than you thought you would when you began. Jack London, for example, expected to complete *The Call of the Wild* as a 5000-word story. Within five weeks he had produced the 32,000-word novel we now consider a classic.

THE HABIT OF WRITING

When professional writers sit down to their day's work, they do not always have a good idea of what they are going to write. More often, getting started is difficult and frustrating—ideas seem to disappear, words will not flow, pessimism and depression set in. But this need not happen.

Some writers develop their own systems to get their work going. Ernest Hemingway used to stop work each day *just before he ran out of things to say*, so that when he resumed work the following morning at six, he wouldn't have to start cold. Once he had started by completing the previous day's work, he was ready for additional writing.

Other writers play out their string before they quit work each day. To get them started again the next morning, almost anything they put down on paper will serve. They may begin to write and find that what is appearing before them is a letter to a friend or a rebuttal to a newspaper editorial. They may merely blow off steam about the cruelty of life. No matter. Writing anything leads to more writing and, finally, to the writing they must do.

Some colleges offer courses that encourage students to develop the habit of writing in just this fashion. These writing courses give credit for a certain number of words a day, every day, on any subject.

THE TECHNIQUE OF FREE WRITING

When you have no idea what to write about, try *free writing*. Soon enough your mind will move you into productive work. The discipline that comes from writing regularly makes you a better writer, just as hours of practicing scales and easy pieces improve a pianist's work. Many important writers, Hemingway among them, started out as journalists. The pressure of deadlines and regular assignments on many subjects taught them to report concisely and clearly. Ben Hecht, a Chicago newspaperman who went to Hollywood, was able to write the movie *Underworld* in two weeks, even though it was the first screenplay he had ever tackled. His newspaper experience had made him a disciplined writer.

For each session of *free writing*, set a goal of a certain number of words, just as you would if you were taking a course or if your city editor told you to bring in one story a day every day. If possible, set aside the same time each day at the same desk. That time slot and that desk will help to establish the mood for writing. No planning, no thinking. Let the words flow. Dream. Complain. Write a letter to a friend. Plan for the future. Rebuild society. Shape the world. Tell a story. Write anything. Write. Soon enough you will begin writing the paper you are supposed to write.

In this process, don't look for polished writing. As you write each day, your writing will flow more smoothly. In time it will also be more persuasive, more gripping, more expressive of you. But when you have finished writing the paper you are supposed to write, you have completed your first draft. No matter whether it is anything you are proud of. The process of *free writing* has enabled you to make a good start toward the production of a good paper.

AFTER THE FIRST DRAFT

Once you have a first draft and feel confident that what you have written will eventually be worth reading, your next job begins. You must read through your draft carefully to delete where necessary, to reorganize where necessary, and to make whatever improvements in style are necessary to be sure you have written as well as you can. You want to check for clarity and for logical ordering of ideas. You want to make sure that your argument will convince your reader. You want to make certain you have used the most appropriate words for your subject and your audience. You want to double-check all spellings and other essential details.

The checklist that follows spells out what to look for in reviewing a draft and preparing for the final draft.

CHECKLIST FOR WRITERS

Information
1. Have I stated my purpose clearly?

2. Have I presented all my arguments convincingly and in logical order?

3. Have I omitted any important arguments that should be presented to convince the reader?

4. Have I kept to the point and been specific?

5. Have I answered opposing points of view, or have I merely attacked them?

6. Have I reasoned logically in every detail of the discussion?

7. Have I stated my conclusion clearly?

Style

1. Have I written as directly and clearly as I can, always speaking to the same reader and using language appropriate for that reader?

2. Have I written in the liveliest and most interesting style I can manage? Are my verbs as strong as possible? Do they convey the meaning I want? Are my adjectives and adverbs doing the job I want them to do?

3. Can I delete any words and thereby strengthen my writing?

Structure

1. Have I written an opening paragraph that makes clear what I am going to say and makes the reader want to go on?

2. Have I organized each paragraph logically and provided smooth transitions between paragraphs?

3. Have I closed my report with a section or paragraph that ties my argument tightly together and leaves the reader convinced of the strength of my argument?

4. Have I deleted all sentences that add nothing to my meaning or to the strength of my argument?

WRITING EFFECTIVELY

Be sure that any important writing you do—whether one page or many pages long—is tightly structured. Each sentence you write must assist in the development of the paragraph of which it is a part. Each paragraph you write must deal with a single topic. Finally, the topic treated in each paragraph must relate directly to the subject of the entire work. When you have finished all your work—from your first vague thoughts on the subject through final rewriting, typing, and proofreading—you must make certain that you have covered your subject to your own satisfaction and the satisfaction of your reader. For these reasons, the thought processes underlying your writing are of greatest importance.

The writing you produce will satisfy your reader only if it shows the same sense of organization displayed in each well-organized paragraph and sentence. Thus, all your writing must be directed toward the theme you are discussing, and you must check your work after you complete your first draft to see that you have not strayed from that theme.

Good Structure Pays Off

Just as you can most easily organize an individual paragraph by writing a topic sentence, you can best organize an entire paper—whether a student theme, a memorandum, a report, an important letter, or a proposal—by having your theme in mind before you begin to write. Knowing what you are trying to convey enables you to write confidently and easily. You may not know yet the precise conclusions you will reach, but you ought to have clearly in mind the general goal you are trying to reach. For example, do you intend to make recommendations dealing with recent developments in electronics or with plans for further attractive technological innovations? Do you intend to propose plans for a local community development? Or do you wish to propose a restructuring of your company's personnel policies?

Whatever you intend to accomplish, if you do not have some idea of what you want to say before you begin to write, you may make a number of false starts before you fully understand just what you want to tell your reader. This explains why many people waste a great deal of time writing their opening sentences again and again—and many of them despair of ever becoming competent writers. What to do about this?

When you do not have a detailed understanding of just what you intend to say, it is far better to begin to write without knowing where your thoughts will lead you than to sit and stare at a blank page while waiting for inspiration to strike or for your thinking to sort itself out. If you begin by writing down anything that comes to mind and keep on writing, without regard for how good your writing is, sooner or later a theme will emerge. This theme will organize your thinking and make it possible for you to write effectively. It is in the subsequent rewriting that you will sharpen your writing, making it unified and cohesive.

A well-organized piece of writing will fall roughly into three parts. These may be thought of as the introduction, the body, and the conclusion.

Writing an Effective Introduction

An introduction tells the reader what your paper will discuss and stirs the reader's interest in the subject. The first purpose can be accomplished in several ways. You may state the theme of the entire paper, you may state the questions you are going to deal with, or you may give the background of the questions or problems you are going to discuss. You may accomplish the second purpose—supplying the reader with good reasons to go on—by beginning with a striking quotation from a respected source, by citing a pertinent newspaper headline, by offering a statement by a public official or expert in your subject, or by stating facts that call attention to the importance of the subject.

One of the best ways to interest your reader in going on is to make the boldest claim you can. (Be sure to substantiate it later on.) By the time the reader has come to the end of the introduction— whether a single paragraph or several pages long—you will have made clear what the subject is and why the reader should continue reading.

The Body Tells It All

The body of any paper develops and supports the theme established in the introduction, supplying the information that will convince the reader to accept the writer's point of view. Many types of paragraphs are appropriate to explain and expand and support the theme convincingly. To develop a particular point, you may relate facts or incidents chronologically, you may classify information, you may compare or contrast two ideas, and you may supply definitions. You may also divide large topics into their logical parts, and you may illustrate the truth of what you are saying by providing specific examples to support your points.

Writing the Conclusion

In a long report a conclusion may be fairly detailed, summarizing for the reader every important point, but especially the overall theme. Without such a summing up, the reader is left with the burden of putting together the full meaning of the paper. Instead of forcing readers to think back over everything they have read, any good writer supplies a summary of what has been discussed.

A short paper does not usually require a detailed conclusion. Because little information has been presented, the reader would be bored with repetitive details. Nevertheless, readers should not be abandoned abruptly once the body of the paper comes to an end. All that is necessary in a short piece is for you to state once again—in different words, of course—what the introduction raised as the subject of discussion and what you have said about it. Having read this restatement of the theme, the reader will know that the writer did not quit suddenly before the end. The reader will also be aware that you have accomplished in the paper what you set out to accomplish.

In a long report, the conclusion plays an equally vital role. It spells out, item by item, just what you have found or are recommending or are formally proposing. Think of such a statement as providing the reader with a complete set of notes on the subject you have been discussing. Even if the reader will not be able to recall all your detailed thinking about your subject, he or she will know its most important aspects—your findings, your recommendations, your proposal.

Let Everything Come Together

When you plan and write your first draft, you risk setting yourself back unnecessarily by being too aware of the final structure of the report. You may find it more useful to leave the final shaping for the rewriting stage, when you can play the role of reader rather than writer. Think about this for a moment. As reader, you can take in what you have written and evaluate the way your report is put together. You can easily make any changes of words, phrases, sentences, and even whole paragraphs to complete your orderly presentation of ideas. You can also move these elements about to increase the effectiveness of your presentation.

What usually begins as a shapeless topic, then, can be polished and repolished until you have a paper you are proud to submit. The necessary polishing takes time and care. It begins when you have completed your first draft and may continue even while you are doing the final typing.

The chief secret of a successful paper is simply this: think before you write, think while you write, think when you revise. And never fool yourself into giving up after preparing just one draft. No matter how carefully you work while preparing your first draft, you will find that the act of writing will sharpen your thoughts and make it necessary for you to rethink, if not the entire topic, at least some of its subsidiary points. A second draft (and sometimes a third) is the way to transfer your best thinking to paper.

– 2 –

Effective Résumés

A résumé supplies the pertinent work and other experience, education, and personal information by which employers judge a job applicant's qualifications. No résumé alone will guarantee a job. But it can do a great deal to get the applicant a favorable hearing. A good résumé opens doors to interviews; a poor one closes them.

Employers usually conduct personal interviews before hiring a person for a position of real responsibility. They want to learn everything they can about an applicant. They want to make certain that the applicant's personal qualities match the requirements of the position that is open. Not least, they want to see the kind of impression the applicant makes in person.

When you look for your first opportunity and as you advance in your career, you probably will have to apply for a job in writing. You will find it helpful, therefore, to learn how to write a résumé that opens doors for you and that represents you in the best possible light, so that employers will be eager to meet you—and to hire you.

There are various ways to set up an effective résumé, but at the least your résumé should meet the requirements of clarity, compactness, and completeness. This is also one area in which neatness counts for a great deal. Some people go to great lengths to have their résumés set in type, making the end result look like an attractive and professional offering. Such an effort, however, is not necessary—in fact, it is not even appropriate except for some extremely experienced and high-priced executives. For all other résumés, a perfectly typed and intelligently arranged listing of qualifications is sufficient. Note that the typing should be perfect—no handwritten corrections or insertions of any kind.

141

Once you have achieved a perfect master copy, however, the tedious work is done: From then on, you will be able to make photocopies of this master copy, and the photocopies are what you will mail out. Keep the master (do not fold it or let it get soiled) in case more copies have to be made. Should you apply for another position a year or two later, this master can easily be updated and retyped.

Depending on whether your résumé is being prepared for an entry-level or a more advanced position, the weight given to the separate elements will vary. All résumés you create, however, will include the following.

1. Your name, mailing address, and phone number where you can be reached during working hours.

2. Your work experience. This category will, of course, list any jobs in the same field in which you are now seeking employment. But any related work experience should also be cited.

3. Your educational background, including any college and advanced degrees and fields of specialization.

4. Any volunteer experience, hobbies, or special skills you have that are pertinent to the job you are applying for.

5. References.

6. In addition, you may want to include a line indicating the type of job you are seeking.

In the past many people included personal statistics on their résumés—birth date, height and weight, marital status, and physical condition. This information is no longer considered relevant. In fact, legislation forbidding discrimination against women, against the handicapped, and so forth makes it inadvisable to include such data.

The two principal ways of setting up the information in the résumé are *chronological* (samples 1 and 2) and *functional* (sample 3). (See pages 145-148.)

In a chronological résumé the separate categories of education and work experience are listed *backward* in the order of occurrence—most recent job first, then the one preceding it, and so forth; latest degree earned or latest school attended first, and so on.

In a functional résumé, work experience is divided not by time but by the kind of work performed—administrative, for example, or work requiring the operation of certain machinery or equipment, and the like. The other categories (such as hobbies) follow the same pattern established for each type of résumé.

Your résumé will also vary somewhat depending on whether you are seeking work for the first time or have a background of related work experience to offer. If you are seeking work for the first time, list your educational background first and in the greatest detail. If you have had jobs in the field in which you are seeking employment, supply your work experience first and make it highly specific. You then may summarize your educational background in a few lines.

Name and Address

It is important that anyone who receives your résumé be able to get in touch with you easily. You will, of course, give your permanent address, but you may also need to include a temporary address (such as a school dormitory). You may also wish to include your home telephone number and, if you are presently employed, your number at work. Make certain that each is clearly labeled. This information generally appears at the top of the résumé, either centered or to one side. When you supply two addresses and phone numbers, it works well to center your name and then place the addresses below it, one on each side.

Work Experience

In the chronological résumé, begin the listing of each previous job with the dates of employment, followed by the job title and then the name and address (city only) of the firm.

In the functional résumé, place the job title first, and make the dates of employment the final item in the entry, following the name and address of the firm. Your listing may also include a brief description of the work you performed, skills involved, and responsibilities assigned. Part-time and summer jobs also have their place in this section. The salary you received has no place in a résumé.

Education

If you attended more than one college and university, or trade schools, make a separate listing for each. Besides mentioning the degree or certificate obtained and your major field of study, you may find it useful to include minor fields and related course work. If you have just been graduated and have little or no work experience, you may wish to include your grade-point average.

Include high-school attendance only if it is relevant or if it calls attention to outstanding achievement. For example, if the job you are applying for requires special speaking and writing ability, you may wish to supply information relating to this. Any potential employer can assume that someone who has been accepted by a college has successfully completed earlier educational requirements.

Special Abilities

This category will include all knowledge of languages—foreign languages as well as computer languages. (Current practice treats them equally.) Skill on any machinery also belongs here; this includes office machines (such as computers) and heavy machinery if any of these are within your experience and are applicable to the kind of work you are looking for.

Volunteer work, club associations, and participation in charity drives should be listed if they relate to the kind of work you are seeking. Ringing doorbells to collect contributions to the March of Dimes, for example, gives some preliminary training for various kinds of sales work. Experience as president of a glee club or other campus group means that you have already demonstrated ability in organizing and motivating others for a common purpose—a requirement for any job in which you will be supervising a work force of any size.

Not all your hobbies may be worth mentioning. Concentrate on hobbies that may be interesting to an employer. The fact that you love to bake, for instance, and have won your local 4-H Bake-Off cannot impress an employer who is looking for someone to coordinate a large payroll, but it may give you the edge you need if you are applying for a position in restaurant management.

References

Before you begin to compile your résumé, you would do well to let a few people know you are looking for a job and ask them if they would be willing to give you a good reference, should any prospective employer get in touch with them. If they are willing to write letters of recommendation for you, you are free to make photocopies for further use.

On the résumé itself, however, it is current practice not to list the names and addresses of people willing to supply references. On your résumé, instead, supply a line reading "*References supplied on request,*" "*References available upon request,*" or similar wording.

To illustrate all these points, some sample résumés are supplied below. The first is for a young woman trying to improve her present situation; the second represents a recent college graduate; and the third is the résumé of an older woman returning to the work force after some years of inactivity.

Sample 1

Joan Daily
831 Elm Street
Chatterbrook, New Jersey 07771
(201) 555-1234

Previous Work Experience

July 1988 to present: Animal Health Technician, Chatterbrook Veterinary Group. Assisting in four-person mixed practice. Duties include laboratory work, surgical assistance, emergency treatment, and medical records. Practice limited to small animals.

Summer 1987: Animal Health Technician, Downe County Animal Hospital, Downe, Pennsylvania. Full range of duties, especially client contact and inventory control. Large animal practice, specializing in brood mares.

September 1985 to May 1987 (part time): Animal Health Technician, County Emergency Clinic for Animals, Downe, Pennsylvania. All emergency services, including client contact and telephone advice.

Education

    M.A., 1987, Erie University, Microbiology.

    B.S., 1986, Pennsylvania State University. Biology major, anthropology minor. Graduated with honors.

Professional Qualifications

    Member, American Academy of Veterinary Technicians

    Licensed, Pennsylvania

    Certified, New Jersey

Additional Skills

    Speaking and writing knowledge of Spanish

    Basic accounting (payroll, inventory)

References

    Available on request

Sample 2

JAMES DUNPHY

<u>Current Address</u>
1607 Harris Hall
Community University
Seaside, NJ 07070
(201) 497-8749

<u>Permanent Address</u>
783 Elm Street
Chatterbrook, NJ 07771
(201) 555-1234

<u>Position Desired</u>
An entry-level position in the field of business
administration.

<u>Education</u>
Seaside Community College, Seaside, NJ, B.A., 1993
    Major: accounting; minor: retailing. Grade point
    average: 3.5 in major; 3.0 overall.
Central High School, Chatterbrook, NJ, 1989
    Scholastic Honor Society. National Merit Scholar.

<u>Other Skills</u>
Languages: Spanish; Polish; C and Fortran.
Pilot, licensed for small aircraft.

<u>Extracurricular Activities</u>
Campus Correspondent, <u>Newark Star-Ledger,</u> 1991-1993.
    Regularly reported on sports events, other
    newsworthy events as they occurred.
President, Student Political Union, 1992-1993.
    Organized monthly lecture series open to all
    students; ran Board of Directors' meetings;
    instituted faculty-student debates in conjunction
    with 1988 elections.

<u>Work Experience</u>
Summer 1992—Office floater, Worldwide Electronic
    Conglomerate, Inc., Trenton, NJ. Handled various
    bookkeeping and accounting duties in payroll
    department for 27 branch offices.
Sept. 1989—June 1991—Bookkeeper, Garden State Realty,
    Trenton, NJ (part time). Responsible for all books
    of two-person real-estate firm.
Summer 1988—Sales clerk, Gentlemen's Emporium,
    Chatterbrook, NJ. Retail sales in men's clothing
    store.

References furnished on request.
Willing to relocate.

Sample 3

MABEL LAWRENCE
324 Oak Street
Chatterbrook, NJ 07771
(201) 555-1234

OBJECTIVE   Administrative/supervisory position,
             preferably in art-related field.

SKILLS   <u>Administrative</u>
             Managed art gallery, supervised staff of
             seven, installed exhibitions.
             Organized annual arts fairs for community.
             <u>Personal and Written Communication</u>
             Fund raising by mail and telephone.
             Interviewed applicants for arts grants.
             Worked with teenagers on specific projects.
             <u>Other</u>
             Fluent in French and Italian, both spoken
             and written.
             Word processing, stenography, dictaphone.

EDUCATION   <u>Wellesley College</u>, Wellesley, MA
             B.A., art history major, mathematics
             minor, 1968
             <u>Trenton Community College</u>, Trenton, NJ
             M.A. business administration, 1985

EXPERIENCE   <u>Modern Art Gallery</u>, New York, NY, 1968-1970.
             Manager. Arranged for exhibitions,
             supervised opening parties, dealt with staff
             and clients.
             <u>Art Department</u>, Wellesley College, 1967-
             1968. Research assistant. Worked with
             professor on funded monograph, checking
             references, organizing footnotes and
             bibliography, arranging for permissions
             (elaborate correspondence).
             <u>Chatterbrook Arts Fair</u>, Chatterbrook, NJ
             1969-1992. Originated, established, and
             managed annual fair to raise funds for
             Chatterbrook Public Library. Artists
             included painters, musicians, craftspeople.
                                        (continued)

MABEL LAWRENCE
page 2

> New Jersey Arts Council, 1982-1985.
> Interviewed applicants for arts grants in
> the Trenton area. Wrote detailed opinions
> and reviews for state agency.
> Northern New Jersey Women's Clubs, 1986-
> 1988. Local representative for yearly fund
> drive. Raised money through letter campaign
> and follow-up phone calls and personal
> appeals.
> Chatterbrook Public School System, Volunteer
> Arts Program, 1989-1992. Worked with seventh
> graders to paint murals on walls of new
> school building; with high-school sophomores
> on originating and carrying through a poster
> contest to celebrate Chatterbrook
> Centennial.

HONORS AND
AFFILIATIONS

> Graduated from college summa cum laude
> Corresponding secretary, Chatterbrook
> Women's Club.
> Member, New Jersey Art Association.
> Member, Alpha Rho Tau (professional
> fraternity in art field).

REFERENCES   Credentials and references upon request.

– 3 –

Effective Letters

LETTERS OF APPLICATION

With your résumé you will send a covering letter, introducing yourself as a person. Such a letter usually begins by explaining why you are getting in touch with the particular company or other organization—whether you have heard of a specific job opening (through a newspaper advertisement, for example) or whether you are initiating a contact in the hope that a position will become available soon.

You may want to use your second paragraph to say something specific about the particular company or organization and indicate the contribution you feel you can make to its operation. If you are answering an advertisement, for example, you may wish to point out that in a previous position you gained experience in the same skills that are being sought.

Finally, express your hope for a personal interview. If you are applying for a position that will require you to travel to the interview, you may wish to suggest a time when it will be convenient for you to be there and volunteer to telephone for an appointment.

Like your résumé, your letter of application should reflect your seriousness and your ability to do a good job. Such a letter, however, can be more personal, and it can show some confidence and warmth. There are many ways of wording and organizing a letter of application. The following sample shows one of them.

1105 Plane Avenue
Chicago, Illinois 60614

May 7, 1993

Ms. Willa Caruther, Employment Supervisor
Cornwell, McCormick, and Drake
Certified Public Accountants
409 Third Avenue
New York, New York 10017

Dear Ms. Caruther:

I would like to apply for the position of junior
accountant specializing in retail practice that
you advertised in today's *New York Times*. The
enclosed résumé gives details on my background
and experience, showing my qualifications for the
position you describe. I can think of nothing
better than launching my career with a firm as
fine as Cornwell, McCormick, and Drake.

My two years in the accounting department of a
large retail chain have given me complete
familiarity with accounting requirements of
retail businesses, and I have written many
letters and reports of the types you mention in
your advertisement. I also played an active role
in assisting our auditors in performing two
annual audits, so I am thoroughly familiar with
current audit procedure.

I have enjoyed my work during the past two years
and intend to make my career in accounting. I am
leaving my present position because opportunities
are limited in so small an office. In addition
I wish to broaden my knowledge of accounting
practice and qualify as a CPA, so I can move
ahead in the field as far as my talents permit.

If you wish, I shall ask Prairie State to forward
my undergraduate transcript as soon as I complete

my final semester's work ten days from now.
I believe it will show that I have taken all the
accounting courses offered at Prairie State and
have never received any grade but "A" in all 32
credits. If you wish to write to any of my
employers or teachers for personal evaluation,
please do so. They have all indicated their
willingness to supply evaluations of my
qualifications.

Sincerely yours,

Jane Marquesee

BUSINESS LETTERS

People who work in offices find that letters occupy much of their
work time, both in writing and in reading them. As a reader, you
probably appreciate letters that get directly to the point. As a writer,
therefore, you must learn to please your own readers, who want you
to come quickly to the point.

There are many types of business letters: inquiries, orders, re-
sponses, remittances, acknowledgments; personal letters to employees, personal letters to clients; form letters for personnel matters
and public relations; customer service letters, sales promotion letters, sales letters; letters asking for credit, letters extending credit,
letters refusing credit; letters offering payment, letters asking for
payment, letters explaining why payments are late. All these share
certain characteristics: They are polite, direct, clear, correct, and as
brief as possible.

Many parts of this book deal with good writing, so the remainder
of this chapter will not repeat any of the suggestions presented elsewhere. Instead, some examples of good business letters are provided. Each example presents only the salutation, body, and
complimentary close. The correct spacing and punctuation of the
inside addresses, date, and name of the writer are shown in the
sample letter of application provided above.

Letter of Inquiry

Dear Mr. Cauthen:

I am conducting a study for the National
Insurance Association of current underwriting
practices followed by its members. This study
will be reported in a volume scheduled for
publication early next year. Because your company
for many years has led the New England area in
underwriting volume, I would not consider my
study complete without consulting one or more
members of your Underwriting Department.

I plan to be in Hartford during the first two
weeks of October and would appreciate the
opportunity to spend two days with anyone you
designate from Providence Mutual to talk with me
about your underwriting practices. I anticipate
that I will need at least that amount of time to
cover all the items I am planning to include in
my study.

For the convenience of your staff, I am enclosing
a list of the topics I plan to cover during my
stay with you. I know I am asking for a great
deal of time with your staff, but I hope the
information developed in this industry-wide study
will compensate you for the expenditure of time.

The report will be distributed to you, of course,
as a member of the NIA, and your cooperation will
be recognized in the foreword.

I look forward to an affirmative reply at your
convenience.

Sincerely,

Evan Caldwell

Response to an Inquiry

Dear Mr. Caldwell:

We at Providence Mutual are always eager to do our share in any program sponsored by your organization. We recognize the benefit we all receive from active cooperation in studies such as the one you describe in your recent letter.

We will, therefore, make available to you during the first two weeks in October several senior underwriters on our staff, who will be requested to supply you with any underwriting information you require. The information you sent with your letter has been distributed for study by our underwriting staff.

To help us in scheduling, I would appreciate a telephone call as soon as you have selected the days you will actually spend with us. My administrative assistant knows of your request, of course, and will be ready to set firm dates with you if you call while I am away from my office. She will also be glad to assist you in making hotel and travel reservations.

I hope you will find time to lunch with me and members of my staff on the days you spend with us.

Please let me know if I can be of further assistance.

Cordially,

George Cauthen

Complaint

Gentlemen:

I am not writing this letter to complain about the promptness or efficiency of your customer service. In the past two months we have had to make nine emergency requests for repair of your 8840 photocopying machine. In each case your staff responded promptly and accomplished the needed repair within a few hours.

What I am complaining about is that we had to call on you so many times within so short a period for assistance with a machine only three months old. You know as well as I that a machine we depend on for reliable service should not require such frequent repair.

You also know as well as I that we do not own the machine but are merely leasing it. The terms of the lease call for automatic renewal of the lease unless we notify you of our intention to terminate our agreement at least one month before the end of the lease.

Since the current lease period ends six weeks from today, I hereby notify you that we will not renew unless your machine suddenly shows signs of giving better service than it has so far.

Sincerely yours,

Greta Pastor

Reply to Complaint

Dear Mrs. Pastor:

Your letter arrived at my desk half an hour ago and left me red-faced with embarrassment but eager to help with the service problem you describe. You are entirely justified in feeling the way you do, and I am eager to do everything I can to see that the problem is resolved as promptly as possible. Eagle Industries does not want to lose your valuable business.

I have initiated the following actions in hope of returning you to our list of satisfied customers.

1. By now you have had a telephone call from me, asking permission to inspect and overhaul your present 8840 photocopier on your premises. This work will be performed at no cost to your company, and our service personnel will be directed, with your permission, to accomplish all necessary work over the weekend or after the close of your business day, so there will be no interruption of your work.

2. I have instructed the head of our service department to conduct a component-by-component study of the machine you are leasing to determine whether we have delivered to you a machine that fails to meet our quality requirements. This is especially important to us, since we have experienced great customer satisfaction with the 8840 line. Of more than 4000 machines now in use, yours is the only one that has required anything but routine maintenance.

3. If we discover any fundamental flaws in the machine you now are using, we will replace it with a new machine from our assembly line and credit you in full for the time you have had the present machine.

I hope this reply is satisfactory. I will be calling you on the telephone as soon as our actions are complete to determine whether everything we have done meets with your approval.

Please accept my apology for any inconvenience we have caused and my assurance that we will remedy the situation quickly and completely.

Sincerely,

Paul Stark

Sales Letter

Dear Dr. Sammis:

You are one of many physicians in the Dallas—Fort Worth area who were interested enough in new developments in automated diagnosis to stop at our booth during the recent Texas Medical Society Convention. At that time you indicated you might profit from subscription to our computerized diagnostic laboratory service, now used by more than 44,000 California physicians.

We are preparing to offer our service to physicians in your area within the next 60 days and would appreciate the opportunity to call on you and explain the low cost and high reliability of our automatic diagnosis.

Our presentation will take only 15 minutes of your time, and we would be glad to schedule the presentation to meet your convenience.

I shall be telephoning your office on Wednesday, October 14, to set up an appointment. On conclusion of the meeting, I shall leave with you the necessary agreements to be completed if you wish to subscribe to our service. Be assured there will be no obligation on your part to make any commitment at the time of the presentation.

Sincerely yours,

Bill Townes

Collection

Dear Mr. Townes:

I am writing to remind you that your account with us shows an unpaid balance of $1204 for merchandise shipped to you on January 5, almost three months ago.

The summer buying season is about to begin and, before going on to Chicago to show our new designs, we are eager to clear up outstanding accounts. If there is some reason why you cannot make the payment, please don't hesitate to call me. If your payment is late because of some oversight, please oblige by putting the payment in the mail.

I look forward to receiving your check and to continuing doing business with you, as we have done over the years.

Sincerely,

Victor Johns

Recommendation

Dear Mrs. Brown:

Nothing can give me more pleasure than having the opportunity to reply to your letter requesting information about James Lockner, an applicant for employment with your firm.

James worked for us for three years while he was a student, and in all that time he was punctual, reliable, courteous, and efficient. No part-time employee we have had in all my years with our company has been quicker to learn or more willing to work.

I hope you will see fit to offer James employment. All of us at Acme are rooting for him.

Sincerely yours,

Sara Trumbull

Employment Offer

Dear Mr. Lockner:

We have completed our evaluation of your interviews and our study of your excellent qualifications and outstanding references. It is my pleasure to offer you a position as sales representatives in our heavy equipment division at an annual salary of $26,000, as explained in our discussion on June 28.

If your interest in the position is firm, we would like to have you report here at the Personnel Office by 8:30 a.m. on the first of August. You will be assigned to headquarters for three months of training. On satisfactory conclusion of training, you will work out of our Minneapolis office, as you requested.

Please complete the enclosed Acceptance of Employment form and return it to us as soon as possible. In addition I would appreciate your taking the time to telephone me collect today to say whether you are going to join us.

The sales manager, Mrs. Alice Holness, whom you met at our office, joins me in extending congratulations to you at the start of what we hope will be a highly successful career with Farm Equipment, Inc.

Cordially,

Rita Brown

As all these examples show, good business letters are polite, direct, clear, correct, and as brief as possible. Since careers in business usually include the writing of many letters, it is never a waste of time to practice the skill. Letters are written by people and read by people. The good letters you write will help you make good impressions on others. Any poor letters you write may have the opposite effect.

– 4 –

Business Reports

Business reports may be brief replies—less than a page long—to questions that can be answered easily. For example, what are the company's sales in the Northeast in the current quarter, broken down by states, and how do they compare with the previous year's results in the corresponding period? How does the company's wage scale for office workers compare with wages paid by other firms in the area?

Business reports may also be elaborate—covering many pages and supplying answers to questions that require a great deal of research. Why are the company's sales dropping in the Northeast? What are the company's principal product deficiencies, as reported by customers and sales staff? Can you recommend a program to improve the company's product line and recapture market leadership? What internal changes will be necessary to upgrade the company's sales effort? What changes in promotion and marketing do you recommend to support the sales campaign?

Each of these questions may be the subject of a brief, individual report. Together they become the subject of a long report.

No matter how simple or complex, a business report is intended to answer a specific question or set of questions. The company sales manager or president needs information for long-range planning. The marketing or accounting department needs information before establishing new procedures. The company must supply information to stockholders in an annual report. Whatever the need, a report will be written and submitted.

Business reports resemble college research papers except that the subject of the report is usually spelled out clearly and assigned to the writer. An exception to this is a report you may wish to write on your own initiative, recommending changes of some kind or pointing out the need for action in a certain area of the company's operations. Based on observations made during your day-to-day work, you decide to write a special report: *Our department can improve efficiency by computerizing our billing procedures . . .* or *Incoming orders can be processed within 24 hours if we . . .* Most companies encourage this kind of initiative by employees, but before you begin to write, you would do well to find out whether your manager looks with favor on such writing.

ACQUIRING INFORMATION

When a report is assigned to you, your first decision will concern the best way to collect the necessary information. The principal sources of business information are

- observation

- interviews

- questionnaires

- library research

All these sources can yield the data that form the basis of a report.

Observation

If your report deals with a subject you have been considering for some time, you have probably observed enough so that you need only organize your thoughts, outline a report, and begin to write. Most often, however, you will have to make firsthand observations to find the information you need. For example, you may initiate a time-motion study of office procedures, shipping procedures, or production methods in order to gather data for a report on company operations. You may accompany sales representatives or customer-service personnel on their field trips if you are studying sales or service problems. Whatever the subject, whatever the type of observation you intend to make, you will need to keep careful records of what you learn.

If you know in advance what you are looking for, you will find it helpful to establish a format for your observations, so that the process of note-taking will be as easy as possible. If you have prepared a checklist of items to be observed, your notes will consist of check marks or number ratings corresponding to the qualities of the activities under observation. This method is less time-consuming than narrative writing. To avoid disturbing the people you are observing, you may decide to write your notes after each observation is complete. If you do, be sure to make your notes promptly after each observation so as not to overlook important information.

Interviews

Interviews are an excellent method of collecting information. Your company may employ many people who, together, know a great deal about the company's business. Such people are usually pleased to help you collect the information you need. All that is necessary to get their cooperation is a polite request along with an explanation of what you are seeking and why. If you give people ample notice before approaching them for the information, and if your attitude makes it clear that you are seeking help from knowledgeable sources, you will have no trouble getting the facts you need. If you interrupt people while they are doing their own work, or if your attitude is less than open and respectful, you may get little from them.

Just as you will find it useful to develop a format for observations, you should have a list of specific items to cover in interviews. Make the final item in your checklist an invitation to the persons interviewed to speak on any topic related to your subject. You may find that a person you are interviewing on ways to improve office procedures, for example, has given much thought to the subject and has ideas you would never hear anything about if you rely only on a fixed series of questions you design yourself. By offering people the chance to speak freely, and by being a good listener, you may gain much more than you ever thought possible. You may also make friends with people who can assist you further in other work assignments.

Questionnaires

Questionnaires are most useful when you cannot speak directly with people who have information you need for a report. There are a few requirements to keep in mind when preparing a questionnaire:

- Make your inquiry personal and warm, so that the people you write to will be inclined to answer willingly.

- Limit the number of questions you ask, and make the questions brief and clear. People have work to do and will show no sympathy for a researcher who makes excessive or vague demands.

- Explain exactly why you are asking for information and how the people you are polling will benefit from answering your request.

- Supply a self-addressed, stamped envelope, so as to make replies easier for your respondents.

- Just as in planning an interview, make the last item in the questionnaire an invitation to respond freely on topics you may have overlooked.

- Express your thanks in advance.

Library Research

Library research on business topics often begins with a request to a company librarian to perform a search for printed sources of information. If your company does not have its own library, you will have to conduct your own search. You may find it helpful to employ such reference works as *Business Periodicals Index* and *Encyclopedia of Business Information Sources*. The *Index* guides the reader to approximately 165 periodicals in all fields of business. The *Encyclopedia* covers books and reports as well as periodicals.

COMPILING THE REPORT

Once you have collected all the information you need—whether through observation, interviews, questionnaires, library research, or a combination of several methods—you are ready to plan and write your report.

As you begin writing, keep in mind the assigned question that is the focus of the report. Remember that you are writing for a busy reader, and while that reader may want to know every important bit of information you have found, no reader has unlimited reading time. You must write your report in such fashion that if the reader stops at any point, the most important information up to that point has been covered. In this sense, a good business report is much like a well-written newspaper article, putting the most important information first. If possible—and good business writers always find it possible—abstract the entire report in the opening sentences of the report. Here are three examples of such openers:

> Our sales in every state of the Northeast declined in the current quarter, the largest decline being 38% in New York, the smallest 2% in Vermont.
>
> The company's median secretarial pay falls 3% above the median wage reported by ten companies of our size in our geographic labor market. Only among junior clerks, for whom our scale is 10% below the median, are we experiencing abnormally high personnel turnover.
>
> Interviews conducted with all six members of our economic analysis section and responses to questionnaires distributed among our principal customers in the Southwest region indicate that our sales decline during the past six months resulted from our decision to defer redesign of our product line despite increased competition from McAndrew, Inc. and from D'Arcy Bros.

Such opening comments tell the reader exactly what a report will document, and the reader can expect the report to back up the opening statement completely.

Following the opening sentence, which you may think of as an *abstract*, you may want to write an *introduction*, citing the reasons for conducting the study and supplying other information that prepares the reader to understand the report fully. You may then write various sections with such titles as *Data Sources, Study Procedures, Findings, Analysis,* and *Conclusions and Recommendations*. You will usually reserve charts, tables, and other detailed information for an *appendix*, knowing that only the most careful reader will want to read such information. When a graph or other form of easily interpreted visual display can be used to summarize the central findings of your report, you may wish to make it part of your abstract. Business readers are accustomed to interpreting visuals.

A brief report need not include actual titles for the various sections, but the arrangement of material would remain the same. Whether you write a long report or a short one, however, your objective is to present your thinking directly, clearly, compactly, and completely.

Section III

DICTIONARY OF USAGE

Usage is defined as the manner in which a language is commonly written or spoken. The suggestions and preferences offered here deal with problems most often encountered in personal, academic, and business writing.

A

a, an. The article *a* is used before a word beginning with a consonant sound: *a part; a heart*. The article *an* is used before a word beginning with a vowel sound: *an elephant; an hour*.

The rule is based on sound. The word *heart* begins with the consonant sound *h*. The word *hour* begins with a vowel sound, as though it were spelled *our*. Write *a history*, not *an history*. *History* begins with a consonant sound. Write *an historical novel* and *an historic event* because the consonant sound *h* is almost completely lost in these phrases.

absolute, absolutely. These words are often misused as intensifiers (strengtheners) of terms that need no strengthening. *She is absolutely the most beautiful woman I know* is no stronger than *She is the most beautiful woman I know*. Absolute means perfect, complete, pure, unconditional. Save *absolute* for such expressions as *absolute monarch* and *absolute zero*, which do not have the same meanings as *monarch* and *zero*. Use *absolutely* only when the word it modifies needs strengthening and there is no chance you are wrong: "I will show that the accused *absolutely* was not in the room when the shot was fired," the defense attorney said. See also *definitely; very*.

167

accept, except. The verb *accept* means receive: I will *accept* your resignation. *Except* appears most often as a preposition meaning excluding: Everyone will be welcome *except* John. The verb *except*, used far less often, means exclude: Late reports *are excepted* (excluded) from consideration.

adapt, adopt. *Adapt* means become accustomed: Chelsea quickly *adapted* to her new school. *Adapt* also means make suitable to conditions or requirements: After considerable effort the engineers were able to *adapt* the old engine to increase its torque. *Adopt* means take up or practice, or choose to take: The sisters *adopted* a style of dress that displeased their parents.

adverse, averse. Unfavorable situations and conditions are *adverse*: An *adverse* school environment may make learning difficult for all but the most gifted students. People who are opposed to a course of action are *averse* to it: I am not *averse* to your suggestion but I need more time to make up my mind.

advice, advise. *Advice* is a noun: I cannot act on your *advice*. *Advise* is a verb: My physician *advised* me to stop smoking.

affect, effect. The verb *affect* means influence: Your eloquent words *affected* me deeply. The verb *effect* means cause: Imposition of a prison sentence *effected* a welcome change in his habits. The noun *affect* is reserved for use by psychologists and students of psychology. It means feeling: My client showed strong *affect* during her early months of therapy. The noun *effect* means result: Your loss had no *effect* on me.

aggravate. The verb *aggravate* means worsen: Rough play late in the season *aggravated* his old knee injury. The meaning of annoy or exasperate—as in You *are aggravating* me, Fred—is considered colloquial by many teachers and editors.

agree to, agree with. One *agrees to* a proposal. One *agrees with* a person.

ain't is used only, if it is used at all, in highly informal speech. It is best to avoid *ain't* in writing. See also *contractions*.

all, all of. *All* is all that is needed except when a pronoun or noun is the object of the preposition *of*: Wes wasted *all* his energy. Judith knew *all* her clients by name. *All of* us agreed to join the club.

allusion, illusion, delusion. An *allusion* is an indirect reference, a reference in which the object referred to is not named: His poem on the seasons makes many *allusions* to life and death that go unnoticed by unsophisticated readers. The chairman *made an allusion to* (or *alluded to*) your absence when he said, "Some of our most talkative members are not here today." An *illusion* is a false impression created by wishful thinking or by faulty perception: The love he saw in her eyes proved to be an *illusion*. The children were fascinated by the magician's optical *illusions*. A *delusion* is a mistaken belief resulting from self-deception: Psychopaths frequently exhibit *delusions* of persecution.

already, all ready. *Already* means previously or before: She was *already* showing signs of suffocation. *All ready* means completely prepared: Are you *all ready* to have dinner?

alright is an incorrect spelling of *all right.*

also should not be used in place of the conjunction *and*: John, Jane, *and* (not *also*) Dick attended the book fair. You may use *also* as an adverb: As John Milton wrote, "They *also* serve who only stand and wait."

alternately, alternatively. *Alternately* means in turn: The pianist and the violinist played *alternately* through the evening; while one rested, the other performed. *Alternatively* means instead: You may study physics now; *alternatively,* you may defer your science requirement until next semester. The noun *alternative* means choice: You have two *alternatives*: accept the transfer or resign from the company.

altogether, all together. *Altogether* means entirely: We were *altogether* disgusted by her lack of team spirit. *All together* means in a group: When we are *all together,* we manage to have a good time.

among, between. *Among* is most often used for three or more, *between* for two: *among* all the contenders for the nomination; *between* the two brothers. *Between* is also used to indicate a relationship of any two members of a group of three or more: New disagreements began to arise *between* the nations of the Middle East.

amount, number. *Amount* refers to things that cannot be counted: Even a small *amount* of debris is unacceptable. *Number* refers to things and people that can be counted: There are a *number* of errors in the report. We expected a large *number* of people to attend. *Amount* is always singular. *Number* is singular when it refers to a particular quantity, plural when it means several or many: That *number* is too great for most people to grasp. A large *number* of my dinner guests become ill every time I cook.

A.M., P.M., a.m., p.m. These abbreviations are never used as nouns. See me at *6 p.m.* (not *6 in the p.m.*). See me at *six in the morning* (not *six in the a.m.*). Capitals and small letters are equally correct in typing these abbreviations, but be consistent within a paper, report, or other writing.

an, a. See *a, an.*

and etc. is an example of redundancy, saying the same thing twice. The Latin *et* in *etc.* means and. The entire Latin expression for which *etc.* is the abbreviation is *et cetera,* meaning *and the rest. Etc.* applies only to things, not people. Except where space is a limitation, *etc.* should not be used. Substitute such expressions as *and so forth, and the like,* and *and others.* See also *et al.*

and/or. In most instances, either *and* or *or* expresses the intended meaning. It is worth rephrasing a sentence to avoid the awkward *and/or.*

angry at, angry with. If you must be angry, be *angry with* people, *angry at* anything else: I am *angry with* my sister. I am *angry at* the way you were treated. See also *mad, angry.*

ante-, anti-. The prefix *ante-* means before and appears in such words as *antecedent* and *antebellum.* The prefix *anti-* means against and appears in such words as *antipathy* and *antihistamine.* Never say or write that you are *anti* anything. Say you are opposed to it.

anxious, eager. *Anxious* means fearful, apprehensive, concerned: I became increasingly *anxious* as the operation dragged on and the surgeons sent no reassuring word. *Eager* is used when an anticipation is joyous: I am *eager* to attend the concert with you.

anybody, anyone, everybody, everyone, nobody, somebody, someone. These pronouns all are single words: *Anybody* who has a ticket will be admitted to the reception. *Anyone* can learn to spell correctly. *Everybody* must be considered. *Everyone* is welcome. *Nobody* was late. Notice that all these pronouns are singular: *Somebody has stolen* my driver's license. *Someone has* to pay for the tickets. When written as two words, the resulting phrases have different meanings: There is *no body* of knowledge I like more. *Every body* in the temporary morgue has now been identified.

anyways is incorrect. Use *anyway*: I am not being paid but I will do the work *anyway*. *Anyway* and *any way* have different meanings: I will do the work *any way* you want me to.

appraise, apprise. *Appraise* means estimate the value of: I am certain the jeweler *will appraise* your ring without charge. *Apprise* means inform: *Have* you *apprised* your parents of the terrible accident you were in?

around is an inadequate substitute for *about* or *near*: I will see you *about* (not *around*) nine o'clock. Play *near* (not *around*) the school until I get home from work. Use *around* to mean on all sides: He walked *around* the block twice to cool off.

as is an awkward substitute for *because, since,* or *for*: They asked not to be disturbed *because* (not *as*) they were studying for their examinations. *As* can be understood to relate to time; in the example just given, *as* can be misread to mean *while*.

as best, as best as are incorrect replacements for *as well as*: I am doing *as well as* (not *as best as*) I can. I am doing *my best* (not *as best I can*).

as good or better than. Insert *as* after *good*: I want one *as good as or better than* hers. The second *as* is needed in any comparative expression of this type: She had done *as well as or better than* any man in the class.

as regards is an incorrect substitute for *about* or *concerning*: I am writing *about* (not *as regards*) the radio I ordered. See also *regarding*.

as well as does not have the same meaning as *and*; in addition, it does not make a singular subject plural: The bicycle, *as well as* the other toys you ordered, *is* not appropriate for Sonja. The bicycle *and* the other toys you ordered *are* not appropriate for Sonja.

at about has one word too many: *about* or *at* is enough: They will be here *about* noon. They will be here *at* noon.

at the same time that means no more than *while*: I entered *while* (not *at the same time that*) he was speaking. Though we expect speech to have a certain amount of extra verbiage, writing should be as tight as possible.

at this point in time means no more than *now*. *At that point in time* means no more than *then*. One meaning of *point* is a particular time. As an alternative to *then*, you may write *at that point*: I decided *at that point* to leave the company. By *then* (not *At that point in time*) we knew the Senate would not be willing to take part in a whitewash. See also *point in time*.

author is always a noun, never a verb. *Thackeray authored many novels* is unacceptable. Instead: *Thackeray was a prolific author* or *Thackeray wrote many novels*. Resist the urge to make verbs of such nouns as *critique* and *gift*. See also *critique*.

averse, adverse. See *adverse, averse*.

awful is a weak substitute for *bad* or for more descriptive terms: How *disappointed* (not *awful*) I felt! It was a *disappointment* (not *an awful disappointment*). Do not use *awful* as a vague intensifier (strengthener): *I felt cheated* is better than *It was an awful shame*. Use *awful* when you want to describe something that is extremely disagreeable: *The execution was awful. The smell of death after the earthquake was awful*. Loose use of *awful* will rob the word of its meaning of inspiring dread, terror. Use *awesome* to describe something that inspires awe—a feeling of overwhelming reverence, admiration, or fear: *Her grasp of linguistics was awesome*. See also *very*.

B

badly, an adverb, is often misused as a complement of the linking verb *feel*. Correct: *I feel bad* (not *badly*) about her loss. Adverbs cannot complement (complete) linking verbs. Nor is *badly* a proper synonym for *very much*: Huck wanted *very much* (not *badly*) to do what was right for Jim.

Badly is used correctly to mean improperly or excessively: We found that the children had been treated *badly*. The testing service found the radio to be *badly* defective. See also *feel bad, feel badly, feel good, feel well*.

basic has become an overworked adjective: The *basic* truth is evident. Truth is truth; what does *basic* add? The adjective *essential* is also overworked, as are the adverbs *basically* and *essentially*. These words often appear to be sly attempts to support questionable claims: *Essentially*, Ron is a decent fellow. Is Ron decent or isn't he? Adding *essentially* makes the reader wonder whether the writer is being snide. *Basically*, their position is valid. Is it valid or isn't it?

beautiful is another overworked adjective. The meaning of *beautiful* is well understood, but the word has been applied indiscriminately in speech and writing: He is a *beautiful* person. There is nothing wrong with seeing beauty in persons and ideas, but constant repetition of *beautiful* robs the word of meaning and marks the user as a lazy or imprecise writer. Write *He thinks only of others* (not *He is a beautiful person*). I admire Fred and Mary (not *Fred and Mary are beautiful people*) because they treat their children well. See also *meaningful* and *viable*.

because is sometimes misused as a replacement for *that* in introducing noun clauses: The excuse they gave for being late was *that* (not *because*) their train was delayed. The noun clause *their train was delayed* serves as the complement of the linking verb *was*. The pronoun *that* introduces the noun clause.

They were late *because* their train was delayed. The subordinate clause *their train was delayed* serves as modifier of the main clause, *They were late*. The conjunction *because* introduces the modifying clause. See also *fact that; being as, being that; as*.

being as, being that are incorrect replacements for *because* or *since*: I am leaving *because* (not *being as* or *being that*) you refuse to cooperate. See also *as*.

beside, besides. *Beside* is a preposition meaning by the side of: She knelt *beside* me to pray. *Besides* is an adverb meaning in addition: *Besides*, they were unaware of the effect of their words.

best. See *as best as*.

better can be used with *had* to mean ought: You *had better* (not *You better*) learn to listen to reason.

better than is not used to mean more than: We took *more than* (not *better than*) an hour to dress. *Better than* is correct only in comparisons: She is *better than* her sister in many ways. Your dish tastes *better than* mine.

between, among. See *among, between*.

between you and I is incorrect for *between you and me. Between* is a preposition requiring the objective case, and *you* and *me* are objects of the preposition *between*.

burst should not be confused with *bust*: The pipes will *burst* (not *bust*) if they are not drained completely. Our pipes have *burst* (not *busted*). The verb *bust* is colloquial, and the noun *bust* has entirely different meanings.

but, hardly. Because both these words are negative in meaning, they must not be used with other negatives. Instead of *I didn't have but one* or *I didn't hardly have any time,* write: *I had but one* and *I hardly had any time.*

> Watch out as well for *only* and *scarcely,* which can also have negative meanings. See also *hardly; scarcely; only.*

but what is a regional (colloquial) spoken substitute for *that*: I cannot believe *that* (not *but what*) he will not make the team. I believe he will make the team.

buy is a good verb: I *buy* my fruit at the corner store. As a noun, *buy* is limited to slang and business writing: It was a good *buy*.

C

can, may. *Can* suggests the ability to do something: I *can* climb that hill. *May* suggests permission or intention: You *may* leave the room. I *may* return tomorrow if the weather is good.

cannot, can not. *Cannot* is commonly used except when it is advantageous to place special emphasis on *not*: I *cannot* find my keys. You really *can not* expect your friends to put up with such atrocious behavior.

cannot but is an awkward locution. One *must* (not *cannot but*) admire her. See also *but what.*

capitol, capital. A *capitol* is a building that serves as the seat of government: We have our offices in the *Capitol. Capital* is the spelling used for all other meanings, including money and a city that contains the seat of government: He could recite the *capitals* of all fifty states. They lack sufficient *capital* to start a business of that size.

> *Capital* is also used as an adjective with several meanings: That is a *capital* crime in South Carolina. He is a *capital* fellow.

censor, censure. As verbs, *censor* and *censure* have different meanings. *Censor* means examine and remove objectionable parts of a work: The mayor *censors* all films shown in our city. *Censure* means criticize strongly: After the Senator's improprieties were revealed, the Senate *censured* him.

childish, childlike. *Childish* carries a negative connotation of immaturity: Oscar's wife accused him of being *childish*. *Childlike* has the approving connotation of innocence, purity—all that is good in children: We all admired the *childlike* trust Sister Mary showed.

climactic, climatic. Two often confused words. *Climactic*, the adjectival form of *climax*, refers to decisive acts or events: The trial was approaching its *climactic* phase. *Climatic* is the adjectival form of *climate*: We are told we can anticipate major *climatic* changes in the next century.

close proximity. This phrase says the same thing twice. Either word alone will do. The stars appeared *close* to one another. Its *proximity* to the beach made the property desirable. Even better: The property was desirable because it was only twenty feet from the beach.

compare to, compare with, contrast with. To show that one thing is like another in an unreal, or metaphoric, sense, *compare to* is used: "Shall I *compare* thee *to* a summer's day?"

To analyze real, or literal, likenesses or differences between people, objects, and ideas, *compare with* is used: Why *compare* the boy *with* his older brother? To emphasize differences, *contrast with* is used: Mother was always *contrasting* my erratic behavior *with* my brother's steady habits.

Avoid comparing or contrasting anything or anybody with anything or anybody inappropriate: I *compared* him *with her* (not *with her manners*). I *contrasted* her novel *with his* (not *with his ability as a writer*).

complement, compliment. The verb *complement* means fill out or complete: Her hat *complemented* her dress perfectly. A bottle of fine wine *complemented* the meal. The verb *compliment* means praise: I wonder why he *complimented* me so extravagantly on my work?

As nouns, these words retain the difference in meanings: A *complement* is needed after a linking verb. His exaggerated *compliments* made me uncomfortable.

consensus of opinion. The words *of opinion* are superfluous. *Consensus* means general agreement in belief or opinion: The class was unable to reach a *consensus*. (Notice the spelling: *Consensus* has nothing to do with a census.)

contact in the sense of *communicate* is an overused verb. It is best replaced with a more precise verb: *ask, inform, speak, write, telephone,* and so forth. When the form of communication cannot be specified, it is better to use *get in touch with* or *communicate with*.

contemptible, contemptuous. Acts worthy of contempt or scorn are *contemptible*: I find cheating *contemptible*. People showing contempt are *contemptuous*: Why is he always *contemptuous* of me?

continual, continuing, continuous. *Continual* means repeated but frequently interrupted: We were annoyed by his *continual* sneezing. *Continuing* means existing over a long period: The architect said he had a *continuing* interest in the design of small homes. *Continuous* means uninterrupted and ongoing: The *continuous* action of the waves enables shellfish to find the food they need.

contractions. Such everyday contractions as *don't* (for do not), *let's* (for let us), and *you're* (for you are) should be avoided in formal reports and papers: We are (not We're) convinced that it is (not it's) crucial to run further tests before going into production.

contrast with. See *compare to, compare with, contrast with*.

could of is a colloquial spoken variant of *could have*: We *could have* (not *could of*) danced all night. See also *of*.

council, counsel, consul. *Council* means governing board: Take your petition to the City *Council*. *Counsel* means attorney: I suggest you retain *counsel*. *Counsel* also means advice: Have you had the advantage of her *counsel?* The verb *counsel* means advise: He *counseled* caution. A *consul* is a foreign-service officer: Burton served Britain as *consul* in several African countries.

counterproductive is an overused bureaucratic word meaning tending to hinder attainment of a desired end: Their *self-defeating* (not *counterproductive*) protests brought even greater repression. They finally abandoned their *fruitless* (not *counterproductive*) campaign.

credible, credulous. *Credible* means believable: The jury thought her testimony *credible*. *Credulous* means easily deceived, gullible: How can anyone with that much experience be so *credulous?*

Incredible* and *incredulous* also have different meanings: I find his account *incredible* (unbelievable). Why is he always *incredulous* (skeptical)?

criteria, criterion. The plural noun *criteria* means standards of judgment: Have you met all the *criteria* for admission? The organization does not reveal its principal *criteria* for admitting members. The singular noun *criterion* means standard of judgment: I do not understand the first *criterion* you established for selecting an administrative assistant. Age may not be applied as a *criterion* in judging applicants.

There must always be noun-verb agreement when either the singular or the plural noun is used.

critique is a good noun but a poor verb: I agreed with the *critique* (or *criticism* or *review*) printed in the newspaper. Now we will have a chance to *criticize* or *review* (not *critique*) her latest poem.

D

data is a plural noun, the plural form of *datum* (though the singular is almost never seen except as a modifier in, for example, *datum point*). Careful writers use a plural verb with *data*: His *data* were convincing.

deduce, deduct. *Deduce* means draw a conclusion: Sherlock Holmes *deduced* that the crime had been committed by a monkey. *Deduct* means subtract: Social security payments *were deducted* from our salaries for seven months.

Notice that the noun *deduction* has both the above meanings: Holmes made many clever *deductions* (inferences). Social Security *deductions* (subtractions) unfairly affect poorly paid workers.

definitely is an empty and overworked modifier. *She was interested* means just as much as *She was definitely interested.* See also *absolute, absolutely.*

delusion. See *allusion, illusion, delusion*.

dependent, dependant. *Dependent* is the most frequent spelling. It is the only acceptable one when the word is used as an adjective: My children are *dependent* (not *dependant*) on me. It is also the preferred spelling for the noun: My only *dependent* is my mother. While *dependant* is an acceptable spelling for the noun, it is rarely used and best avoided.

desirable, desirous. Desirable objects or people are sought after: I find her *desirable*. Desirous people yearn for something: Tillie was *desirous* of achieving wealth. Even better: Tillie *desired* wealth.

device, devise. *Device* is a noun: She has every kitchen *device* a cook needs. *Devise* is a verb: They *devised* a far better solution.

differ from, differ with. *Differ from* is used to express dissimilarity: Your painting *differs from* his in treatment of color. *Differ with* is used to express disagreement: I may occasionally *differ with* you on small matters, but we always agree on important affairs.

discreet, discrete. *Discreet* means prudent in speech or behavior: Be *discreet* about our firm's plans if you want to succeed here. *Discrete* means separate: Do you know that there are seven *discrete* steps in the solution to that problem?

disinterested, uninterested. Though these words may sometimes be considered synonyms, careful writers give them different meanings. They use *disinterested* to mean impartial: A good referee is always *disinterested*. *Uninterested* means showing lack of interest: You appear to be *uninterested* in mathematics, and I know why.

dissemble, disassemble. *Dissemble* means pretend: A successful poker player must be prepared to *dissemble* now and then during a game. *Disassemble* means take apart: Once you have *disassembled* the motor, be sure to retest every part.

distinctive, distinguished. *Distinctive* means readily identifying: Lord Fawn's *distinctive* lisp marked him as an idle aristocrat. *Distinguished* means eminent or marked by excellence: His *distinguished* sister was promoted to company president only five years after she joined our company.

don't is the correct contraction of *do not*, but not for *does not*: He *doesn't* (not *don't*) know the way home. In writing, contractions are best avoided except for informal letters, notes, and the like.

due to the fact that. Why use this lengthy expression when *because, due to,* and *since* carry the same meaning? Her success was *due to* her perseverance (not *due to the fact that* she persevered). See also *fact that.*

E

eager. See *anxious, eager.*

early on is a fad expression, meaning no more than *early* or *soon.*

ecology, environment are frequently confused nouns. *Environment* means conditions surrounding a living organism: Pollution can damage our *environment. Ecology* means the study of the interactions of plants or animals with their environments: Many college students take courses in *ecology.*

effect. See *affect, effect.*

e.g. This abbreviation for the Latin locution *exempli gratia* (for the sake of example) is used in scholarly footnotes, charts, and the like. In straight text, it should always be replaced with *for example* or *for instance.* See also *i.e.*

either, neither. These words refer to one of two items or groups of items, never to more than one or two: *Either* you play a strong role in our community organization, or I resign. *Neither* the magazines nor the newspapers reported the incident accurately. Joan, Alice, or Fred (not *Either Joan, Alice, or Fred*) must be home in time to prepare dinner. See also *neither.*

elicit, illicit. *Elicit* is a verb meaning draw forth: The chairman decided to remain silent in order to *elicit* helpful suggestions from the group. *Illicit* is an adjective meaning unlawful: *Illicit* drugs soon disappeared from the campus.

emigrate, immigrate. The prefixes *e-* (out of) and *im-* (into) are the keys to these verbs. *Emigrate* means leave a country to settle elsewhere: Large numbers of young men and women *emigrated* from Ireland during the nineteenth century. *Immigrate* means enter a country to make one's home: She *immigrated* to Canada to find a peaceful life. Emigrants *emigrate*; once they have *immigrated*, they become immigrants.

Migrants and migratory workers travel from place to place, seeking work or a place to settle down. When they do settle down, they are no longer migrants or migratory workers.

eminent. See *imminent, eminent.*

enormity. The primary meaning of *enormity* is excessive wickedness: Who can grasp the *enormity* of genocide? *Enormity* should not be used to indicate a large quantity or high level: The degree (not *enormity*) of her generosity was never forgotten by the town.

enthuse is a colloquial verb and should be avoided in papers and reports. More formal wordings are *be enthusiastic* and *show enthusiasm for*: Once he had seen the campus, he *was enthusiastic* (not *enthused*) about everything connected with the college.

environment. See *ecology, environment.*

epithet, epitaph. An *epithet* is an expression that characterizes a person or object—for example, *first lady* for the wife of a president, *the Oval Office* for United States Presidential power. *Epithet* also is a contemptuous expression: I have never heard *epithets* that surpass the ones she uses when she loses her temper. An *epitaph* is a tombstone inscription: *Here lies an honest man.*

equally as. Such expressions as *equally good, equally bad,* and *equally wrong* do not need *as*: All their mathematical proofs are *equally* (not *equally as*) time-consuming.

essential is an overworked and usually unnecessary adjective. *The essential truth* means no more than *the truth*. See also *basic.*

et al. is the abbreviation for the Latin locution *et alii*, meaning *and others*. It is generally found only in scholarly bibliographies to indicate multiple authorship: Jones, Arthur, *et al., A History of Nepal*. In straight text it should always be replaced with *and others* or a similar phrase. Notice that *et* in *et al.* is not an abbreviation and therefore is not followed by a period. *Et* in Latin means *and*.

etc. is the abbreviation for *et cetera*, a Latin locution meaning *and the rest*. It is not used to refer to people and is appropriately used in lists, charts, and the like. In straight text it should always be replaced with *and others, and so forth,* or a similar phrase. See also *et al.*

everybody, everyone. See *anybody, anyone, everybody, nobody, somebody, someone.*

every day, everyday. *Every day* is a phrase that functions as an adverb: We perform certain chores *every day. Everyday* is an adjective: *Everyday* affairs can be boring.

every so often can profitably be replaced with *often, infrequently, occasionally,* or the like. If these words do not adequately convey the intended meaning, more specific wording—such as *every two days, weekly, once a month*—should be used.

except. See *accept, except.*

expect means anticipate. It does not mean suppose: We *expect* you for lunch. I *suppose* (not *expect*) she knows the way to our house.

F

fact that. This phrase is frequently misused in claiming as fact something that is unworthy of such claim: The *fact that* the Yankees may not win has not crossed Billy's mind. Such a slight thought is too obvious to be classified as fact. Rewrite: *That the* Yankees may not win has not crossed Billy's mind. Again: *That* (not *The fact that*) she may be pregnant seems a possibility. This thought has not been established as fact. But: The *fact that* Napoleon was born in Corsica has never left Frenchmen's memories. Napoleon's birthplace is a fact that can be verified. See also *due to the fact that.*

farther, further. The distinction between these two words, though badly smudged, is nevertheless still observed by careful speakers and writers. *Farther* applies to distance: You will travel *farther* in a day if you start early in the morning. *Further* is more often used to mean more or additionally: I have no *further* interest in your career. She will question me *further* tomorrow morning.

feel bad, feel badly, feel good, feel well. Of these four common expressions, only the second is inappropriate. The linking verb *feel* takes a predicate adjective as its complement—for example, *bad, good, well, strong, weak*: I *felt bad* (sad) about her failure. I *felt good* (happy) about her success. I *felt well* (healthy) all day. (*Well* is also an adverb: He *dances well*.)

Feel badly is a misguided attempt to find an adverb for the linking verb *feel*, since linking verbs cannot be modified.

fewer, less. *Fewer* refers to things that can be counted: *Fewer* people attended than we had anticipated. *Less* refers to things that cannot be counted: This cereal contains *fewer* (not *less*) calories. He eats *less* than he once did. This cereal contains *less* sugar than most. See also *more, less.*

finalize. See *-ize words.*

financial, monetary. *Financial* refers to money matters: He had no *financial* skill. We used to have a *financial* interest in that business. All of us should manage our own *financial* affairs.

Monetary refers to banking and to management of money by governments: The Federal Reserve Board establishes *monetary* policy in the United States. Ordinary individuals play no role in establishing *monetary* policy.

fine is a vague and overused modifier. A more descriptive modifier can usually be found: Sam is a *generous* (not *fine*) man. The weather was *clear* (not *fine*). I *like you* (not *like you fine*).

flaunt, flout. *Flaunt* means show off: My dentist appeared eager to *flaunt* her skills. *Flout* means show contempt for: Too many members of past administrations *flouted* the laws of our country.

flunk is slang and therefore inappropriate in formal writing. I am afraid I will *fail* (not *flunk*) the final examination.

foot, feet. *Foot* is singular, *feet* is plural. In such phrases as *a six-foot rule, foot* correctly functions as an adjective. *Feet* is always a noun. The shelf measures three *feet.*

for example. See *such as.*

for real. *For real* and the countless other *for* expressions waiting to be coined should be avoided. No one will be admitted *free* (not *for free*). No one will be admitted *without paying*. The slang expression *Is he for real?* has its charm but means no more than the slang expression *Is he real?*

former, latter are words used to indicate one of two: I read Crane and Pound, the *former* when I wanted to enjoy myself, the *latter* when I wanted to fall asleep. After examining the ranch house and the Tudor, I wanted to buy the *latter.*

When referring to one of more than two, *first* and *last* are used. After examining the ranch house, the Tudor, and the Cape Cod, I selected the *first* (not the *former*). See also *later, latter.*

forthcoming is incorrectly considered a substitute for *forthright* or *candid.* He was *forthright* (or *candid,* not *forthcoming*) in his testimony.

Forthcoming means approaching or available when promised: The *forthcoming* debate is attracting great interest. Will the necessary funds be *forthcoming?*

fortuitous, fortunate. These two good adjectives are in danger of losing their separate identities. *Fortunate* means lucky: We are *fortunate* in having an interesting speaker with us. *Fortuitous* means unplanned, accidental: The bombing of the hospital was *fortuitous:* the bomb was intended for a nearby target. A *fortuitous* encounter sometimes gives more pleasure than a thoroughly planned date.

fulsome. This adjective has nothing to do with *full.* It means disgustingly insincere: I found his *fulsome* praise unflattering and unworthy of the man.

funny is used only to mean amusing: I find few comedians *funny. Funny* is not a synonym for such words as *odd, strange, queer,* and *unusual*: His behavior at the party was *strange* (not *funny*), since he claims that he had not had a drink.

further See *farther, further*

G

good is an adjective, not an adverb: The car runs *well* (not *good*). As a predicate adjective, *good* serves as a complement of linking verbs: *seem good; be good; feel good.* A person who helps other people *does good; do-gooder* is a twentieth-century coinage that has gained many advocates. See also *feel bad, feel badly, feel good, feel well.*

got to is an inappropriate substitute for *have to, has to, had to*: I *have to* (not *got to*) leave now.

graduate. More and more the once frowned-upon use—*she graduated from college*—is seen instead of the older *she was graduated from college*.

However, the form that omits *from*—as in *I graduated high school*—is still frowned upon and probably will be frowned upon for a long time.

graffiti is a plural (the singular is *graffito*). Subway *graffiti* are so colorful that I envy the artists' skill.

grievous presents a spelling and pronunciation problem. The word has only one *i*. There is no word that is spelled or pronounced *grievious*.

H

had of, had ought. *Had* should be used instead of the colloquial *had of*: I wish I *had* (not *had of*) bought that car. *Should* or *ought* takes the place of *had ought*: You *should* (not *had ought to*) be more careful in the future. You *ought to* (not *had ought to*) practice more. See also *of*.

hanged, hung. *Hanged* is used for executions, *hung* for everything else. They *hanged* the poor man. They *hung* all their paintings. The sides of beef *hung* for a month.

hardly should not be used with a negative expression, since *hardly* itself carries a negative meaning: You *can* (not *can't*) *hardly* blame him. They *hardly* (not *don't hardly*) ever come to see us anymore. See also *but, hardly; only; scarcely*.

healthful, healthy. Food and climate can be *healthful*; people are *healthy*. When asked why he was so *healthy*, he replied that he ate only *healthful* dishes.

himself. See *myself, yourself, himself, ourselves, yourselves, themselves*.

historic, historical. *Historic* means history-making: The *historic* attack on Pearl Harbor is commemorated each year in the United States. *Historical* means relating to history or pertaining to history: She is best known for her exciting *historical* novels.

hopefully. The use of this adverb is changing. Again and again it is appearing in sentences in which *hopefully* has nothing to modify. *Hopefully, you will be home by ten* is replacing *I hope you will be home by ten.*

Hopefully is traditional in such constructions as *she said hopefully* and *they peered hopefully.* In these constructions, *hopefully* has verbs to modify: "My life is over," he said *hopelessly.* "My life is just beginning," she said *hopefully.*

hung. See *hanged, hung.*

I

i.e. is the abbreviation for the Latin locution *id est,* meaning *that is.* (Do not confuse it with *e.g.,* which means *for example.*) The abbreviation *i.e.* is appropriately used in scholarly works and in some other formal writing. In other writing it should always be replaced with *that is.*

if and when means no more than either *if* or *when* alone: I shall see him *when* (not *if and when*) he is ready to see me. *If* (not *If and when*) you hear any news, be sure to call me at once.

illicit. See *elicit, illicit.*

illusion. See *allusion, illusion, delusion.*

imaginary, imaginative. These adjectives are frequently confused. *Imaginary* means unreal: My daughter had an *imaginary* playmate whom she described as a blue boy with wings. *Imaginative* means showing powers of imagination: *Imaginative* literature, particularly stories for children, was my editor's principal interest.

immigrate. See *emigrate, immigrate.*

imminent, eminent. *Imminent* means about to occur: We have been told that the birth of the child is *imminent. Eminent* means outstanding, distinguished: They were unable to find an *eminent* scientist who was willing to praise the research.

implement is a favorite verb of bureaucrats, who use it as a replacement for *do, carry out, authorize, conduct, accomplish, apply, perform,* and many other verbs. The engineers wanted to *do* (not *implement*) the work as quickly as possible. They decided that they would *carry out* (not *implement*) the plan as soon as they found the money for it.

imply, infer. *Imply* means suggest: The witness *implied* in her testimony that the company books had been kept dishonestly, but the prosecutor could not get her to say so directly. *Infer* means conclude from evidence: From what Beatrice said, we *inferred* that her marriage was far from happy.

Speakers and writers *imply*; listeners and readers *infer*. The nouns associated with *imply* and *infer* are, respectively, *implication* and *inference*.

in all probability means nothing more than *probably*: Juan will *probably* (not *in all probability*) be elected.

in case usually means nothing more than *if*: Go to the library *if* (not *in case*) you have time.

incidence, incidents. *Incidence* means rate of occurrence: The *incidence* of crime is growing in some rural areas. *Incidents* are events: Two ugly *incidents* were reported last night.

incredible, incredulous. See *credible, credulous.*

infer. See *imply, infer.*

ingenious, ingenuous. *Ingenious* means clever: Edison was an *ingenious* inventor. *Ingenuous* means naive, frank: Aware that Emily was *ingenuous*, her brother and sister-in-law never confided in her or expected her to understand the subtleties of their relationship.

Disingenuous, the antonym of *ingenuous,* means lacking in candor.

in, into. *In* refers to position or location: He was put *in* charge of the department. The child is *in* her crib. *Into* refers to motion from outside to inside: The patient was moved *into* the intensive care unit.

innumerable, numerous. *Innumerable* means too many to be counted: We found *innumerable* insects inside the closet. *Numerous* means many: *Numerous* guests left before the party ended. Better: *Many* guests left before the party ended.

in regards. The *s* must be deleted. *In regard to* or *with regard to* will serve the purpose. Better yet, use *about*: I am writing *about* my unfilled order, which I placed with your company two months ago. See also *as regards.*

inside of means nothing more than *inside* or *within*: They remained *inside* (not *inside of*) the house. I shall be there *within* (not *inside of*) two hours.

in terms of. This phrase is overused and misapplied. The sentence He considered the plan in terms of its merits and its risks means nothing more than *He weighed the merits and risks of the plan*. *In terms of* has become a grand expression, a darling of pretentious speakers and writers.

In terms might best be restricted to such uses as *in loving terms* and *in terms of endearment*, in which *terms* is a synonym for *words* and has a few other meanings. He spoke *in terms* (words) too difficult for me to understand. The *terms of employment* (conditions of employment) were never made clear. *Prison terms* (periods of confinement) do not always reflect the nature of the crimes committed by felons.

interpersonal. This word, used by some social scientists as an elaborate substitute for *personal*, has inevitably become a favorite of many laymen. To make matters worse, *interpersonal* almost always appears with *relationship*, the meaning of which is already implicit in the word *interpersonal*. They enjoyed a close *interpersonal relationship* means nothing more than They enjoyed a close *relationship* or They were good friends.

in the event that means nothing more than *if*: If (not *In the event that*) he attends the meeting, we can expect complete chaos. *If* it rains (not *In the event that it rains*), the game will be postponed.

in the not too distant future. See *near future*.

in view of the fact that means nothing more than *because* and probably misrepresents as fact a statement that is unproven or trivial. See also *fact that*.

irregardless is incorrect for *regardless*: They will continue their struggle *regardless* (not *irregardless*) of the consequences.

it is, there is, there are are indirect, word-wasting ways to open sentences. Such sentences waste the subject position on the empty expletive *it* or *there*. The linking verbs that follow—*is, are, were, was, will be*—add nothing. We end up with *It is childish of you to behave in such a manner* instead of the forceful and direct *Your behavior makes you appear childish*. By avoiding *it is* we have six words in place of eleven. See also *there is, there are.*

It's I, it's me. Who now will answer *It's I* when asked *Who's there?* Even though *It's I* has grammatical correctness on its side, *It's me* is universally acceptable.

its, it's. The possessive of *it* is *its*: I think *its* battery should be replaced. The contraction of *it is* is *it's*: I assure you *it's* beyond me. See also *contractions.*

-ize words. The suffix *-ize* affords almost unlimited possibilities for new verbs—*criticize, ostracize, plagiarize,* and so on—but it does not give license to create verbal monsters. Some *-ize* coinages are welcome, enabling us to express in a single word thoughts that might otherwise require a phrase. Other *-ize* verbs are pretentious replacements for existing verbs that convey the same meaning—*finalize* for *complete, optimize* for *perfect, conceptualize* for *conceive* or *think, formularize* for *formulate.*

J

judicial, judicious. *Judicial* refers to matters of law: The *judicial* process must not be disrupted. *Judicious* refers to careful judgment: Be *judicious* in choosing a life partner.

just is a weak replacement for *completely, simply, quite, only, merely*: The boredom of household duties *completely* (not *just*) exhausted me. I was *simply* (not *just*) incapable of studying last semester. (Better yet: The boredom of household duties *exhausted* me. I was *incapable* of studying last semester.) The book costs *only* (not *just*) eleven dollars.

just exactly. This gushing phrase appears in such sentences as This is *just exactly* what I want. Better: This is *exactly* what I want. This is *precisely* what I want. Best: *This is what I want.*

K

kind, type are both singular: This *kind* (not *these kind*) of behavior; these *kinds* of behavior; that *type* of furniture; those *types* of furniture. When using *kind* or *type*, the verb that follows must agree in number with its subject: This *kind* of behavior *is* objectionable. Those *types* of furniture *are* suitable for any home.

The word *such* can usually replace *type* and *kind*: *Such* behavior wins one no friends.

kind of, sort of are poor substitutes for *somewhat* or *rather:* I was *somewhat* (not *kind of* or *sort of*) disappointed. Even *somewhat* and *rather* are vague modifiers, candidates for deletion: *I was disappointed.*

Kind of and *sort of* apply to variety or type: What *sort of* man is he? What *kind of* cereal do you prefer?

Do not use *a* after *sort of* and *kind of:* She is the *sort of* (not *sort of a*) person who will do well in any job she takes.

L

lack. As a verb, *lack* does not need *for*: We *lack* (not *lack for*) ambition. As a noun, *lack* is usually followed by *of*: They suffered from a *lack of* money.

large part is a weak substitute for the weak adjectives and pronouns *many* and *most*: I think *many* (not *a large part*) of the books were damaged. *Large part* can be used to mean *much* when referring to a structure: *A large part* of the building was destroyed by fire.

Large part shares the disadvantages of vagueness with *much, many,* and *most.* What is *a large number, a large portion, a large proportion,* or *a large share?* Where possible, be specific. *All but three* of the books were damaged. *One wing* of the building was destroyed. He has spent *all but three hundred dollars* of the money his mother left him.

later, latter. *Later* is the comparative form of *late*: He was habitually *later* than I. One of his *later* works was banned in Boston. *Latter* means the second of two: As for the problems of cost and time, the *latter* can easily be resolved, but not cost. See also *former, latter.*

laudable, laudatory. *Laudable* means deserving of praise: The critics said her early performances were *laudable* for their strong dramatic interpretation. *Laudatory* means giving praise: The *laudatory* speeches given during Edna's retirement dinner pleased everyone but Edna herself.

lay, lie. The principal parts of *lay* are *lay, laid, laid.* The principal parts of *lie* are *lie, lay, lain.* *Lay* means place: *Lay* the books on the table. He *is laying* bricks. He *laid* the linoleum. The hens *have laid* eggs all winter. *Lie* means incline or rest. *Lie* on the beach. She *is lying* on the couch. The books *have lain* there unread for a month.

Lie, meaning to tell an untruth, has still other forms—*lie, lied, lied.*

lead, led are the present and past forms of the verb *lead*: General Patton *led* his troops across the Rhine. I think it is time to *lead* the fans in a cheer.

The metal is *lead*: Pewter is an alloy of tin and *lead*.

learn, teach. *Learn* means acquire knowledge: Students *learn*. *Teach* means impart knowledge: Some college professors *teach* little.

leave, let are frequently confused verbs. *Leave* means depart from: *Leave* the room at once. *Let* means permit: *Let* me go. Exception: *Let me* (equally correct, *Leave me*) *alone*. In formal writing, *Let me alone* is preferred.

less. See *fewer, less; more, less.*

let's us in effect uses the same word twice. *Let's* is the contraction of *let us*: *Let's* (not *Let's us*) go to the theater. See also *contractions.*

liable is a weak substitute for *likely* in expressing probability: Mike was *likely* (not *liable*) to lose his job because of his frequent absences. *Liable* (with *for*) expresses legal responsibility: Are you *liable* for damages?

In addition, be sure not confuse *liable* with *libel*, a legal term meaning defamation of a person: *Libel* is difficult to prove in United States courts.

lie. See *lay, lie.*

lightning, lightening. *Lightning* is a natural phenomenon: We sought shelter during the *lightning* storm. *Lightening* is a reduction in weight or severity: We ought to consider *lightening* our packs. The verb *lighten* also has the meaning of make lighter: Joyce will not consider *lightening* her hair color.

like in one of its functions is a preposition: Anyone *like* Tom has a good chance of succeeding. *Like* is not used as a conjunction: Tom ran as though (not *ran like*) the law were after him. The recent expression *tell it like* (instead of *as) it is* is a forceful misapplication of *like.*

likely. As an adjective, *likely* is appropriately used to say that something is probable or suitable: A *likely* story! This is a *likely* source for your research. As an adverb, however, *probably* is more appropriate: He will *probably* (not *likely*) arrive before lunch.

literally, figuratively. *Literally* means actually: By the fifteenth of the month, we *literally* had no money left. *Figuratively* means metaphorically, not actually: We *figuratively* fell through the floor when the foreman made his announcement. In this cliché no one actually (literally) fell through anything. The writer was exaggerating to show a degree of surprise. If he had written *We literally fell through the floor in surprise,* he either would have been wrong or we would know that termites had been hard at work for a long time.

loath, loathe. *Loath* (also spelled *loth*) is an adjective that means reluctant: He was *loath* to show his cards, since he had such a poor hand. *Loathe* is a verb that means despise: One cannot help but *loathe* a bully.

look good, look well. One can *look good* and one can *look well.* The former refers to appearance, the latter to health. See also *feel bad, feel badly, feel good, feel well.*

loose, lose. *Loose* is an adjective: My collar is *loose.* *Lose* is a verb: I hope you do not *lose* your way.

lot of, lots of are weak substitutes for *many* or *much.* See also *large part; innumerable, numerous.*

M

mad, angry. *Mad* means insane: Ophelia went *mad.* I am *angry with* (not *mad at*) you. See also *angry at, angry with.*

many, much, most. *Many* is used for things and people that can be counted: *Many* dogs run loose. *Much* is used for things that cannot be counted: *Much* trouble can be avoided. *Much* sugar was used in her recipes. *Most* is used for everything: *Most* dogs eat well. *Most* trouble cannot be avoided. *Most* sugar is wasted. See also *most.*

may. See *can, may*.

may be, maybe. *May be* is a verb form: We *may be* there on time. *Maybe* is an adverb: *Maybe* she did not hear us.

may of, might of, must of. See *of*.

mean for is a colloquialism for *mean that*: We did not *mean that* you should stay home (not We *did not mean for* you to stay home).

meaningful. This overworked adjective usually serves little purpose unless accompanied by an explanation: We found his statement *meaningful* in that it clarified his beliefs and supported them logically. Since the word *meaningful* is vague, the sentence is best reworded: His statement *clarified and supported his beliefs*. Expressions such as *meaningful relationship* and *meaningful discussion* tend to be empty. More specific terms will improve any sentence.

media. This word is plural (the singular is *medium*): Many people feel the news *media are* (not *is*) creating stories instead of reporting and interpreting them. My favorite news *medium* is the newspaper. *Medium* and *media* do not refer to newspapers, television, and the rest unless specified (*the news media*) or so understood in context. *Medium* means instrument or means: there are entertainment *media*, instructional *media*, and many other types of *media*.

might of. See *of*.

monetary. See *financial, monetary*.

moral, morale. The adjective *moral* refers to morality, the standards of human conduct: You pose a *moral* question that only you may answer. The noun *morale* means mental outlook or condition: Team *morale* had never been lower before an important game.

more, less are superfluous as modifiers of comparatives: In important ways you are *better* (not *more better*) than I am. I am not *as hungry as you are* (not *I am less hungrier than you are*). See also *fewer, less*.

most is not an appropriate substitute for *almost*: We understood *almost* (not *most*) everything the speaker said. *Most* may be used to mean the greater amount: We understood *most* of what you said.

More and *most* cannot modify adjectives that do not allow modification. *Unique,* for example, cannot become *more unique* or *most unique,* since *unique* means one of a kind. See also *many, much, most.*

much. See *many, much, most.*

must of. See *of.*

myself, yourself, himself, ourselves, yourselves, themselves. The *-self, -selves* pronouns are used as intensifiers (strengtheners): I *myself* bear no ill will. They also serve as reflexives: They act as though they hate *themselves.*

The most common misuses of these pronouns are corrected in the following examples. She gave *me* (not *myself*) a box of cigars. I am no taller than *she* (not *herself*). My parents asked my sister and *me* (not *myself*) to go with them. The correct form of the third person plural is *themselves,* not *theirself* or *theirselves.* See also *ourself.*

N

near future is a weak substitute for *soon.* Even weaker is *in the not too distant future,* which also means *soon.* Whenever possible, use specific expressions: *tomorrow; two days from now; next week.*

needless to say is merely a space-filler. Whatever is needless to say need not be said and should be left out.

neither is used for one of two: He *neither* drinks *nor* smokes. I will recommend *neither* Joe *nor* Al. Since *neither* is negative, *either* is used when the sentence already contains a negative: *I will not buy either* (not *neither*) *car. I will buy neither car.* See also *either, neither.*

nice is a weak substitute for adjectives that carry specific meanings: *starry sky* means more than *nice sky; generous person* means more than *nice person.* Vague modifiers are best avoided.

noisome, a rarely used word, has nothing to do with *noisy;* it means disgusting: The chemistry experiment gave off *noisome* fumes that drove us from the laboratory.

nowheres is a colloquialism for *nowhere: Nowhere* (not *Nowheres*) we looked did we find land at a price we could afford.

number. See *amount, number.*

numerous. The preposition *of* is not used after *numerous*. *Numerous* (not *Numerous of*) manuscripts were sold at auction yesterday. In most sentences, *many* conveys the same meaning as *numerous* and has the advantage of simplicity. See also *innumerable, numerous.*

O

obviate the necessity of. This expression uses unnecessary words. *Obviate* means make unnecessary: By finishing his tables with fine steel wool and tung oil, he *obviates* (not *obviates the necessity of*) frequent polishing.

of. Informal speech and writing sometimes substitute *of* for *have* in such expressions as *may have, might have, could have, should have, ought to have, would have,* and *will have.* The use of *of* for *have* in formal speech or writing is always incorrect.

of between is an awkward substitute for *of* in such expressions as *a crowd of between ten and fifteen thousand.* Better: *a crowd of ten to fifteen thousand.*

off of uses one word too many. Harry jumped *off* (not *off of*) the diving board. Stay *off* (not *off of*) the roof.

on account of is an inadequate substitute for *because* or *because of*: He was rejected *because* (not *on account of*) his aptitude test scores were low. She was given a seat *because of* her age.

only should not be used with negatives: I wanted *only* to avoid hurting her (not *I wanted only not to hurt her*). See also *but, hardly; hardly; scarcely.*

opt for is a bureaucratic and pretentious substitute for *choose* or *decide*: They *chose* (not *opted for*) direct action. She *decided on* (not *opted for*) a policy of cordial cooperation.

oral, verbal. See *verbal, oral.*

ordinance, ordnance. *Ordinance* refers to decrees or laws: The city council establishes fire *ordinances. Ordnance* refers to military weapons and ammunition: The troops spent many hours making sure their *ordnance*—especially their 105mm howitzers—remained combat-ready.

ought to is never preceded by *had*: They *ought to* (not *had ought to*) keep better records. They *ought to* (not *had ought to*) have kept better records. See also *had of, had ought.*

ourself. Only a monarch, judge, or editorial writer may use *ourself*: We *ourself* find no problems in the proposed equipment.

The rest of us must write *ourselves*: We found *ourselves* encumbered with debts and responsibilities we had never wanted. See also *myself, yourself, himself, ourselves, yourselves, themselves.*

out loud is a colloquial substitute for *aloud*: Mother read *aloud* (not *out loud*) to us every evening during those harsh winters.

outside of. *Of* is an unnecessary addition: They remained *outside* (not *outside of*) the house during the party. See also *inside of.*

owing to the fact that. This phrase is a cumbersome substitute for *because*: *Because* (not *Owing to the fact that*) we had so little money, we were forced to do without everything but the essentials. *Owing to* is another unfortunate substitute for *because*: *Because of* (not *Owing to*) her illness, she could not compete in the games. See also *fact that.*

P

party. This noun should not be used to refer to an individual: *Joseph* (not *That party*) made a serious error. Such usage is acceptable only in contracts and similar documents: *the party of the first part.*

The word is also properly used in the sense of *participant*: I am not a *party to* (a participant in) the dispute.

past. Expressions containing words that refer to the past do not need the additional adjective *past*. *Past experience* means no more than *experience,* and *past history* means no more than *history.* Ralph's *record* (not *past record*) hurts his chances for employment.

per is effective only in combination with Latin words: *per diem,* not *per day*; *per capita,* not *per person.* With English equivalents of these words, *a* sounds better: Many consultants are paid $750 *a day.* The admission fee was $20 *a person,* $30 *a couple.* The price is 10 cents *a hundred.*

Per se is Latin for *by itself* and the like. We do not oppose hard work *per se*, but we do reject meaningless work. More effective: *We reject meaningless work, not hard work.*

percent, percentage. *Percentage* is used when numbers are not specified: *a small percentage. Percent* is used after numbers: 15 *percent*; 20 *percent*.

persecute, prosecute. *Persecute* means harass: Minority groups *have* often *been persecuted. Prosecute* means pursue or—rarely—persist in: District attorneys *prosecute* criminal cases. Governments *prosecute* wars.

phenomena is a plural noun: *These phenomena are* (not *This phenomena is*) disturbing. *Phenomenon* is the singular form: Lightning is a natural *phenomenon*.

plenty is a colloquialism for *quite* or *very*: The yellow one is *quite* (not *plenty*) good. Since *quite* and *very* are vague and overused—is *quite* good or *very good* better than *good*?—both words can usually be omitted to improve effectiveness: The yellow one is good. The blue one is excellent. See also *very*.

point in time is an overworked fad expression that means no more than *time* or *stage*: By that *point* (not *point in time*) the evil plot had gone so far that nothing could stop it. See also *at this point in time*.

poorly is a colloquialism for *poor* in expressions dealing with health: The cow appears *sick* (not *is feeling poorly*).

practicable, practical. *Practicable* means capable of being accomplished: Your plan is *practicable* if you have enough capital to carry you through the first year of operations. *Practical* means sensible or aware of results: She is a *practical* person, always concerned with getting a job done as inexpensively as possible.

An *impractical* person is unconcerned with how much things cost. An *impracticable* plan should be discarded because it will not work.

pre-. Words such as *recorded* and *planned* should not be burdened with the prefix *pre-*, since they already denote actions that have been completed earlier: The preceding program was *recorded* (not *prerecorded*). A vacation is *planned* (not *preplanned*). *Pre-* is sensibly used in such words as *precede*, which has a meaning entirely different from that of *cede*, and *prejudge*, which means more than *judge*.

precipitate, precipitous. *Precipitate* means overly hasty: Guard against *precipitate* action. *Precipitous* means steep: The riverbank is *precipitous* near the falls.

Precipitate is also a verb meaning bring about prematurely: Discovery of the embezzlement *precipitated* the bank officer's dismissal.

preclude. *Preclude* means make impossible. Actions can be *precluded*: Their poverty *precluded* buying a house (not *precluded them from buying a house*) even though the monthly payments would be low. People cannot be *precluded*: Her handicap grew steadily worse and finally *precluded* all physical activity (not *precluded her* from performing all physical activity).

previous to, prior to are weak, pompous substitutes for *before*: She was appointed *before* (not *prior to* or *previous to*) earning her doctorate.

principal, principle. The adjective *principal* means chief: My *principal* concern is your safety. The noun *principal* usually refers to the head of a school or officer of an organization: She was a *principal* in the engineering concern for many years. *Principal* also means capital: The bank demanded payment of the entire *principal* as well as all earned interest.

Principle is always a noun referring to truth or standards: The person on trial appeared to be completely lacking in *principles*. In *principle* you are entirely correct, but you have neglected important considerations in assessing the problem.

probably. See *in all probability; likely.*

prophecy, prophesy. *Prophecy* is a noun: Most of her *prophecies* inevitably proved incorrect. *Prophesy* is a verb: The astrologer *prophesied* a marriage blessed with many children.

prosecute. See *persecute, prosecute.*

Q

questionable, questioning. *Questionable* means open to doubt: The so-called Iraqgate investigation concerned itself primarily with *questionable* official acts. *Questioning* means quizzical: Her *questioning* attitude made me so uncomfortable that I decided to find another administrative assistant.

question as to whether. *Question as to* adds nothing to *whether* in such sentences as The *question as to whether* the indictment was properly drawn was raised by the grand jury. Better: The grand jury did not *question whether* the indictment was properly drawn. *Whether* the indictment was properly drawn was not discussed by the grand jury.

quite a. *Quite a bit, quite a few,* and other such expressions are vague. Explicit expressions are always more effective: *50 percent; more than half; the majority; three; fourteen.* The sentence He took *quite a bit* of time to answer tells little. More informative: *He took five minutes to answer.* See also *very.*

quote cannot function as a noun in formal speech and writing. The noun is *quotation*: Were you able to find a suitable *quotation* (not *quote*)? *Quote* is an accepted verb: Did you *quote* enough from the published record to give your conclusions validity?

R

raise, rise. As a transitive verb, *raise* takes a direct object: I *raise* corn and alfalfa. He *raised* his sisters and brothers. Each year the landlady *raises* our rent. As an intransitive verb, *rise* does not take a direct object: Can you actually see the cake *rise*? The sun *rose* after eight. They *have risen* early all their lives.

rarely if ever is a lightweight substitute for *rarely. Rarely ever* is just as pointless. You will *rarely* (not *rarely if ever* or *rarely ever*) find me in the library. *Seldom* is close to *rarely* in meaning and can provide welcome variety: I am *seldom* found in a library.

rather. See *kind of, sort of.*

ravage, ravish. *Ravage* means destroy: Fire *ravaged* our village. The poor child *was ravaged* by fever. *Ravish* has several meanings, among them rape and carry off by force. Both meanings are directed at people rather than property: All the young women of the village *were ravished* by enemy soldiers.

really, real. Like *very, really* is used too often as a vague strengthener (intensifier). While *really* means in reality or truly and can be applied to many thoughts, it can almost always be omitted without damaging meaning: Cats are *useless* (not *really useless*) in a modern apartment. Habitual use of *really* leads to such gushing sentences as *She did really well* and *I really like you*. Yet sentences do benefit from use of *really* when the word strengthens the intended meaning: He *really* was at home when he said he was.

The distinction between *real* and *really* is important to note. *Real* is an adjective; *really* is an adverb: *real events,* not fiction; *really sick,* not pretending.

reason is because is not a logical formulation. The accepted form is *reason is that*: The *reason* I am angry *is that* (not *because*) you neglected to call on time. *Reason* may often be omitted: I am angry *because* you neglected to call on time. See also *because*.

refer should not be followed by *back*. The prefix *re-* provides the meaning of again or back: *Refer* (not *Refer back*) to my first letter on this topic.

regarding. This word and all its cousins—*in regard to, in respect to, with respect to, relating to, relative to,* and the old-fashioned *as regards*—can be replaced by *about* or *concerning*: I am writing *concerning* your advertisement for a computer programmer. We have no doubt *about* her ability to do excellent work.

regretful, regrettable. People can be *regretful*: Since you clearly intended no harm, why be *regretful* over what happened? Only actions or the results of actions can be *regrettable*: The stockholders found your unprovoked outburst *regrettable*. Consumer attitudes toward recent price rises were considered *regrettable* by large corporations.

relation, relationship. *Relation* describes a connection of things or abstractions: No one fully understands the *relation* between unemployment and inflation. *Relationship* describes a connection based on friendship or association of people: The business *relationship* they enjoyed was the envy of their competitors. See also *meaningful*.

respectfully, respectively. *Respectfully* means with respect: They speak *respectfully* of you. *Respectively* means singly in the order mentioned and usually appears in such awkward sentences as *John and Jim were eight and ten years old respectively.*

Respectively is seldom needed. Such sentences can usually be rewritten: *John was eight years old and Jim was ten.*

right is a colloquialism for *very, somewhat,* or *extremely*: I am *very* (not *right*) proud of you. Yet, no matter which intensifier is used, the thought is not strengthened by its inclusion. *Very* *proud* is no stronger than *proud*: I am *proud* of you. See also *very*.

rise. See *raise, rise.*

S

said. This verb form is sometimes used as an adjective by lawyers and others who deal with legal matters: The *said contracts* were deemed void. Thus, whenever *said* is used as an adjective, it conveys the impression of legality, usually inappropriately: The *said faulty instrument* must be returned to the tool crib. Better: *Return the faulty instrument to the tool crib.*

says. As the past tense of *say, says* is a colloquialism: She *said* (not *says*) yesterday that she would attend the meeting.

scarcely cannot be used with negatives: I *scarcely* had time (not *scarcely had no time*) to finish the work. See also *hardly, neither.*

seldom. See *rarely if ever.*

-self, -selves. See *myself, yourself, himself, ourselves, yourselves, themselves.*

sensory, sensual, sensuous. *Sensory* refers to the senses or sensation: The experiment calls for isolating the subject so that all *sensory* stimuli are blocked. *Sensual* usually refers to gratification of physical or sexual appetite: He spent his time pursuing *sensual* pleasures rather than devoting himself to his studies. *Sensuous* applies most often to aesthetic enjoyment: The critic responded favorably to the *sensuous* music played last night.

set, sit. These verbs are sometimes confused. *Set*, a transitive verb, means place (something) in position: *Set* the vase on the table. *Sit*, an intransitive verb, means be seated: *Sit* wherever you wish.

To confuse matters, it must be noted that the moon, planets, stars, hens, and concrete—correctly—*set.*

shall, will. At one time these words had separate meanings and uses, but the distinction is fast disappearing, with *will* winning out for most uses. Traditionally, formal writing showed the future by *I shall; we shall; you will; he, she, it,* and *they will.* Determination, necessity, and duty still are indicated by *I will; we* *will; you shall; he, she, it,* and *they shall.* In your formal writing, you ought to observe these distinctions.

should of. See *of.*

similar. This adjective means resembling, not same: Joe's father's reaction was *similar* to mine, but I managed to control my response.

simple, simplified, simplistic. *Simple* means easy to understand: She was able to solve *simple* problems without using paper and pencil. *Simplified* means made less complex: *Simplified* concepts are useful in textbooks written for children. *Simplistic* refers to oversimplification of complex matters by ignoring complexities: Voters are frightened by the *simplistic* solutions some politicians propose for complex economic problems.

 Simplistic condemns; *simple* and *simplified* carry no judgments.

since. Although *since* may be used to mean because, such use requires care. The problem is that *since* can also refer to time past. Within a sentence, the meanings may be distinguished by use of a comma when *since* means *because.* Time: He has lived in New York City *since* 1960. Cause: He considers himself a New Yorker, *since* he has lived in the city for many years.

sit. See *set, sit.*

so. *So* is an invaluable adverb in such formulations as She was *so intelligent* that I stood in awe of her. But when *so* is used as a conjunction—We were late, *so* we took a taxi—a sagging sentence may result. Rewriting invariably produces a stronger construction: *Because we were late,* we took a taxi. We took a taxi *because we were late.*

someplace, some place. *Someplace* is a poor substitute for the adverb *somewhere*: My dog is hiding *somewhere* (not *someplace*) between your house and mine. *Some place* refers to an unspecified position or location: *Some places* in the administration were still unfilled three months after the mayor took office.

somewhat. See *kind of, sort of.*

sort of. See *kind of, sort of.*

specie. *Specie* refers to coined money: Gold *specie* is highly valued. It is not the singular of *species*, which has the same form in the singular and plural: She wrote her thesis on a rare plant *species*. Those *species* are rapidly approaching extinction.

stationary, stationery. *Stationary* means not moving: A *stationary* target is easy to hit with a rifle. *Stationery* means writing paper and related items: My father's *stationery* store was known throughout the city.

stayed, stood. *Stayed* is the past tense of *stay*: They *stayed* at the reception long after they should have gone home. We *stayed* in bed. *Stood* is the past tense of *stand*: We *stood* at attention while the anthem was played. The building *stood* near the town green.

stimulant, stimulus. A *stimulant* temporarily arouses organic activity: According to an article I read, most *stimulants* are not addictive. A *stimulus* may result in a response: Her remark provided the *stimulus* we needed to complete our project.

stood. See *stayed, stood*.

such as. The phrase *such as* introduces the listing of a few examples or illustrations: The children were given a variety of toys, *such as* dolls, jacks, and board games. The phrase indicates that what follows is an incomplete selection, so it is misleading to add *and others* or *and so on* at the end of the sentence. The same rule applies to any list following *for example*.

such that. Even when correctly used, *such that* leads to awkward and vague sentences: Their position was *such that* we could not meet their demands. Better: *They asked for so much money that we could not come to an agreement. They asked for more money than we could afford to give them.*

Such that is not used before a clause that indicates result: They made a strong protest *such that* the city changed its policy. Better: *They made such a strong protest that the city changed its policy. They made so strong a protest that the city changed its policy.*

sure. *Sure* is an adjective, not an adverb: One *sure way* to fail is to neglect your studies. In formal writing, *sure* is not a substitute for *certainly* or *surely*: You *surely* (not *sure*) cannot mean that.

sure and is a colloquial substitute for *sure to*: Be *sure to* (not *sure and*) sit in the bleachers if you want to be among baseball fans who know the game.

suspicion is a noun, not a verb: They *suspect* (not *suspicion*) everything we do. He cannot overcome his *suspicion* that the chief executive officer wants to ease him out of the company.

swell is not an acceptable substitute for *good* and similar words except in informal speech: Johnson's dictionary had a *good* (not *swell*) initial sale. Since I met Lily, I have felt *elated* (not *swell*).

T

talk to, talk with. *Talk to* means inform: Tomorrow I shall *talk to* the men and women on the assembly line about the new safety regulations. *Talk with* means converse: I want to *talk with* you about our plans for completing the project.

teach, learn. See *learn, teach*.

than, then. *Than* is a conjunction: Her work is no better *than* yours. *Then* is an adverb: I *then* decided to return to my office and finish some work.

theirself, theirselves. Both are incorrect. See *myself, yourself, himself, ourselves, yourselves, themselves*.

their, there. *Their* is the possessive form of *they*: *Their* taxes were so high that they were forced to sell their home. *There* is an adverb: She went *there* on her own. *There* is also an expletive: *There* is no use in arguing further. See also *it is, there is, there are*.

themselves. See *myself, yourself, himself, ourselves, yourselves, themselves*.

there is, there are. *There is* is followed by a singular: *There is* only one shirt left in my drawer. *There are* is followed by a plural: *There are* two shirts left in my drawer. *There is* and *there are* should not be used habitually to start sentences. To understand why, see *it is, there is, there are*.

these kind, those kind. See *kind, type*.

thusly. Since *thus* is an adverb, it does not need the *-ly* ending: *Thus*, he was unable to finish the work he had started. Caruso sang the note *thus* (not *thusly*).

to, too. *To* is a preposition: I gave the package *to* the receiving clerk. *Too* is an adverb: We found the book *too* difficult. She is *too* ill to perform tonight. *Too* is not always a good substitute for *very*: He is not *very* (not *too*) ill. See also *very*.

try and is colloquial for *try to*: *Try to* (not *Try and*) find the part quickly.

type. As a noun, *type* requires addition of *of* in such expressions as *type of novel*: That *type of* business (not *type* business) requires too much capital. In technical expression, *type* is often included unnecessarily. An automatic transmission (not *automatic-type*) used to require frequent repair. *Type* is singular, *types* plural: *this type; that type; these types; those types.* See also *kind, type.*

U

unbend, unbending. The verb *unbend* means relax: After a long flight, the crew *would* often *unbend* in the airport coffee shop before returning home. The crew *was unbending* in the airport coffee shop. (In the second example, *was unbending* is in the past progressive tense of *unbend*.)

   The adjective *unbending* means incapable of compromise: On questions of personal conduct, the minister was *unbending*. She was *unbending* in her insistence on high standards of scholarship. (In these two examples, the adjective *unbending* is the complement of *was*.)

underneath. It is incorrect to follow *underneath* with *of*: The beads were *underneath* (not *underneath of*) the table.

uninterested. See *disinterested, uninterested*.

unique means one of a kind. It does not mean unusual. Since few things are unique, the word should be used with care, and modifiers should be used with utmost care: The helicopter provides *unique* (not *most unique* or *very unique*) air transportation.

   Some people or things may be *nearly unique, perhaps unique, probably unique, apparently unique,* and so on, but never *most unique, very unique,* or *entirely unique*.

unless and until. These three words together accomplish no more than the single words *unless* or *until*: I will not see you again *unless* (or *until*, but not *unless and until*) you give me a written apology. See also *when, as, and, if.*

usage. This word is properly used for matters involving customs and standards: English *usage* is difficult for the foreign-born. It is a poor substitute for *use*: He noted the increasing *use* (not *usage*) of alcohol by high-school students.

use, utilize. These words have the same meaning. Many speakers and writers mistakenly think *utilize* raises the intellectual appeal of their discourse. Why not use the shorter word?

V

various. This word is not followed by *of*: *Various* (not *Various of*) useful techniques are being developed. *Various* (not *Various of*) ideas were discussed before the final decision was taken. Since *various* implies a number of different items, *some, several,* or *certain* may serve better in many sentences: *Several* (not *Various*) employees are being considered for promotion.

verbal, oral. Though the difference between these words is disappearing, their original meanings can be useful. *Verbal* means in spoken or written words: Helen Keller's *verbal* skills were extraordinary in one who was born deaf, mute, and blind. *Oral* means spoken or referring to the mouth: *Oral* communication has been made easier by widespread use of the telephone. The dentist told me I would have to consult an *oral* surgeon.

The sentence *We reached a verbal agreement* means no more than *We used words to reach an agreement.* Better: *We reached an agreement. We reached a written agreement. We reached an oral agreement.* Oral agreements are verbal agreements, but for careful writers and speakers verbal agreements are not necessarily oral.

very. The greatly overused adverb *very* can profitably be omitted as the modifier of an adjective or adverb. In innumerable cases, the word modified is just as strong without *very.* A *very special person* means nothing more than a *special person.* A *very beautiful woman* is no more attractive than a *beautiful woman. Tired,* for example, can stand without *very* unless *exhausted, sleepy,* or some other precise meaning—which can be stated— is intended.

Though *very pleased* and *very interested* are commonly seen and heard, *very* should not be used to modify other past participles, such as *defeated* or *used. Very nearly defeated* and *very widely used* convey meaning (in these phrases, *very* modifies the adverbs *nearly* and *widely*), but you can do as well without *very*: *nearly defeated; widely used. Very* is also an adjective and can be used to heighten meaning: He decided to visit her on the *very day* she was to leave for her new job. See also *unique.*

viable is a currently favored adjective that is used when *practicable* or *workable* is more apt: We consider the plan a *workable* (not *viable*) solution to our problems. *Viable* is appropriate in specialized uses: A *viable fetus*, for example, is one capable of surviving after birth. While *viable* has many applications, we risk overusing it by putting it to petty uses: *The menu you propose for the awards dinner is viable* may be intended to mean that we can afford pork and beans for eleven players and the coach.

W

wait up is a colloquialism for *wait*: She was running so swiftly that I had to ask her to *wait* (not *wait up*) for me.

In idiomatic English, anxious parents *wait up* for inconsiderate children—the parents do not go to bed before their children come home. See *anxious, eager.*

want for. *Want for* means lack: I hope we never *want for* food and shelter again. The locution is not an acceptable substitute for *want*: I *want* (not *want for*) you to do the work right now.

ways. *Ways*, the plural of *way*, has many uses: She found faster *ways* of designing microcircuits. I do not like his *ways.* Ways is not a substitute for *way* in the sense of distance: We were a long *way* (not *ways*) from home.

when, as, and if is a useless phrase: I will see her *when* (or *if*, but not *when, as, and if*) she returns. See also *unless and until.*

where should not be confused with *that*: We read *that* (not *where*) Italy is changing its monetary policy.

where . . . at. This phrase is popular slang in such sentences as *I didn't know where I was at*, meaning *I was confused.* Use this charming expression only in informal speech and writing.

whether or not. *Whether* is usually enough: I do not know *whether* (not *whether or not*) he will be there. The longer expression can be used to add emphasis: I will do this *whether or not* he agrees. I will do this *whether* he agrees *or not.*

which. The pronoun *which* is used to refer to things: My coat, *which* I had worn for eight years, was too shabby to wear any longer. *Which* is not used to refer to people: Customers *who* (not *which*) pay their bills promptly are given good service.

Which should not be used without a clear antecedent. In the sentence *I decided to go to the game on the spur of the moment, which I did,* the antecedent of *which* is vague. It can refer to the decision or to the trip to the game. Better: *I went to the game on the spur of the moment.*

who, whom. *Who* is subjective and *whom* is objective, but it is often difficult to determine whether the subjective or objective case is correct in certain uses.

In the sentence *She is the manager (who* or *whom) spoke to us last week,* the correct pronoun is *who.* This is so because in the dependent clause *who spoke to us last week,* the pronoun *who* is the subject of the verb *spoke.* In the sentence *I know (who* or *whom) she spoke with yesterday,* the correct pronoun is *whom.* This is so because in the dependent clause *whom she spoke with yesterday,* the pronoun *she* is the subject of the verb *spoke,* and *whom* is the object of the preposition *with.* The same rule functions for the pronouns *whoever* and *whomever.*

Always ask yourself what function—subject or object—any of these four pronouns performs.

whoever, whomever. See *who, whom.*

who's, whose. *Who's* is the contraction of *who is*: Do you know *who's* missing? Guess *who's* coming to dinner. *Whose* is the possessive of *who*: Do you know *whose* book is missing? *Whose* little boy are you? *Whose* refers usually to people: The convict *whose* parole has been denied has vowed to fast until he dies. See also *contractions.*

will. See *shall, will.*

-wise. Many awkward words are being coined by adding the suffix *-wise* to any noun willy-nilly: *moneywise, voterwise, opinionwise,* and so on. This suffix does not mean *with respect to,* as such coinages imply. It does mean *in the manner of* or *in the direction of,* as in *otherwise, likewise, lengthwise.*

In certain established idioms, *wise* is used with the meaning of *having wisdom*: *streetwise children; penny-wise and pound-foolish*. See also *-ize words*.

would like is a weak substitute for *want*: I *want* (not *would like*) you to try milk instead of coffee. *Would like for* and *want for* should not be used in place of *want*: I *want* (not *would like for* or *want for*) you to try milk. See also *lack*.

would of. See *of*.

Y

you know. This expression is frequently used inappropriately in speech as a time-filler, suggesting to listeners a lack of suitable words or thoughts. See also *meaningful*.

yourself, yourselves. See *myself, yourself, himself, ourselves, yourselves, themselves*

Section IV

READY REFERENCE

– 1 –

Abbreviations

UNITED STATES OF AMERICA

Ala.	**AL**	Alabama	Mo.	**MO**	Missouri
Alas.	**AK**	Alaska	Mont.	**MT**	Montana
Ariz.	**AZ**	Arizona	Nebr.	**NE**	Nebraska
Ark.	**AR**	Arkansas	Nev.	**NV**	Nevada
Calif.	**CA**	California	N.H.	**NH**	New Hampshire
Colo.	**CO**	Colorado	N.J.	**NJ**	New Jersey
Conn.	**CT**	Connecticut	N.Mex.	**NM**	New Mexico
Del.	**DE**	Delaware	N.Y.	**NY**	New York
D.C.	**DC**	District of	N.C.	**NC**	North Carolina
		Columbia	N.Dak.	**ND**	North Dakota
Fla.	**FL**	Florida	Ohio	**OH**	Ohio
Ga.	**GA**	Georgia	Okla.	**OK**	Oklahoma
Haw.	**HI**	Hawaii	Oreg.	**OR**	Oregon
Ida.	**ID**	Idaho	Pa.	**PA**	Pennsylvania
Ill.	**IL**	Illinois	R.I.	**RI**	Rhode Island
Ind.	**IN**	Indiana	S.C.	**SC**	South Carolina
Ia.	**IA**	Iowa	S.Dak.	**SD**	South Dakota
Kans.	**KS**	Kansas	Tenn.	**TN**	Tennessee
Ken., Ky.	**KY**	Kentucky	Tex.	**TX**	Texas
La.	**LA**	Louisiana	Ut.	**UT**	Utah
Me.	**ME**	Maine	Vt.	**VT**	Vermont
Md.	**MD**	Maryland	Va.	**VA**	Virginia
Mass.	**MA**	Massachusetts	Wash.	**WA**	Washington
Mich.	**MI**	Michigan	W.Va.	**WV**	West Virginia
Minn.	**MN**	Minnesota	Wis.	**WI**	Wisconsin
Miss.	**MS**	Mississippi	Wyo.	**WY**	Wyoming

COUNTRIES OF THE WORLD

Afg.	Afghanistan	Eng.	England
Alb.	Albania	Eth.	Ethiopia
Alg.	Algeria	Fin.	Finland
And.	Andorra	Fr.	France
Ang.	Angola	G.B.	Great Britain
Ant.	Antigua	Ger.	Germany
Arg.	Argentina	Gr.	Greece
Austral.	Australia	Guat.	Guatemala
Austr.	Austria	Guin.	Guinea
Bah.	Bahamas	Hond.	Honduras
Bahr.	Bahrain	Hung.	Hungary
Bangla.	Bangladesh	Ice.	Iceland
Barb.	Barbados	Ir.	Ireland
Belg.	Belgium	Isr.	Israel
Bhut.	Bhutan	Ital.	Italy
Bol.	Bolivia	Jam.	Jamaica
Bots.	Botswana	Jap.	Japan
Braz.	Brazil	Jor.	Jordan
Brun.	Brunei	Lux.	Luxembourg
Bulg.	Bulgaria	Madag.	Madagascar
Burk.	Burkina Faso (formerly Upper Volta)	Mal.	Malaysia
		Mex.	Mexico
		Mozamb.	Mozambique
Bur.	Burma (now called Myanmar)	Myan.	Myanmar
		Neth.	Netherlands
Buru.	Burundi	N.Z.	New Zealand
Camb.	Cambodia (also called Kampuchea)	Nor.	Norway
		Pan.	Panama
		Pol.	Poland
Camer.	Cameroon	Port.	Portugal
Can.	Canada	PRC	People's Republic of China
C.A.R.	Central African Republic		
		ROC	Republic of China (Taiwan)
Col.	Colombia		
C.R.	Costa Rica	Rum.	Rumania
Czech.	Czech Republic	Scot.	Scotland
Den.	Denmark	S. Afr.	South Africa
Dom.	Dominica	Sp.	Spain
Dom. Rep.	Dominican Republic	Swed.	Sweden
Ecua.	Ecuador	Switz.	Switzerland

Syr.	Syria	USA, U.S.	United States of
Tun.	Tunisia		America,
Turk.	Turkey		United States
U.A.E.	United Arab	Vat.	Vatican City
	Emirates	Venez.	Venezuela
U.K.	United Kingdom	Yugo.	Yugoslavia
Uru.	Uruguay		

PERSONAL, CIVIL, AND MILITARY TITLES AND HONORS

Adj. Gen.	adjutant general
Adm.	admiral
Asst. Prof.	assistant professor
Assoc. Prof.	associate professor
Brig. Gen.	brigadier general
Capt.	captain
CO	commanding officer
Col.	colonel
Comdr.	commander, commodore
cpl.	corporal
CPO	chief petty officer
CWO	chief warrant officer
Dr.	doctor
Ens.	ensign
Esq.	esquire
Flt. Adm.	fleet admiral
Gen.	general
Gov.	governor
Hon.	honorable
Insp. Gen.	inspector general
J.P.	justice of the peace
Jr.	junior
Judge Adv. Gen.	judge advocate general
Lt.	lieutenant
M.	monsieur
Maj.	major
Messrs.	messieurs, gentlemen
Mlle.	mademoiselle
Mme.	madame

M.P.	Member of Parliament
Mr.	mister
Mrs.	mistress
Ms.	blend of *Miss* and *Mrs.*
Msgr.	monsignor
Pfc.	private first class
PO	petty officer
Pres.	president
Prof.	professor
Pvt.	private
Rep.	representative
Rev.	reverend
Sen.	senator
Sfc.	sergeant first class
Sgt.	sergeant
Sr.	senior
WO	warrant officer

UNITS OF MEASUREMENT

Note that square (area) or cubic (volume) measurements are most often abbreviated with exponents—for example in^2, square inches; or m^3, cubic meters.

A	ampere	emf	electromotive force
Å	angstrom	eV	electron volt
a	acre	F	farad
AU	astronomical unit	°F	degree Fahrenheit
bbl	barrel	ft	foot
Btu	British thermal unit	g	gram
bu	bushel	gal	gallon
C	Coulomb	gr	grain
°C	degree Celsius	GRT	gross registered tonnage
cal	calorie	H	henry
cd	candela	ha	hectare
cg	centigram	hl	hectoliter
cl	centiliter	hp	horsepower
cm	centimeter	hr	hour
dB	decibel	Hz	hertz
dl	deciliter	in	inch
dm	decimeter	j	joule
dr	dram	K	kelvin
DWT	deadweight tonnage	kcal	kilocalorie

kg	kilogram	MW	megawatt
kHz	kilohertz	N	newton
kl	kiloliter	naut mi	international nautical
km	kilometer		mile
km/h	kilometers per hour	oz	ounce
kW	kilowatt	π	pi
kWh	kilowatt hour	pH	measure of acidity or
l	liter		basicity
lb	pound	pk	peck
m	meter	psi	pounds per square inch
mg	milligram	pt	pint
MHz	megahertz	qt	quart
mi	mile	rd	rod
min	minute	rpm	revolutions per minute
ml	milliliter	sec	second
mm	millimeter	tn	ton
μm	micrometer	V	volt
mo	month	W	watt
mol	mole	yd	yard
mph	miles per hour	yr	year

MEDICINE, SCIENCE

AC	alternating current
ACTH	adrenocorticotropic hormone
AI	artificial intelligence, artificial insemination
AIDS	acquired immune deficiency syndrome
AM	amplitude modulation
BP	boiling point, blood pressure
CGS	centimeter-gram-second
CPR	cardiopulmonary resuscitation
CT scan	computerized axial tomography
CVA	cerebrovascular accident (stroke)
D & C	dilation and curettage
DDT	dichlorodiphenyltrichloroethane
DNA	deoxyribonucleic acid
EEG	electroencephalogram
EKG, ECG	electrocardiogram
EMG	electromyography
FAS	fetal alcohol syndrome
FM	frequency modulation
FSH	follicle-stimulating hormone
GI series	gastrointestinal series

HDL	high-density lipoprotein
HGH	human growth hormone
HIV	human immunodeficiency virus
IUD	intrauterine device
IV	intravenous
IVF	in vitro fertilization
LDL	low-density lipoprotein
LSD	lysergic acid diethylamide
MCH	mean corpuscular hemoglobin
MCHC	mean corpuscular hemoglobin concentration
MCV	mean corpuscular volume
MKSA	meter-kilogram-second-ampere
MP	melting point
MRI	magnetic resonance imaging
MS	multiple sclerosis, mean square
MSG	monosodium glutamate
NMR	nuclear magnetic resonance
OB-GYN	obstetrics-gynecology
OD	overdose
PKU	phenylketonuria
PET	positron emission tomography
PMS	premenstrual syndrome
PTSD	post traumatic stress disorder
REM	rapid eye movement
RF	radio frequency
Rh factor	rhesus factor
RNA	ribonucleic acid
SD	standard deviation
SE	standard error
SI	International System of Units
SIDS	sudden infant death syndrome
sq	square
STD	sexually transmitted disease
STP	standard temperature and pressure
temp	temperature
TNT	trinitrotoluene
TSS	toxic shock syndrome
UA	urinalysis
UV	ultraviolet (light)
VD	venereal disease

ORGANIZATIONS

AA	Alcoholics Anonymous
AAA	Agricultural Adjustment Administration
	American Automobile Association
	Amateur Athletic Association
AAAL	American Academy of Arts and Letters
AAAS	American Academy of Arts and Sciences
	American Association for the Advancement of Science
AARP	American Association of Retired Persons
AAU	Amateur Athletic Union
AAUP	American Association of University Professors
ABA	American Bar Association
ABT	American Ballet Theatre
ACLU	American Civil Liberties Union
ACP	American College of Physicians
ACS	American Chemical Society
	American Cancer Society
	American College of Surgeons
ADA	American Dental Association
AEC	Atomic Energy Commission
AFC	American Football Conference
AFDC	Aid to Families with Dependent Children
AFL-CIO	American Federation of Labor-Congress of Industrial Organizations
AFM	American Federation of Musicians
AFSCME	American Federation of State, County, and Municipal Employees
AFT	American Federation of Teachers
AFTRA	American Federation of Television and Radio Artists
AHA	American Heart Association
	American Historical Association
	American Hospital Association
AIA	American Institute of Architects
AIAA	American Institute of Aeronautics and Astronautics
AIBS	American Institute of Biological Sciences
AIC	American Institute of Physics
AKC	American Kennel Club
AL	American League (baseball)
ALA	American Library Association

AMA	American Medical Association
ANA	American Nurses Association
ANPA	American Newspaper Publishers Association
ANZAC	Australian and New Zealand Army Corps
AOH	Ancient Order of Hibernians
AP	Associated Press
APO	Army Post Office
APS	American Physical Society
	American Philosophical Society
ASCAP	American Society of Composers, Authors, and Publishers
ASPCA	American Society for the Prevention of Cruelty to Animals
BBB	Better Business Bureau
BBC	British Broadcasting Corporation
BPOE	Benevolent and Protective Order of Elks
BSA	Boy Scouts of America
CAB	Civil Aeronautics Board
CBC	Canadian Broadcasting Corporation
CBS	Columbia Broadcasting System
CENTO	Central Treaty Organization
CIA	Central Intelligence Agency
Comecon	Council for Mutual Economic Assistance
DAR	Daughters of the American Revolution
EC	European Community
EPA	Environmental Protection Agency
FAA	Federal Aviation Agency
FAO	Food and Agriculture Organization
FBI	Federal Bureau of Investigation
FCA	Farm Credit Administration
FCC	Federal Communications Commission
FDA	Food and Drug Administration
FDIC	Federal Deposit Insurance Corporation
FHA	Federal Housing Administration
FSA	Farm Security Administration
FTC	Federal Trade Commission
GATT	General Agreement on Tariffs and Trade
GOP	Grand Old Party (Republican Party)
GSA	Girl Scouts of America
HUD	Department of Housing and Urban Development
ICC	Interstate Commerce Commission
ILA	International Longshoremen's Association
ILGWU	International Ladies' Garment Workers' Union

ILO	International Labor Organization
IMF	International Monetary Fund
INTERPOL	International Criminal Police Organization
IOC	International Olympic Committee
IRA	Irish Republican Army
IRS	Internal Revenue Service
IWW	Industrial Workers of the World
KKK	Ku Klux Klan
L.C.	Library of Congress
LPGA	Ladies Professional Golf Association
MLA	Modern Language Association
NAACP	National Association for the Advancement of Colored People
NAM	National Association of Manufacturers
NARA	National Archives and Records Administration
NAS	National Academy of Sciences
NASA	National Aeronautics and Space Administration
NATO	North Atlantic Treaty Organization
NBA	National Basketball Association
NBC	National Broadcasting Company
NBS	National Bureau of Standards
NCAA	National Collegiate Athletic Association
NCAI	National Congress of American Indians
NCC	National Council of Churches
NCCJ	National Conference of Christians and Jews
NEA	National Education Association
	National Endowment for the Arts
NEH	National Endowment for the Humanities
NFC	National Football Conference
NFL	National Football League
NFO	National Farmers Organization
NFU	National Farmers Union
NHL	National Hockey League
NIH	National Institutes of Health
NL	National League (baseball)
NLRB	National Labor Relations Board
NOAA	National Oceanic and Atmospheric Administration
NORAD	North American Air Defense Command
NOW	National Organization for Women
NRA	National Rifle Association of America
NSC	National Security Council
NSF	National Science Foundation
NYSE	New York Stock Exchange

OPEC	Organization of Petroleum Exporting Countries
OSHA	Office of Safety and Health Administration
OSS	Office of Strategic Services
PAL	Police Athletic League
PBA	Policeman's Benevolent Association
PEN	International Association of Poets, Playwrights, Editors, Essayists, and Novelists
PGA	Professional Golfers Association
PHS	Public Health Service
PLO	Palestine Liberation Organization
PTA	Parent Teacher Association
PWA	Public Works Administration
RCMP	Royal Canadian Mounted Police
ROTC	Reserve Officers Training Corps
SAC	Strategic Air Command
SAR	Sons of the American Revolution
SEC	Securities and Exchange Commission
SSA	Social Security Administration
SSI	Supplemental Security Income
SSS	Selective Service System
TVA	Tennessee Valley Authority
UAR	United Arab Republic
UAW	United Automobile Workers
UMW	United Mine Workers
UN	United Nations
UNESCO	United Nations Educational, Scientific, and Cultural Organization
UNHCR	United Nations High Commissioner for Refugees
UNICEF	United Nations Children's Fund
USAF	United States Air Force
USDA	United States Department of Agriculture
USMC	United States Marine Corps
USN	United States Navy
VA	Veterans' Administration
VFW	Veterans of Foreign Wars
VISTA	Volunteers in Service to America
WCC	World Council of Churches
WCTU	Women's Christian Temperance Union
WHO	World Health Organization
YMCA	Young Men's Christian Association
YMHA	Young Men's Hebrew Association
YWCA	Young Women's Christian Association
YWHA	Young Women's Hebrew Association

BOOKS OF THE BIBLE

Old Testament		**New Testament**	
Gen.	Genesis	Matt.	Matthew
Exod.	Exodus	Mark	Mark
Lev.	Leviticus	Luke	Luke
Num.	Numbers	John	John
Deut.	Deuteronomy	Acts	Acts of the Apostles
Josh.	Joshua	Rom.	Romans
Jud.	Judges	1 Cor.	1 Corinthians
Ruth	Ruth	2 Cor.	2 Corinthians
1 Sam.	1 Samuel	Gal.	Galatians
2 Sam.	2 Samuel	Eph.	Ephesians
1 Ki.	1 Kings	Phil.	Philippians
2 Ki.	2 Kings	Col.	Colossians
1 Chron.	1 Chronicles	1 Thes.	1 Thessalonians
2 Chron.	2 Chronicles	2 Thes.	2 Thessalonians
Ez.	Ezra	1 Tim.	1 Timothy
Neh.	Nehemiah	2 Tim.	2 Timothy
Esth.	Esther	Tit.	Titus
Job	Job	Phil.	Philemon
Ps.	Psalms	Heb.	Hebrews
Prov.	Proverbs	Jas.	James
Eccles.	Ecclesiastes	1 Pet.	1 Peter
Sol.	Song of Solomon	2 Pet.	2 Peter
Isa.	Isaiah	1 John	1 John
Jer.	Jeremiah	2 John	2 John
Lam.	Lamentations	3 John	3 John
Ezek.	Ezekiel	Jude	Jude
Dan.	Daniel	Rev.	Revelation
Hos.	Hosea		
Joel	Joel		
Amos	Amos		
Obad.	Obadiah		
Jon.	Jonah		
Mic.	Micah		
Nah.	Nahum		
Hab.	Habakkuk		
Zeph.	Zephaniah		
Hag.	Haggai		
Zech.	Zechariah		
Mal.	Malachi		

Commonly Misspelled Words

Despite the increasing popularity of spelling check programs for those who use personal computers, reponsibility for correct spelling still rests with the writer. Thus, it behooves all of us who wish to write well to become as proficient in spelling as possible.

The following list of about 1500 commonly misspelled words is provided so that you can identify your own problem words. Once you have found your problem words, practice is the only technique that will make you a proficient speller.

A

absence
absent
absolutely
abundant
abutting
academic
academically
academy
accept
acceptability
acceptable
acceptance
accepting

accommodate
accommodating
accompanied
accompaniment
accompany
accomplish
accuracy
accurate
accuser
accustom
achievement
acknowledge
acknowledgment
acquaint
acquaintance

acquire
acquisition
acre
across
activity
actual
actuality
actually
additional
additionally
address
adequately
adjournment
adjustment
administer

administration
administrative
admission
admittance
adolescence
adolescent
advantage
advantageous
advertisement
advertising
advice
advise
aeroplane
affect
affectionately

affirmative
afraid
against
aggravate
aggregate
aggressive
agitation
airplane
aisle
allay
alleviate
alley
alleys
allies
all right
all together
allude
allusion
ally
already
altar
alter
altogether
amateur
ambulance
ambulatory
amendment
among
amount
analysis
analyze
ancient
announce
announcement
announcing
annually
another
anticipate
antique
anxious
apologetically
apologies

apologize
apology
apostrophe
apparatus
apparently
appeal
appearance
appetite
applies
apply
appointment
appreciate
approaches
appropriate
architecture
arctic
areas
argue
argument
arise
arising
arouse
arousing
arrangement
arrival
arrive
article
artistic
artistically
artistry
ascend
ascendant
ascent
assassin
assent
assistance
assistants
assured
atheist
athlete
athletic
attack

attempt
attendance
attendants
attorney
audience
author
authoritative
authority
authorize
auxiliary
availability
available
avalanche
average
aviator
awfully

B

bachelor
baggage
banana
bankruptcy
banquet
bar
barbarous
bare
bargain
baring
barrel
basement
basic
basically
basis
beautifully
beautify
becoming
before
began
beggar
begin
beginning
behavior

belief
believe
believing
beneficence
beneficent
beneficial
benefit
benefited
berth
bicycle
bidding
bigger
birth
biscuit
boring
born
borne
boundary
breadth
breakfast
breath
breathe
bridal
bridle
brief
brilliant
Britain
Briton
bruise
budget
buoy
buoyant
bureau
burglar
burglaries
burglarize
business
busy

C

cabbage
Caesar

cafeteria	characterize	committing	conscientious
calendar	charity	communal	conscious
campaign	chauffeur	communist	consequence
candidacy	chief	community	consequently
candidate	chieftain	companies	considerable
canvas	children	comparative	consist
canvass	chimney	compare	consistency
capability	choice	comparison	consistent
capable	cholera	compatible	conspicuous
capital	choose	compel	contemporary
capitalism	choosing	compelled	contempt
capitol	chose	compete	contemptible
captain	Christian	competitive	contemptuous
career	cigarette	competitor	continual
carefully	Cincinnati	complement	continuous
carelessness	circle	complete	contribution
carried	circular	complexion	control
carry	cite	compliment	controlling
carrying	civil	compulsion	controversial
castle	client	concede	controversy
catastrophe	climate	conceivable	convenience
category	clothes	conceive	cool
caucus	cloths	concentrate	coolie
cavalry	coarse	conception	coolly
ceases	coherence	condemn	cooly
ceiling	collar	condemnation	cooperate
cellar	colonel	condescend	corollary
cemetery	color	confer	coronary
censer	column	conference	corps
censor	comfortable	conferred	corpse
censure	comfortably	conferring	correlate
censurious	coming	confidence	counterfeit
century	comma	confident	country
certainly	commence	confidential	county
challenge	commencement	confidently	course
chancel	commerce	congressional	courteous
chancellor	commercial	Connecticut	courtesy
change	commission	connotation	cousin
changeable	commit	connote	crazy
changing	commitment	conquer	create
chapel	committed	conqueror	credible
characteristic	committee	conscience	credulous

criminal
crisis
criticism
criticize
cruel
cruelly
cruelty
cubic
cupola
curiosity
curious
currant
current
curriculum
curtain
curtsy
custard
customary
cylinder
cylindrical
cynosure

D

dairy
damage
dangerous
deal
dealer
dealt
debauch
debouch
debris
debt
deceit
deceive
decent
decentralize
deception
decide
decision
default
defendant

defense
defer
deference
deferral
deferred
define
definitely
definition
deity
delegate
deliberately
deliver
dependant
dependent
depth
deputy
descend
descendant
descent
describe
description
desert
desirability
desirable
desire
desirous
despair
despatch
desperation
despicable
despite
dessert
destruction
detriment
devaluate
devastate
develop
developed
development
device
devise
diary

die
different
difficult
dilemma
diligent
dining
dinning
dirigible
disagreeable
disappear
disappearance
disappoint
disapprove
disaster
disastrous
disciple
disciplinary
discipline
discriminate
discriminatory
disease
disgust
disillusion
dispatch
disposal
dissatisfied
dissent
dissimilar
dissipate
divinity
division
doesn't
dominant
dominate
dormitory
dough
dropped
due
dully
duly
duped
during

dye
dyeing
dying

E

eager
earnest
easily
economical
economically
economics
ecstasy
edge
edgy
editor
editorial
effect
efficiency
efficient
egress
eight
eighth
eighty
electoral
electrical
elicit
eligible
eliminate
elude
emanate
embarrass
embassies
embassy
emigrant
eminent
emperor
emphasis
emphasize
emphatic
empirical
employee
encouragement

endeavor
enjoyment
enlightenment
enough
enterprise
entertain
entirely
entrance
envelop
envelope
environment
equal
equality
equally
equip
equipment
equipped
escapade
especially
everything
evidently
exactly
exactness
exaggerate
exaggeration
excavation
exceed
excellence
excellent
except
exceptionally
excessive
excitable
excitement
exclusively
excursion
executive
exercise
exhaust
exhaustive
exhibit
exhibition

existence
existent
exorcise
exorcism
expedite
expedition
expense
experience
experiment
explanation
extraordinarily
extraordinary
extravagant
extremely

F

facility
fallacious
fallacy
familiar
familiarity
fantasy
fascinate
fashion
favorable
favorite
February
federal
federated
feminine
fictitious
filial
Filipino
finally
financial
financier
finial
folios
forehead
foreign
forewarn
foreword

forgive
formally
formerly
forth
fortunate
forty
forward
fourth
franchise
fraternally
fraternity
frequently
friendliness
friendship
frontage
fulfill
fulfillment
fundamental
further

G

gaiety
gallant
garage
gasoline
general
generally
generate
generation
genius
gilt
goddess
government
governor
gradually
grammar
grammatically
grieve
grievous
grocery
group
guarantee

guardian
guidance
guilt
gymnasium

H

handkerchief
handled
handsome
happened
happiness
headache
health
hear
heard
heavily
height
herald
herd
here
heroes
heroic
heroin
heroine
hinder
hindrance
holly
holy
honorable
hop
hope
hopeful
hopeless
hoping
hopping
horizon
hose
hosiery
hospital
hospitalization
humor
humorist

humorous	inevitable	island	lengthen
hundred	inevitably	isle	level
hundredth	infinite	its	leveled
hunger	infinitesimal	it's	liberally
hungrily	influence		library
hypnotism	influential	**J**	license
hypnotize	ingenious		lighten
hypocrisy	ingenuity	janitor	lightened
hypocrite	ingenuous	janitorial	lightening
	ingredient	jealously	lightning
I	inhabitant	jealousy	likelihood
	initiative	jewelry	likely
icicle	injunction	journey	lily
idea	innocence	judge	limb
ideally	innocent	judgment	linen
ideate	inquire	justifiable	listening
ignorance	inquiry	justification	literary
illegal	insistent	justify	literature
illicit	installment		livelier
illusion	instance	**K**	liveliest
illusory	insurance		livelihood
illustrate	intellect	kindergarten	liveliness
image	intellectual	knight	lively
imaginary	intelligence	knowledge	loath
imagine	intelligent	kowtow	loathe
immediately	intentionally		location
immense	interest	**L**	loneliness
immigrant	interference		lonely
immigrate	interior	laboratory	loose
importance	interlocutor	laborer	lose
incidentally	interpretation	laborious	losing
increasing	interruption	laid	loss
incredible	intimate	language	lovable
indebted	introducing	larynx	luncheon
indefinite	inveigle	later	lynch
independence	investigation	latter	
independent	involve	launch	**M**
indicate	ironic	lawyer	
indispensable	irony	leather	machination
individually	irrelevant	led	machinery
industrial	irresistible	legacy	magazine
industries	irritable	legend	magnificence
industry		legible	magnificent
		legitimate	
		leisure	

maintain
maintenance
manage
management
maneuver
manufacture
marine
marriage
marriageable
Massachusetts
mater
material
mathematics
matter
may be
maybe
meanness
meant
mean time
meantime
mechanical
medal
medallion
medical
medicinal
medicine
medieval
melancholy
memorable
mere
metal
metallic
metallurgy
methodical
military
militia
miner
miniature
minimum
mining
minor
minority

minute
misappropriate
mischief
mischievous
misdemeanor
missionary
Mississippi
misspell
monoplane
moral
morale
morally
mortgage
mosquitoes
movable
muscle
muscular
museum
mutilate
mysterious
mystery

N

narrative
nationality
native
naturally
necessarily
necessary
negative
nevertheless
nickel
niece
ninetieth
ninety
notice
noticeably
notoriety
notorious
novel
nuclear
nucleus

O

obligatory
oblige
obliged
obliging
obstacle
obtainable
occasion
occasionally
occur
occurred
occurrence
occurring
officer
official
officially
omission
omit
omitted
operate
opinion
opportunity
oppose
opposite
optimism
optimist
orchard
ordinarily
ordinary
organism
organization
organize
original
originally
outrage
outrageously
owing

P

package
pageant

paid
pamphlet
pamphleteer
papal
parachute
paradigm
paradox
paradoxical
paradoxically
paragraph
parallel
parallelogram
paralysis
paralytic
paralyze
parentheses
parenthesis
parliament
parliamentarian
parliamentary
partial
partially
particle
particular
particularity
particularly
particulate
passage
passed
past
patient
patriot
patriotic
patriotically
peaceable
peaceful
peasant
peculiar
peculiarity
peculiarly
Pennsylvania
perceive

percentage
perception
performance
permanence
permanent
permissible
permission
permitted
persistence
persistent
personal
personality
personally
personnel
perspiration
persuade
persuasion
Philippines
philosopher
philosophical
philosophy
physical
physically
physician
physiological
physiology
pianos
picnic
picnicker
picnicking
piece
pillar
pillow
planed
planned
plausible
playwright
pleasant
pledge
poem
poetic
poetry

polar
polarity
polish
Polish
political
politician
politics
pollen
pollinate
portion
possess
possession
possessive
possibility
possible
possibly
potatoes
poultry
practicable
practical
practicality
practice
prairie
prayer
precede
precedence
precedent
precedents
preciosity
precious
predominant
prefer
preference
preferential
preferred
preferring
prejudice
prejudicial
premium
preparation
preparatory
prepare

presence
presidency
president
pressure
prestige
prevalence
prevalent
priest
primitive
principal
principle
prisoner
privilege
probability
probable
probably
procedural
procedure
proceed
professional
professor
prohibitive
prohibitory
promenade
prominent
pronounce
pronouncement
pronunciation
prophecy
prophesy
proprietary
proprietor
psychoanalysis
psychoanalytic
psychology
psychopath
psychosomatic
punctuation
punish
pupil
purchase
purchased

pursue
pursuing

Q

qualification
qualified
qualify
qualitative
quality
quiescence
quiet
quite

R

rabid
rabies
racing
racy
radical
reality
realization
realize
really
reasonable
reasonably
rebellious
recede
receipt
receive
receiving
recession
recognition
recognize
recollect
recommend
recommendation
recruit
reduction
refer
reference
referred
referring

regularly
reign
rein
relative
reliability
reliable
relief
relieve
religion
religious
remember
remembrance
reminisce
repeat
repetition
representation
representative
require
requisition
residence
resistance
resource
resourceful
respectful
respectfully
response
responsive
restaurant
restaurateur
reunion
reunite
reveal
reveille
revelation
rewrite
rewritten
rhetoric
rhetorical
rheumatism
rhyme
rhythm

ridicule
ridiculous
roommate
routine

S

sacrifice
sacrificial
sacrilege
sacrilegious
safety
salary
sanitary
satire
satisfaction
satisfactory
satisfy
saving
scarcely
scenery
scenic
schedule
schism
scholar
science
scientific
scissors
scrutinize
seamstress
seance
secede
secretary
sectional
security
seize
semicolon
senator
sense
sentence
sententious
separate

separation
sergeant
series
several
sew
shepherd
shining
shoulder
siege
sieve
significance
significant
similar
similarity
simile
simplicity
simultaneous
sincerely
skillful
skillfully
socialism
socialistic
society
sociology
solemn
soliloquy
sophomore
source
sow
specimen
spiritual
sponsor
stability
stabilize
stable
standard
stationary
stationery
statistical
statistics
statuary

statue
stature
statute
stenographer
stepped
stories
straight
stratagem
strategy
strength
strenuous
stricture
structure
studying
subjunctive
substance
substantial
subtle
subtlety
succeed
succession
successor
suddenness
suffice
sufficient
suicidal
suicide
summarily
summons
superintendent
suppose
suppress
surgeon
surprise
surprising
surround
susceptible
suspicious
syllable
symbol
sympathize

sympathy
synonym
synonymous

T

tableau
tailor
tariff
taxation
technical
technique
telephone
telephonic
temperament
temperature
temporary
tempt
tendency
than
theater
their
then
theory
there
therefore
they're
thorough
thought
through
to
tomorrow
too

topic
topically
toured
tournament
traffic
trafficked
trafficking
tragedy
tragic
transfer
transference
transferral
transferred
transitive
traveler
tried
tries
troop
trough
troupe
truly
Tuesday
turkey
turnkey
twelfth
twelve
two
typical
typically
tyrannical
tyranny
tyrant

U

unanimity
unanimous
unconscious
undoubted
undoubtedly
unmanageable
unnecessary
unprecedented
unprecedentedly
until
unusual
unusually
urgent
useful
usefully
usual
usually

V

vacuous
vacuum
valley
valleys
valuable
variety
various
varying
vegetable
vegetation
vegetative
vengeance

vengeful
vicinity
village
villain
villainous

W

warrant
weather
Wednesday
weird
welcome
whether
whiskey
whisky
wholly
wired
woman
women
woolen
woolly
worse
worst
wound
write
written

Y

yacht
yield
your
you're

– 3 –

Time Change

Many modern businesses operate worldwide. Government and military personnel, too, often must communicate with others in many foreign countries. As a result there is often a need to know the time of day in other time zones. The listings on the pages that follow will enable you to quickly determine the time in other locations.

In the listing, if all of a country is in one time zone, only the name of the country is given. Where a country's boundaries extend over more than one zone, the principal cities of the country are given along with their time zones.

The *Eastern Standard Time Zone* in the United States is used as a base. If you are in that zone, you need only add or subtract the number of hours indicated after the name of the country or city whose time you are determining.

For example, if you are in New York or New Jersey or any other Eastern Standard Time Zone area, and wish to know the time in Rome, Italy, look up *Italy*. You will find it has only one time zone, indicated as +6, which means that the time in Italy is six hours later than Eastern Standard Time. So all you need do to determine the time in Italy is add 6 hours to your time. In other words, if it is 12 noon where you are, it is 6 p.m. in Rome.

If you are not in the Eastern Standard Time Zone, follow these steps:

1. In the list, find the name of the country or city *where you are* or are near.

2. Reverse the sign given *for your location*. For example, change a +3 to a -3. Then add or subtract that number from the actual time where you are.

3. Find the name of the country whose time you wish to know and add or subtract the figure you arrived at in step 2 above.

For example, consider that you are in San Francisco and the time is 2 p.m. You wish to know the time in Hong Kong:

1. Locate San Franciso on the list. You find that San Francisco is given as -3.

2. Change the -3 to +3 and add that amount to your actual time: your time, 2 p.m., plus 3 = 5 p.m.

3. Look up Hong Kong on the list. It shows +13. Add that amount to the time from step 2 above: 5 p.m. +13 hours = 6 a.m. (You arrive at this time by counting: 7 hours to midnight plus 6 more to 6 a.m.) Thus, when the time is 2 p.m. in San Francisco, it is 6 a.m. in Hong Kong.

Note: If Daylight Savings Time is in effect in your time zone, *subtract* one hour from the result you found by following the steps above. In the example above, you would subtract one hour from 6 a.m., making it 5 a.m.

Afghanistan +9½
Algeria +6
Angola +6
Argentina +2
Armenia +9
Australia
  Adelaide +14½
  Melbourne +15
  Perth +13
  Sydney +15
Austria +6
Azerbaijan +9

Bangladesh +11
Barbados +1
Belarus +8
Belgium +6
Bolivia +1
Botswana +7
Brazil
  Brasilia +2
  Campo Grande +1
  Rio de Janeiro +2
  Sao Paulo +2
Bulgaria +7

Burma +11½
Burundi +7
Cambodia +12
Cameroon +6
Canada
  Ottawa 0
  Vancouver -3
  Winnipeg -1
Central African
  Republic +6
Chad +6
Chile +1

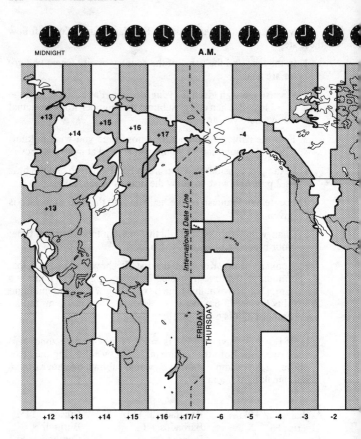

Note: Standard Time in some countries is offset by a half hour from the appropriate time zone. Always check the accompanying list for the exact time change for a country.

China +13	Cuba 0	Dominican Republic 0
Columbia 0	Cyprus +7	Ecuador 0
Congo +6	Czech Republic +6	Egypt +7
Costa Rica -1	Denmark +6	El Salvador -1

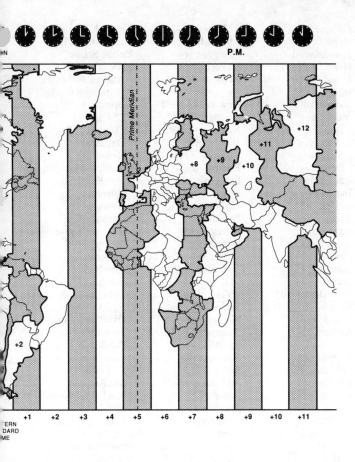

Equatorial Guinea +6	Gabon +6	Greece +7
Ethiopia +8	Gambia +5	Greenland +2
Finland +7	Germany +6	Guatemala -1
France +6	Ghana +5	Guinea +5

Guyana +2
Haiti 0
Honduras -1
Hong Kong +13
Hungary +6
Iceland +5
India +10½
Indonesia
  Djakarta +12
  Irian Jaya +14
  Semarang +13
  Surabaya +12
Iran +8½
Iraq +8
Ireland +5
Israel +7
Italy +6
Ivory Coast +5
Jamaica 0
Japan +14
Jordan +7
Kazakhstan +11
Kenya +8
Korea +14
Kuwait +8
Laos +12
Latvia +8
Lebanon +7
Lesotho +7
Liberia +5
Libya +7
Luxembourg +6
Madagascar +8
Malawi +7
Malaysia +13
Maldives +10
Mali +5
Malta +6
Mauritania +5
Mauritius +9
Mexico
  Guadalajara -1
  Mexico City -1

Monterrey -1
Mazatlán -2
Mongolia +13
Morocco +5
Nepal +10½
Netherlands +6
New Zealand +17
Nicaragua -1
Niger +6
Nigeria +6
Pakistan +10
Panama 0
Paraguay +2
Peru 0
Philippines +13
Poland +6
Portugal +5
Rumania +7
Russia
  Moscow +8
  Omsk +12
  Vladivostok +15
Samoa -6
Senegal +5
Singapore +13
Somalia +8
South Africa +7
Spain +6
Sri Lanka +10½
Sudan +7
Sweden +6
Switzerland +6
Syria +8
Taiwan +13
Tanzania +8
Thailand +12
Togo +5
Trinidad and
  Tobago +1
Tunisia +6
Turkey +7
Uganda +8
Ukraine +8

United Kingdom +5
Uzbekistan +11
United States
  Anchorage -5
  Atlanta 0
  Baltimore 0
  Boston 0
  Chicago -1
  Columbus 0
  Dallas -1
  Denver -2
  Detroit 0
  Fort Worth -1
  Honolulu -5
  Houston -1
  Indianapolis -1
  Kansas City -1
  Memphis -1
  Minneapolis -1
  New York 0
  Los Angeles -3
  Milwaukee -1
  New Orleans -1
  Oklahoma City -1
  Phoenix -2
  Pittsburgh 0
  Philadelphia 0
  St. Louis -1
  San Antonio -1
  San Francisco -3
  Seattle -3
  Washington, D.C. 0
Uruguay +2
Venezuela +1
Vietnam +13
Yemen +8
Yugoslavia +6
Zaire
  Kinshasa +6
  Lumbumbashi +7
Zambia +7

4

Long Distance Telephone Area Codes

Alabama   205
Alaska   907
Arizona   602
Arkansas   501
Bahamas   809
Bermuda   809
California
  Alameda   415
  Anaheim   714
  Bakersfield   805
  Berkeley   415
  Beverly Hills   213
  Burbank   818
  Eureka   707
  Fresno   209
  Hollywood   213
  Huntington Beach   714
  Huntington Park   213
  Livermore   415
  Lodi   209
  Long Beach   213
  Los Altos   415
  Los Angeles   213
  Monterey   408
  Monterey Park   818

Napa   707
Oakland   415
Palm Springs   619
Palo Alto   415
Pasadena   818
Sacramento   916
Salinas   408
San Diego   619
San Francisco   415
San Jose   408
San Rafael   415
Santa Ana   714
Santa Barbara   805
Santa Clara   408
Santa Cruz   408
Santa Monica   213
Stockton   209
Torrance   213

Canada
Alberta   403
British Columbia   604
Manitoba   204
New Brunswick   506
Newfoundland   709

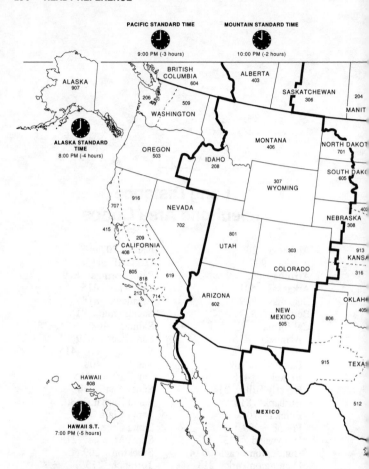

PACIFIC STANDARD TIME
9:00 PM (-3 hours)

MOUNTAIN STANDARD TIME
10:00 PM (-2 hours)

ALASKA
907

ALASKA STANDARD
TIME
8:00 PM (-4 hours)

BRITISH
COLUMBIA
604

206
509
WASHINGTON

OREGON
503

IDAHO
208

ALBERTA
403

SASKATCHEWAN
306

204
MANIT

MONTANA
406

NORTH DAKOT
701

307
WYOMING

SOUTH DAK(
605

916
707

NEVADA
702

415
209
CALIFORNIA
408

805
818
619

213 714

801
UTAH

303
COLORADO

402
NEBRASKA
308

913
KANSA

316

ARIZONA
602

NEW
MEXICO
505

806

OKLAH(
405

915

TEXA

HAWAII
808

HAWAII S.T.
7:00 PM (-5 hours)

MEXICO

512

Nova Scotia 902	Thunder Bay 807
Ontario	Toronto 416
Fort William 807	Prince Edward Isl. 902
London 519	Quebec
North Bay 705	Montreal 514
Ottawa 613	Quebec 418

CENTRAL STANDARD TIME   EASTERN STANDARD TIME   ATLANTIC STANDARD TIME

11:00 PM (-1 hour)   12:00 AM (0 hour)   1:00 AM (+1 hour)

Sherbrooke 819	Grand Junction 303
Saskatchewan 306	Pueblo 719
	Connecticut 203
Colorado	Delaware 302
Colorado Springs 719	Dist. of Columbia
Denver 303	Washington, D.C. 202

Florida
Boca Raton 407
Daytona Beach 904
Fort Lauderdale 305
Gainesville 904
Jacksonville 904
Key West 305
Miami 305
Orlando 407
Palm Beach 407
Panama City 904
Pensacola 904
Tallahassee 904
Tampa 813
Georgia
Albany 912
Athens 404
Atlanta 404
Augusta 404
Columbus 404
Macon 912
Marietta 404
Savannah 912
Hawaii 808
Idaho 208
Illinois
Bloomington 309
Champaign-Urbana 217
Chicago 312
Chicago Hgts. 708
Cicero 708
Decatur 217
Evanston 708
Peoria 309
Skokie 708
Springfield 217
Waukegan 708
Indiana
Bloomington 812
East Chicago 219
Evansville 812
Fort Wayne 219

Gary 219
Indianapolis 317
Kokomo 317
Marion 317
Muncie 317
Terre Haute 812
Iowa
Cedar Rapids 319
Council Bluffs 712
Des Moines 515
Dubuque 319
Iowa City 319
Sioux City 712
Kansas
Kansas City 913
Lawrence 913
Topeka 913
Wichita 316
Kentucky
Fort Knox 502
Frankfort 502
Lexington 606
Louisville 502
Paducah 502
Louisiana
Baton Rouge 504
Lafayette 318
Lake Charles 318
New Orleans 504
Shreveport 318
Maine 207
Maryland
Annapolis 410
Baltimore 410
Ocean City 410
Rockville 301
Massachusetts
Amherst 413
Boston 617
Gloucester 508
Holyoke 413
Lexington 617

Lowell   508
Nantucket   508
Northampton   413
Pittsfield   413
Springfield   413
Worcester   508
Michigan
  Ann Arbor   313
  Battle Creek   616
  Dearborn   313
  Detroit   313
  Flint   313
  Grand Rapids   616
  Kalamazoo   616
  Lansing   517
  Pontiac   313
  Ypsilanti   313
Minnesota
  Duluth   218
  Minneapolis   612
  Rochester   507
  St. Paul   612
Mississippi   601
Missouri
  Independence   816
  Jefferson City   314
  Joplin   417
  Kansas City   816
  St. Louis   314
  Springfield   417
Montana   406
Nebraska
  Lincoln   402
  North Platte   308
  Omaha   402
Nevada   702
New Hampshire   603
New Jersey
  Atlantic City   609
  Elizabeth   201
  Hackensack   201
  Hoboken   201

Jersey City   201
Newark   201
Orange   201
Paramus   201
Princeton   609
Trenton   609
New Mexico   505
New York
  Albany   518
  Amagansett   516
  Amsterdam   518
  Batavia   716
  Binghamton   607
  Bronx   212
  Brooklyn   718
  Buffalo   716
  Ithaca   607
  Jamestown   716
  Long Island   516
  Manhattan   212
  Niagara Falls   716
  North Babylon   516
  Peekskill   914
  Potsdam   315
  Poughkeepsie   914
  Queens   718
  Saratoga Springs   518
  Staten Island   718
  Syracuse 315
  Utica   315
  White Plains   914
  Yonkers   914
North Carolina
  Asheville   704
  Chapel Hill   919
  Charlotte   704
  Durham   919
  Greensboro   919
  Greenville   919
  Raleigh   919
  Winston Salem   919
North Dakota   701

Ohio
  Akron 216
  Cincinnati 513
  Cleveland 216
  Columbus 614
  Dayton 513
  Toledo 419
  Youngstown 216
Oklahoma
  Enid 405
  Oklahoma City 405
  Tulsa 918
Oregon 503
Pennsylvania
  Allentown 215
  Erie 814
  Harrisburg 717
  Lancaster 717
  Philadelphia 215
  Pittsburgh 412
  Reading 215
  Scranton 717
  State College 814
Puerto Rico 809
Rhode Island 401
South Carolina 803
South Dakota 605
Tennessee
  Chattanooga 615
  Kingsport 615
  Knoxville 615
  Memphis 901
  Nashville 615
Texas
  Austin 512
  Brownsville 512
  Corpus Christi 512
  Dallas 214

El Paso 915
Forth Worth 817
Galveston 409
Houston 713
Port Arthur 409
San Antonio 512
Waco 817
Wichita Falls 817
Utah 801
Vermont 802
Virgin Islands 809
Virginia
  Alexandria 703
  Arlington 703
  Charlottesville 804
  Chesapeake 804
  Lynchburg 804
  Norfolk 804
  Richmond 804
  Roanoke 703
  Virginia Beach 804
Washington
  Bellevue 206
  Seattle 206
  Spokane 509
  Tacoma 206
  Walla Walla 509
West Virginia 304
Wisconsin
  Green Bay 414
  Madison 608
  Milwaukee 414
  Oshkosh 414
  Racine 414
  Sheboygan 414
  Superior 715
Wyoming 307

5

Three-Digit U. S. Mail ZIP Code List

006—009
Puerto Rico and Virgin Islands
006 San Juan
007 San Juan
008 San Juan
    (Virgin Islands)
009 San Juan
010—027
Massachusetts
010 Springfield
011 Springfield
012 Pittsfield
013 Springfield
014 Worcester
015 Worcester
016 Worcester
017 Worcester
018 Middlesex-Essex
019 Middlesex-Essex
020 Brockton
021 Boston
022 Boston
023 Brockton
024 Brockton
025 Buzzards Bay

026 Buzzards Bay
027 Providence, RI
    (MA Offices)
028—029
Rhode Island
028 Providence
029 Providence
030—038
New Hampshire
030 Manchester
031 Manchester
032 Manchester
033 Concord
034 Manchester
035 White River
    Junction
036 Brattleboro, VT
    (NH Offices)
037 White River
    Junction, VT
    (NH Offices)
038 Portsmouth
039—049
Maine
039 Portsmouth, NH
    (ME Offices)

040 Portland
041 Portland
042 Auburn
043 Augusta
044 Bangor
045 Portland
046 Bangor
047 Bangor
048 Portland
049 Waterville
050—059
Vermont
050 White River
    Junction
051 Brattleboro
052 Brattleboro
053 Brattleboro
054 Burlington
055 Middlesex-
    Essex, MA
056 White River
    Junction
057 White River
    Junction
058 White River
    Junction

059 White River
    Junction
    060—069
    Connecticut
060 Hartford
061 Hartford
062 Hartford
063 New Haven
064 New Haven
065 New Haven
066 Bridgeport
067 Waterbury
068 Stamford
069 Stamford
    070—089
    New Jersey
070 Newark
071 Newark
072 Elizabeth
073 Jersey City
074 Paterson
075 Paterson
076 Hackensack
077 Red Bank
078 Paterson
079 Summit
080 South Jersey
081 Camden
082 South Jersey
083 South Jersey
084 Atlantic City
085 Trenton
086 Trenton
087 Trenton
088 New Brunswick
089 New Brunswick
    004—149
    New York
004 Mount Vernon
090-098 Military
    (AE)
100 New York
101 New York

102 New York
103 Staten Island
104 Bronx
105 Westchester
106 White Plains
107 Yonkers
108 New Rochelle
109 Rockland
110 Queens
111 Long Island City
112 Brooklyn
113 Flushing
114 Jamaice
115 Western Nassau
116 Far Rockaway
117 Hicksville
118 Hicksville
119 Riverhead
120 Albany (A-J)
121 Albany (K-Z)
122 Albany
123 Schenectady
124 Poughkeepsie
125 Poughkeepsie
126 Poughkeepsie
127 Mid Hudson
128 Glens Falls
129 Plattsburgh
130 Syracuse (A-L)
131 Syracuse (M-Z)
132 Syracuse
133 Utica (A-L)
134 Utica (M-Z)
135 Utica
136 Watertown
137 Binghamton (A-L)
138 Binghamton (M-Z)
139 Binghamton
140 Buffalo (A-L)
141 Buffalo (M-Z)
142 Buffalo
143 Niagara Falls
144 Rochester (A-L)

145 Rochester (M-Z)
146 Rochester
147 Jamestown
148 Elmira
149 Elmira
    150—196
    Pennsylvania
150 Pittsburgh
151 Pittsburgh
152 Pittsburgh
153 Pittsburgh
154 Pittsburgh
155 Johnstown
156 Greensburg
157 Johnstown
158 Du Bois
159 Johnstown
160 New Castle
161 New Castle
162 New Castle
163 Oil City
164 Erie
165 Erie
166 Altoona
167 Bradford
168 Altoona
169 Williamsport
170 Harrisburg
171 Harrisburg
172 Harrisburg
173 Lancaster
174 York
175 Lancaster
176 Lancaster
177 Williamsport
178 Harrisburg
179 Pottsville
180 Lehigh Valley
181 Allentown
182 Wilkes-Barre
183 Lehigh Valley
184 Scranton
185 Scranton

186 Wilkes-Barre	224 Richmond	264 Clarksburg
187 Wilkes-Barre	225 Richmond	265 Clarksburg
188 Scranton	226 Winchester	266 Cassaway
189 Southeastern	227 Culpeper	267 Cumberland, MD
190 Philadelphia	228 Harrisonburg	(WV Offices)
191 Philadelphia	229 Charlottesville	268 Petersburg
192 Philadelphia	230 Richmond	**270—289**
193 Southeastern	231 Richmond	**North Carolina**
194 Southeastern	232 Richmond	270 Greensboro (West)
195 Reading	233 Norfolk	271 Winston-Salem
196 Reading	234 Norfolk	272 Greensboro (East)
213 Philadelphia	235 Norfolk	273 Greensboro (East)
197—199	236 Newport News	274 Greensboro
Delaware	237 Portsmouth	275 Raleigh
197 Wilmington	238 Richmond	276 Raleigh
198 Wilmington	239 Farmville	277 Durham
199 Wilmington	240 Roanoke	278 Rocky Mount
200—205	241 Roanoke	279 Rocky Mount
District of	242 Bristol	280 Charlotte
Columbia	243 Roanoke	281 Charlotte
200 Washington	244 Charlottesville	282 Charlotte
202-205 Government	245 Lynchburg	283 Fayetteville
206—219	246 Bluefield, WV	284 Fayetteville
Maryland	(VA Offices)	285 Kinston
206 Southern	**247—268**	286 Hickory
207 Southern	**West Virginia**	287 Asheville
208 Suburban	247 Bluefield	288 Asheville
209 Silver Spring	248 Bluefield	289 Asheville
210 Baltimore	249 Lewisburg	**290—299**
211 Baltimore	250 Charleston	**South Carolina**
212 Baltimore	251 Charleston	290 Columbia
214 Annapolis	252 Charleston	291 Columbia
215 Cumberland	253 Charleston	292 Columbia
216 Easton	254 Martinsburg	293 Greenville
217 Frederick	255 Huntington	294 Charleston
218 Salisbury	256 Huntington	295 Florence
219 Baltimore	257 Huntington	296 Greenville
220—246	258 Beckley	297 Charlotte, NC
Virginia	259 Beckley	(SC Offices)
220 Northern Virginia	260 Wheeling	298 Augusta, GA
221 Northern Virginia	261 Parkersburg	(SC Offices)
222 Arlington	262 Buckhannon	299 Savannah, GA
223 Alexandria	263 Clarksburg	(SC Offices)

300—319
Georgia
300 North Metro
301 North Metro
302 North Metro
303 Atlanta
304 Swansboro
305 North Metro
306 Athens
307 Chattanooga, TN
   (GA Offices)
308 Augusta
309 Augusta
310 Macon
311 Atlanta
312 Macon
313 Savannah
314 Savannah
315 Waycross
316 Valdosta
317 Albany
318 Columbus
319 Columbus
320—349
Florida
320 Jacksonville
321 Daytona Beach
322 Jacksonville
323 Tallahassee
324 Panama City
325 Pensacola
326 Gainsville
327 Mid-Florida
328 Orlando
329 Orlando
330 South Florida
331 Miami
332 Miami
333 Fort Lauderdale
334 West Palm Beach
335 Tampa
336 Tampa
337 Saint Petersburg

338 Lakeland
339 Fort Myers
340 Military (AA)
342 Manasota
346 Tampa
347 Orlando
349 West Palm Beach
350—369
Alabama
350 Birmingham
   (A-L)
351 Birmingham
   (M-Z)
352 Birmingham
354 Tuscaloosa
355 Birmingham
356 Huntsville
357 Huntsville
358 Huntsville
359 Gadsden
360 Montgomery
361 Montgomery
362 Anniston
363 Dothan
364 Evergreen
365 Mobile
366 Mobile
367 Montgomery
368 Montgomery
369 Meridan, MS
   (AL Offices)
370—385
Tennessee
370 Nashville (A-L)
371 Nashville (M-Z)
372 Nashville
373 Chattanooga
374 Chattanooga
376 Johnson City
377 Knoxville (A-L)
378 Knoxville (M-Z)
379 Knoxville
380 Memphis

381 Memphis
382 McKenzie
383 Jackson
384 Columbia
385 Cookeville
386—397
Mississippi
386 Memphis, TN
   (MS Offices)
387 Greenville
388 Tupelo
389 Grenada
390 Jackson (A-L)
391 Jackson (M-Z)
392 Jackson
393 Meridian
394 Hattiesburg
395 Gulfport
396 McComb
397 Columbus
400—427
Kentucky
400 Louisville (East)
401 Louisville (West)
402 Louisville
403 Lexington (North)
404 Lexington (South)
405 Lexington
406 Frankfort
407 London (West)
408 London (East)
409 London (Central)
410 Cincinnati, OH
   (KY Offices)
411 Ashland (North)
412 Ashland (South)
413 Campton (South)
414 Campton (North)
415 Pikesville (East)
416 Pikesville (West)
417 Hazard (West)
418 Hazard (East)
420 Paducah

421 Bowling Green (East)	453 Dayton	489 Lansing
422 Bowling Green (West)	454 Dayton	490 Kalamazoo
423 Owensboro	455 Springfield	491 Kalamazoo
424 Evansville, IN (KY Offices)	456 Chillicothe	492 Jackson
425 Somerset (North)	457 Athens	493 Grand Rapids (East)
426 Somerset (South)	458 Lima	494 Grand Rapids (West)
427 Elizabethtown	**460—479**	495 Grand Rapids

430—458
Ohio

460—479
Indiana

480—499
Michigan

500—528
Iowa

430 Columbus (North)	460 Indianapolis (North)	496 Traverse City
431 Columbus (South)	461 Indianapolis (South)	497 Gaylord
432 Columbus	462 Indianapolis	498 Iron Mountain (East)
433 Columbus	463 Gary	499 Iron Mountain (West)
434 Toledo (East)	464 Gary	500 Des Moines (A-F)
435 Toledo (West)	465 South Bend	501 Des Moines (G-M)
436 Toledo	466 South Bend	502 Des Moines (N-Z)
437 Zanesville (South)	467 Fort Wayne	503 Des Moines
438 Zanesville (North)	468 Fort Wayne	504 Mason City
439 Steubenville	469 Kokomo	505 Fort Dodge
440 Cleveland	470 Cincinnati, OH (IN Offices)	506 Waterloo
441 Cleveland	471 Louisville, KY (IN Offices)	507 Waterloo
442 Akron	472 Columbus	508 Creston
443 Akron	473 Muncie	509 Des Moines
444 Youngstown	474 Bloomington	510 Sioux City
445 Youngstown	475 Washington	511 Sioux City
446 Canton	476 Evansville	512 Sheldon
447 Canton	477 Evansville	513 Spencer
448 Mansfield	478 Terre Haute	514 Carroll
449 Mansfield	479 Lafayette	515 Omaha, NE (IA Offices)
450 Cincinnati (West)	480 Royal Oak	516 Omaha, NE (IA Offices)
451 Cincinnati (East)	481 Detroit	520 Dubuque
452 Cincinnati	482 Detroit	521 Decorah
	483 Royal Oak	522 Cedar Rapids (A-L)
	484 Flint	523 Cedar Rapids (M-Z)
	485 Flint	524 Cedar Rapids
	486 Saginaw (West)	
	487 Saginaw (East)	
	488 Lansing	

525 Ottumwa
526 Burlington
527 Rock Island, IL
    (IA Offices)
528 Davenport
    530—549
    Wisconsin
530 Milwaukee
    (North)
531 Milwaukee
    (South)
532 Milwaukee
534 Racine
535 Madison
537 Madison
538 Madison
539 Portage
540 Saint Paul, MN
    (WI Offices)
541 Green Bay
    (West)
542 Green Bay
    (East)
543 Green Bay
544 Wausau
545 Rhinelander
546 La Crosse
547 Eau Claire
548 Spooner
549 Oshkosh
    550—567
    Minnesota
550 Saint Paul
551 Saint Paul
553 Minneapolis
554 Minneapolis
555 Minneapolis
556 Duluth (East)
557 Duluth (West)
558 Duluth
559 Rochester
560 Mankota
561 Windom

562 Willmar
563 Saint Cloud
564 Brainerd
565 Detroit Lakes
566 Bemidji
567 Thief River Falls
    570—577
    South Dakota
570 Sioux Falls
571 Sioux Falls
572 Watertown
573 Mitchell
574 Aberdeen
575 Pierre
576 Mobridge
577 Rapid City
    580—588
    North Dakota
580 Fargo
581 Fargo
582 Grand Forks
583 Devils Lake
584 Jamestown
585 Bismarck
586 Dickinson
587 Minot
588 Williston
    590—599
    Montana
590 Billings
591 Billings
592 Wolf Point
593 Miles City
594 Great Falls
595 Havre
596 Helena
597 Butte
598 Missoula
599 Kalispell
    600—629
    Illinois
600 North Suburban
601 North Suburban

602 Evanston
603 Oak Park
604 South Suburban
605 South Suburban
606 Chicago
609 Kankakee
610 Rockford
611 Rockford
612 Rock Island
613 La Salle
614 Galesburg
615 Peoria
616 Peoria
617 Bloomington
618 Champaign
    (North)
619 Champaign
    (South)
620 St. Louis, MO
    (IL Offices)
622 St. Louis, MO
    (IL Offices)
623 Quincy
624 Effingham
625 Springfield
    (East)
626 Springfield
    (West)
627 Springfield
628 Centralia
629 Carbondale
    630—658
    Missouri
630 Saint Louis
631 Saint Louis
633 Saint Louis
634 Hannibal
635 Kirksville
636 Flat River
637 Cape Girardeau
638 Sikeston
639 Poplar Bluff
640 Kansas City

641 Kansas City	684 Lincoln (M-Z)	725 Batesville
644 Saint Joseph	685 Lincoln	726 Harrison
645 Saint Joseph	686 Columbus	727 Fayetteville
646 Chillicothe	687 Norfolk	728 Russelville
647 Harrisonville	688 Grand Island	729 Fort Smith
648 Joplin	689 Hastings	**730—749**
650 Mid-Missouri	690 McCook	**Oklahoma**
651 Jefferson City	691 North Platte	730 Oklahoma City
652 Mid-Missouri	692 Valentine	731 Oklahoma City
653 Mid-Missouri	693 Alliance	734 Ardmore
654 Springfield	**700—714**	735 Lawton
655 Springfield	**Louisiana**	736 Clinton
656 Springfield	700 New Orleans	737 Oklahoma City
(A-L)	701 New Orleans	738 Woodward
657 Springfield	703 Thibodaux	739 Liberal, KS
(M-Z)	704 Hammond	(OK Office)
658 Springfield	705 Lafayette	740 Tulsa
660—679	706 Lake Charles	741 Tulsa
Kansas	707 Baton Rouge	743 Tulsa
660 Kansas City	708 Baton Rouge	744 Muskogee
661 Kansas City	710 Shreveport	745 McAlester
662 Shawnee	711 Shreveport	746 Oklahoma City
Mission	712 Monroe	747 Durant
664 Topeka (A-L)	713 Alexandria	748 Oklahoma City
665 Topeka (M-Z)	(East)	749 Poteau
666 Topeka	714 Alexandria	**750—799**
667 Fort Scott	(West)	**Texas**
668 Topeka	**716—729**	750 North Texas
670 Wichita (A-L)	**Arkansas**	751 Dallas
671 Wichita (M-Z)	716 Pine Bluff	752 Dallas
672 Wichita	717 Camden	753 Dallas
673 Independence	718 Texarkana, TX	754 Greenville
674 Salina	(AR Offices)	755 Texarkana
675 Hutchinson	719 Hot Springs	756 Longview
676 Hays	National Park	757 Tyler
677 Colby	720 Little Rock	758 Palestine
678 Dodge City	(A-L)	759 Lufkin
679 Liberal	721 Little Rock	760 Fort Worth
680—693	(M-Z)	761 Fort Worth
Nebraska	722 Little Rock	762 Denton
680 Omaha	723 Memphis, TN	763 Wichita Falls
681 Omaha	(AR Offices)	764 Fort Worth
683 Lincoln (A-L)	724 Jonesboro	765 Waco

766 Waco	802 Denver	837 Boise
767 Waco	803 Boulder	838 Spokane, WA
768 Abilene	804 Denver	(ID Offices)
769 Midland	805 Longmont	**840—847**
770 Houston	806 Brighton	**Utah**
771 Houston	807 Brighton	840 Salt Lake City
772 Houston	808 Colorado	841 Salt Lake City
773 North Houston	Springs	842 Salt Lake City
774 North Houston	809 Colorado	843 Salt Lake City
775 North Houston	Springs	844 Ogden
776 Beaumont	810 Pueblo	845 Provo
777 Beaumont	811 Alamosa	846 Provo
778 Bryan	812 Salida	847 Provo
779 Victoria	813 Durango	**850—865**
780 San Antonio	814 Grand Junction	**Arizona**
(West)	815 Grand Junction	850 Phoenix
781 San Antonio	816 Glenwood	852 Phoenix
(East)	Springs	853 Phoenix
782 San Antonio	**820—831**	855 Globe
783 Corpus Christi	**Wyoming**	856 Tucson
784 Corpus Christi	820 Cheyenne	857 Tucson
785 McAllen	821 Yellowstone	859 Show Low
786 Austin	National Park	860 Flagstaff
787 Austin	(MT Office)	863 Prescott
788 San Antonio	822 Wheatland	864 Kingman
789 Austin	823 Rawlins	865 Gallup, NM
790 Amarillo	824 Worland	(AZ Offices)
791 Amarillo	825 Riverton	**870—884**
792 Childress	826 Casper	**New Mexico**
793 Lubbock	827 Gillette	870 Albuquerque
794 Lubbock	828 Sheridan	871 Albuquerque
795 Abilene	829 Rock Springs	872 Albuquerque
796 Abilene	830 Rock Springs	873 Gallup
797 Midland	831 Rock Springs	874 Farmington
798 El Paso	**832—838**	875 Santa Fe
799 El Paso	**Idaho**	877 Las Vegas
885 El Paso	832 Pocatello	878 Socorro
800—816	833 Twin Falls	879 Truth or
Colorado	834 Pocatello	Consequences
800 Denver (North)	835 Lewiston	880 Las Cruces
801 Denver (South)	836 Boise	881 Clovis

882 Roswell
883 Carrizozo
884 Tucumcari

889—898
Nevada
889 Las Vegas
890 Las Vegas
891 Las Vegas
893 Ely
894 Reno
895 Reno
897 Carson City
898 Elko

900—966
California
900 Los Angeles
901 Los Angeles
902 Inglewood
903 Inglewood
904 Santa Monica
905 Torrance
906 Long Beach
907 Long Beach
908 Long Beach
910 Pasadena
911 Pasadena
912 Glendale
913 Van Nuys
914 Van Nuys
915 Burbank
916 North
    Hollywood
917 Alhambra
918 Alhambra
920 San Diego
921 San Diego
922 Palm Springs
923 San Bernardino
924 San Bernardino
925 Riverside
926 Santa Ana

927 Santa Ana
928 Anaheim
930 Oxnard
931 Santa Barbara
932 Bakersfield
933 Bakersfield
934 Santa Barbara
935 Mojave
936 Fresno
937 Fresno
938 Fresno
939 Salinas
940 San Francisco
941 San Francisco
942 Sacaramento
943 Palo Alto
944 San Mateo
945 Oakland
946 Oakland
947 Berkeley
948 Richmond
949 North Bay
950 San Jose
951 San Jose
952 Stockton
953 Stockton
954 North Bay
955 Eureka
956 Sacramento
957 Sacramento
958 Sacramento
959 Marysville
960 Redding
961 Reno, NV
    (CA Offices)
962-966 Military
    (AP)

967—968
Hawaii
967 Honolulu
968 Honolulu

969
Guam
969 Agana, Guam

970—979
Oregon
970 Portland
971 Portland
972 Portland
973 Salem
974 Eugene
975 Medford
976 Klamath Falls
977 Bend
978 Pendleton
979 Boise, ID
    (OR Offices)

980—994
Washington
980 Seattle
981 Seattle
982 Everett
983 Tacoma
984 Tacoma
985 Olympia
986 Portland, OR
    (WA Offices)
988 Wenatchee
989 Yakima
990 Spokane
991 Spokane
992 Spokane
993 Pasco
994 Lewiston, ID
    (WA Offices)

995—999
Alaska
995 Anchorage
996 Anchorage
997 Fairbanks
998 Juneau
999 Ketchikan

– 6 –

Metrication Tables

CONVERSION TO AND FROM METRIC UNITS

Linear Measure (Length)

To convert	Multiply by
inches to millimeters	25.4
inches to centimeters	2.54
feet to meters	0.305
yards to meters	0.914
miles to kilometers	1.609

Linear Measure (Length)

To convert	Multiply by
millimeters to inches	0.039
centimeters to inches	0.394
meters to feet	3.281
meters to yards	1.094
kilometers to miles	0.621

Square Measure (Area)

To convert	Multiply by
sq. inches to sq. centimeters	6.452
sq. feet to sq. meters	0.093
sq. yards to sq. meters	0.836
acres to hectares	0.405

To convert	Multiply by
sq. centimeters to sq.inches	0.155
sq. meters to sq. feet	10.764
sq. meters to sq. yards	1.196
hectares to acres	2.471

Cubic Measure (Volume)

To convert	Multiply by
cu. inches to cu. centimeters	16.387
cu. feet to cu. meters	0.028
cu. yards to cu. meters	0.765

To convert	Multiply by
cu. centimeters to cu. inches	0.061
cu. meters to cu. feet	35.315
cu. meters to cu. yards	1.308

Liquid Measure (Capacity)

To convert	Multiply by
fluid ounces to liters	0.03
quarts to liters	0.946
gallons to liters	3.785
imperial gallons to liters	4.546

To convert	Multiply by
liters to fluid ounces	33.814
liters to quarts	1.057
liters to gallons	0.264
liters to imperial gallons	0.220

Weights (Mass)

To convert	Multiply by
ounces avoirdupois to grams	28.35
pounds avoirdupois to kilos	0.454
tons to metric tons	0.907

To convert	Multiply by
grams to ounces avoirdupois	0.035
kilos to pounds avoirdupois	2.205
metric tons to tons	1.102

Temperature

Fahrenheit		Celsius (Centigrade)
32°F	(freezing point of water)	0°C
212°F	(boiling point of water)	100°C
98.6°F	(body temperature)	37°C

To find degrees Celsius, subtract 32 from degrees Fahrenheit and divide by 1.8.

To find degrees Fahrenheit, multiply degrees Celsius by 1.8 and add 32.

TABLES OF WEIGHTS AND MEASURES

Linear Measure

1 mil	= 0.001 inch	= 0.0254 millimeter	
1 inch	= 1.000 mils	= 2.54 centimeters	
12 inches	= 1 foot	= 0.3048 meter	
3 feet	= 1 yard	= 0.9144 meter	
5 1/2 yards	= 16 1/2 feet	= 1 rod	= 5.029 meters
8 furlongs	= 1,760 yards	= 5,280 feet	= 1(statute) mile
1 (statute) mile	= 1.6093 kilometers		
3 miles	= 1 league	= 4.83 kilometers	

Square Measure

1 sq. inch	= 6.452 sq. centimeters	
144 sq. inches	= 1 sq. foot	= 929.03 sq. centimeters
9 sq. feet	= 1 sq. yard	= 0.8361 sq. meter
30¼ sq. yards	= 1 sq. rod	= 25.292 sq. meters
160 sq. rods	= 4,840 sq. yards	= 43,560 sq. feet
	= 1 acre	= 0.4047 hectare
640 acres	= 1 sq. mile	= 259.00 hectares
		= 2.590 sq. kilometers

Cubic Measure

1 cubic inch	= 16.387 cubic centimeters	
1,728 cubic inches	= 1 cubic foot	= 0.0283 cubic meter
27 cubic feet	= 1 cubic yard	= 0.7646 cubic meter
16 cubic feet	= 1 cord foot	= 0.453 cubic meter
128 cubic feet	= 1 cord	= 3.625 cubic meters
		= 8 cord feet

Nautical Measure

6 feet	= 1 fathom = 1.829 meters
100 fathoms	= 1 cable's length (ordinary)

(In the U.S. Navy 120 fathoms or 720 feet, or 219.456 meters)
= 1 cable's length
(In the British Navy, 608 feet, or 185.319 meters)
= 1 cable's length

10 cable's length	= 1 international nautical mile
	= 1.852 kilometers (exactly), 6.076.11549 feet by international agreement

1 international nautical mile = 1.150779 statute miles
(the length of a minute of longitude at the equator)

3 nautical miles	= 1 marine league (3.45 statute mile)
	= 5.56 kilometers
60 nautical miles	= 1 degree of a great circle of the earth
	= 69.047 statute miles

Dry Measure

1 pint		= 33.60 cubic inches	= 0.5506 liter
2 pints	= 1 quart	= 67.20 cubic inches	= 1.1012 liters
8 quarts	= 1 peck	= 537.61 cubic inches	= 8.8098 liters
4 pecks	= 1 bushel	= 2,150.42 cubic inches	= 35.2390 liters

According to U.S. standards, following are the weights avoirdupois for single bushels of the specified grains: for wheat, 60 pounds; for barley, 48 pounds; for oats, 32 pounds; for rye, 56 pounds; for shelled corn, 56 pounds. Some States have specifications varying from these. The British dry quart = 1.032 U.S. dry quarts

Liquid Measure

1 gill	= 4 fluid ounces	= 7.219 cubic inch	= 0.1183 liter
4 gills	= 1 pint	= 28.875 cubic inches	= 0.4732 liter
2 pints	= 1 quart	= 57.75 cubic inches	= 0.9464 liter
4 quarts	= 1 gallon	= 231 cubic inches	= 3.7854 liters

The British imperial gallon (4 imperial quarts) = 277.42 cubic inches = 4.546 liters. The barrel in Great Britain equals 36 imperial gallons, in the United States, usually 31½ gallons.

Apothecaries' Fluid Measure

1 minim	= 0.038 cubic inch	= 0.0616 milliliter
60 minims	= 1 fluid dram	= 0.2256 cubic inch
		= 3.6966 milliliters
8 fluid drams	= 1 fluid ounce	= 1.8047 cubic inches
		= 0.0296 liter
16 fluid ounces	= 1 pint	= 28.875 cubic inches
		= 0.4732 liter

(See table immediately preceding for quart and gallon equivalents.) The British pint = 20 fluid ounces.

Circular (Angular) Measure

60 seconds (")	= 1 minute (')	
60 minutes	= 1 degree	
90 degrees	= 1 quadrant	= 1 right angle
180 degrees	= 2 quadrants	= 1 straight angle
4 quadrants	= 360 degrees	= 1 circle

Avoirdupois Weight

(The grain, equal to 0.0648 gram, is the same in all three tables of weight.)

1 dram	= 27.34 grains	= 1.772 grams	
16 drams	= 437.5 grains	= 1 ounce	= 28.3495 grams
16 ounces	= 7,000 grains	= 1 pound	= 453.59 grams
100 pounds	= 1 hundredweight	= 45.36 kilograms	
2,000 pounds	= 1 ton	= 907.18 kilograms	

In Great Britain, 14 pounds (6.35 kilograms) = 1 stone, 112 pounds (50.80 kilograms) = 1 hundredweight, and 2,240 pounds (1,016.05 kilograms) = 1 long ton.

Troy Weight

(The grain, equal to 0.0648 gram, is the same in all three tables of weight.)

3.086 grains	= 1 carat	= 200.00 milligrams	
24 grains	= 1 pennyweight	= 1.5552 grams	
20 pennyweights	= 480 grains	= 1 ounce	= 31.1035 grams
12 ounces	= 5,760 grains	= 1 pound	= 373.24 grams

Apothecaries' weight

(The grain, equal to 0.0648 gram, is the same in all three tables of weight.)

20 grains	= 1 scruple	= 1.296 grams
3 scruples	= 1 dram	= 3.888 grams
8 drams or 480 grains	= 1 ounce	= 31.1035 grams
12 ounces or 5,760 grains	= 1 pound	= 373.24 grams

THE METRIC SYSTEM

Linear Measure

1 millimeter	= 0.03937 inch		
10 millimeters	= 1 centimeter	= 0.3937 inch	
10 centimeters	= 1 decimeter	= 3.937 inches	
10 decimeters	= 1 meter	= 39.37 inches	= 3.2808 feet
10 meters	= 1 decameter	= 393.7 inches	
10 decameters	= 1 hectometer	= 328.08 feet	
10 hectometers	= 1 kilometer	= 0.621 mile	= 3,280.8 feet
10 kilometers	= 1 myriameter	= 6.21 miles	

Square Measure

1 sq. millimeter	= 0.00155 sq. inch		
100 sq. millimeters	= 1 sq. centimeter	= 0.15499 sq. inch	
100 sq. centimeters	= 1 sq. decimeter	= 15.499 sq. inches	
100 sq. decimeters	= 1 sq. meter	= 1,549.9 sq. inches	
		= 1.196 sq. yards	
100 sq. meters	= 1 sq. decameter	= 119.6 sq. yards	
100 sq. decameters	= 1 sq. hectometer	= 2.471 acres	
100 sq. hectometers	= 1 sq. kilometer	= 0.386 sq. mile	
		= 247.1 acres	

Land Measure

1 sq. meter	= 1 centiare	= 1,549.9 sq. inches	
100 centiares	= 1 are	= 119.6 sq. yards	
100 ares	= 1 hectare	= 2.471 acres	
100 hectares	= 1 sq. kilometer	= 0.386 sq. mile	= 247.1 acres

Volume Measure

1,000 cubic millimeters	= 1 cubic centimeter
	= 0.06102 cubic inch
1,000 cubic centimeters	= 1 cubic decimeter
	= 61.023 cubic inches
	= 0.0353 cubic foot
1,000 cubic decimeters	= 1 cubic meter
	= 35.314 cubic feet
	= 1.308 cubic yards

Capacity Measure

10 milliliters	= 1 centiliter	= 0.338 fluid ounce	
10 centiliters	= 1 deciliter	= 3.38 fluid ounces	
		= 0.1057 liquid quart	
10 deciliters	= 1 liter	= 1.0567 liquid quarts	
		= 0.9081 dry quart	
10 liters	= 1 decaliter	= 2.64 gallons	= 0.284 bushel
10 decaliters	= 1 hectoliter	= 26.418 gallons	= 2.838 bushels
10 hectoliters	= 1 kiloliter	= 264.18 gallons	
		= 35.315 cubic feet	

Weights

10 milligrams	= 1 centigram	= 0.1543 grain
		= 0.000353 ounce (avdp.)
10 centigrams	= 1 decigram	= 1.5432 grains
10 decigrams	= 1 gram	= 15.432 grains
		= 0.035274 ounce (avdp.)
10 grams	= 1 decagram	= 0.3527 ounce
10 decagrams	= 1 hectogram	= 3.5274 ounces
10 hectograms	= 1 kilogram	= 2.2046 pounds
10 kilograms	= 1 myriagram	= 22.046 pounds
10 myriagrams	= 1 quintal	= 220.46 pounds
10 quintals	= 1 metric ton	= 2,204.6 pounds